SURVIVING SANCTITY:

One Young Woman's Journey
from Welfare, to Religion, to Sanity

Janet Cobb

Library of Congress Control Number: 2016901255
Janet Cobb Consulting, Chicago IL
ISBN-10: 0692613315
ISBN-13: 978-0692613313 (Janet Cobb Consulting)

DEDICATION

To those who loved and supported me despite
my holier-than-thou attitudes and actions along the way.

To those who challenged me to always
'act justly, love mercy, and walk humbly ...'

To each young woman searching to find her voice
— regardless of her specific circumstances —
that my story might empower her to keep listening within

To those who struggle with depression; that they continue to
believe their story isn't over yet.

ACKNOWLEDGEMENTS

Working on this manuscript for more than fifteen years, I cannot begin to list all of the individuals who have impacted the final outcome: my husband and children who have put up with my hours in front of a computer and my late nights – leaving me less than amicable during the day. Thank you.

To those who have read pieces and entire manuscript drafts along the way: coworkers, friends, librarians, friends of friends, students, and family members. Thank you.

To the many folks who took interest in my stories, asking why I became a Sister or why I left the convent, guiding me – perhaps unaware – to the truth of my story. Thank you.

I would be remiss to not acknowledge and to thank the many women with whom I shared life during my almost thirteen years in the convent. These women shared their lives and stories with me, some encouraging and others challenging me, but always giving of themselves with the grace they had in the moment. Thank you.

FORWARD

Major life events leave such a mark sometimes, that you never forget exactly where you sat or what you were doing when they happened. They linger, residing just beneath the surface, lest you forget. The shooting of JFK on November 22, 1963. The Loma Prieta Earthquake that shook the Bay Area Giants-A's World Series in 1989. The Tian An Men Square Massacre June 4, 1989. The bombing of the Twin Towers on 9/11.

My father's leaving without a trace, is a moment that forever changed the trajectory of my life, but I have no recollection of where I was or what I was doing when I heard the news. Instead, the details lay buried beneath a dense fog, forever irretrievable – as if my father simultaneously existed everywhere and nowhere, lurking in the curtains and orchestrating the entirety of my drama without ever stepping foot on stage. My drama: a series of sentences that dictated my life and drove me to the convent.

I left home a spontaneous, passionate young woman willing to go anywhere or do anything to bring God's love and forgiveness to the world, but allowed myself to be demeaned, belittled, and destroyed in the process – hoping to somehow make amends for sins I never committed. Until seemingly inconsequential conversations, minor decisions and intangible vibes converged in the center of my soul – creating irreversible, irreconcilable shifts.

My life became unbearable and the illusions that sustained it dissolved, requiring me to begin again. Almost thirteen years later, I returned to the world with a chunk of my life and myself, missing.

Surviving Sanctity is the answer to the why's so many have posed: Why did I enter? Why do I speak Chinese, drink hot water, know nothing of the 1980's, and rarely buy anything for myself? Why did I stay as long as I did? Why did I leave? Why don't I regret one minute?

Surviving Sanctity is my story – a mix of unforgettable moments and insidious twists and turns. My story, shared with the simple hope that any woman who ever believed she is not good enough, needs to be perfect, or deserves to be treated poorly, might find her voice and strength to confront life's toxins, and embrace the spark that has kept her going through years of loneliness, loss and longing.

My story is not the story of every nun, sister, or religious community. The memories I share here are mine as I remember them, not as anyone else might. As anyone with siblings can attest, no two people remember a single event in exactly the same way. I absolutely admire the many wonderful women who have dedicated their lives to the service of children, the elderly, the sick and the poor as vowed religious. I truly believe in the value of individuals offering themselves in the service of others while vowing poverty, chastity, and obedience. I simply could not continue to do so. My choice to leave the convent does not, and should not, invalidate anyone else's choice to stay. To protect the privacy of the Sisters who happened upon my path, I have changed the names of every Sister and the name of the Chicagoland community I explored on my arrival in Chicago. I have also included no photos of any other Sister.

Prequel: Rosaries & Riots

To be perfectly honest, my mother didn't seem all that special to me. Growing up, adults around me, at school and church, called Mom a saint. I learned about and read the lives of the saints, but somehow my mother didn't fit the bill. Sure, our kitchen calendar kept track of which Saturday's we all lined up in the front pew of the darkened church to 'go to Confession'; and we filed into the sixth pew for Mass every Sunday and each Wednesday night for the Novena to Our Lady of Perpetual Help; dry palm branches hung behind each crucifix in the house and beneath every bedroom light switch hung a small dish with holy water or its salty remnants – but didn't every Catholic home in the late 1960's and early 1970's? My earliest memories are of siblings and I kneeling around the furniture, backs straight and hands folded praying the Daily Rosary, and of classmates walking in procession to crown a statue of the Blessed Mother.

One favorite childhood memory I haven't been able to replicate with my own children, despite my efforts, is the Saturday morning ritual of French Toast. With one small frying pan, my mom managed to keep four pieces of French Toast coming hot to my plate as my siblings and I devoured, in six to eight bites, a stack at a time. To this day, nothing quite tastes like Mom's French Toast. Even her white bread, toasted with just the right amount of dark crisp spots, and evenly spread margarine is spectacular. Although I enjoyed every bite, these feasts, in my mind, didn't qualify Mom for sainthood. Moms are supposed to do these things.

Saints didn't leave children in the back seat of the car at the grocery store parking lot, waiting for what seemed to be hours, to catch up on the latest news and gossip; or push them away as they cuddled up on the couch because, at the age of eight, they'd gotten 'too old for that'. Saints didn't hold in-your-face, screaming matches with their teenage sons, threatening to beat them with a belt if they didn't straighten up, stop fighting, and learn respect. I can still feel the fear from the times she packed us smaller children in the car because she wouldn't stand for it any more. We drove a few blocks and arrived back at the house, Mom barging into the living room, pointing her finger in my brothers' faces shouting, 'This is my house. If anyone is going to leave, it won't be me.' Before we knew it, whatever wind stirred up the emotions leading to the outburst died out and we all sat together watching TV or playing Spades, as if nothing happened.

Mom couldn't be a saint. She fell asleep during our Daily Rosary more often than not, and slept more than I imagined anyone could. And she smoked all the time, and even fell asleep sometimes, cigarette in hand – burning holes in the arm of the couch and in the rug beneath her. The smoke rings she blew intrigued and impressed me, but I never understood why she wasted money we didn't have, when she never really inhaled. Seriously. She lit a rolled up paper filled with tiny bits of leaves with a match, sucked on it, held the smoke in her mouth, and blew it back out. This way, she claimed, nothing reached her lungs; she enjoyed the flavor and didn't need the nicotine. Thanks for sharing all the smoke with me, I thought. We ate saltine crackers and butter at the end of the month sometimes, but she sent us to the local P&X to buy her cigarettes.

Each Ash Wednesday, as far back as I can remember, Mom quit smoking for Lent. By the time the smudgy black cross of ashes spread across her forehead and we all piled back into the car, she lit up with the intention of quitting, on Sunday, when the forty days of Lent officially began. By the time we arrived at 11:30 am Mass the following Sunday, finding our usual pew, Mom looked frazzled and worn down. Sure enough, at the end of the hour, as we headed home, she lit up. She would give up cigarettes on Sunday, before 11:30 am Mass, for Lent.

Mom's idea of heaven: *smoking my cigarettes and drinking my tea in peace* – a rare opportunity given she had eight children. Church folks and neighbors who never heard Mom opine on heaven based her sainthood on the fact that she raised eight children in one very small, government housing apartment with four bedrooms and a bathroom upstairs, and a living/dining space, kitchen, and laundry area packed into about four hundred square feet downstairs.

Our tiny apartment stood in Rodeo, a small town along the San Pablo Bay just north of San Francisco, originally the spot to roundup all the area livestock for shipping to slaughterhouses and packing plants. Like many small towns, we boasted ten different churches and eleven bars; two stoplights and three gas stations; two public grade schools and one Catholic; and three distinct parts of town: The Highlands where the wealthy lived; Old Rodeo which housed the blue collar families; and The Projects which contained everything the town considered evil: poverty, drugs, prostitution, violence, and black people. Beyond the borders of the Projects loomed fear and loathing, hatred for everything inside. But my siblings and I called The Projects, home.

Drastically juxtaposed to the incense, holy water, and celestial angels offered at school and church, my day-to-day experiences included riots, SWAT teams, and evil.

"Shut off the lights. Now. Get down. Get out of the window." Mom shouted. Grown men fighting, policemen with billy-clubs, and lots of shouting

4

covered our front lawns. By the end of the night, one policeman left with a broken nose and our neighbor Isaac, a broken arm. Another night, pounding came from the back door, with Ronnie McGhee shouting, "Isaac, let me in or they'll kill me." Ronnie had the habit of walking down the street with a rifle in hand, often seen running from someone. Yet, he never failed to help Mom carry in the groceries. That night, Ronnie mistook our back yard for Isaac's. Dad opened the door, let him in, and for the next few hours we all sat watching TV together, until Ronnie and Dad decided the coast was clear.

A year or so later on Halloween (which just so happens to be my birthday), as we sat eating cake because Dad insisted we sing and eat cake before anyone went trick-or-treating, the cops surrounded the building across the street, SWAT teams and all, to apprehend somebody. So, like it or not, my siblings who usually rushed through the birthday song and devoured the cake, still couldn't go out. Instead, we sat peeking through the curtains, watching the cops with guns in hand, ready to fire. The standoff took about an hour and with the man wrestled to the ground, and no one really hurt, hordes of children, in simple lion and princess costumes, took to the streets searching for as many sweets as little bags could hold.

"Who do you think you are? You can't take my children from me. They are mine. They are good girls. You can't take them, you devil. You came into my house; took my clothes out of my closet; stole all my food. You are the devil. I am God. You are the devil. You!"

I looked up to see Sheila, our mentally ill next-door neighbor, her wild strawberry blonde, disheveled hair, spitting, almost foaming at the mouth, pointing towards me. I vaguely noticed those around me giggling, yelling back at Sheila, and moving indoors. I stood on the narrow pavement, almost frozen, as her frantic screams pierced, not just my ears, but my soul. Sheila was institutionalized and her two young daughters who'd often run naked in the streets at midnight, taken away.

Nate and Sandy, with their son Miles, moved in next. Sandy worked as a prostitute and Nate, her pimp, dealt drugs on the street and beat his wife and child almost daily. We all heard the beatings, but the bedroom activity remained more private, audible only to me because of our shared bedroom wall. Within minutes of Nate getting home, the sounds of tiny bones cracking against the wall and backslaps across the face flooded the backyard where everyone hung out. Miles, almost four, came out regularly covered with bumps and bruises. "I fell down the stairs … I fell off my bike." Everyone knew Miles didn't deserve the beatings, but no one said a word.

When neighbors asked what happened when Mom called us in for "the Rosary", rather than attempt explanation, we invited them in. If we wanted to get outside, we mumbled Our Father's, Hail Mary's and Glory Be's at top speed. If not, the Rosary became the time to share mundane and not so mundane life events, concerns of the heart most families shared around a dinner table. In the middle of a Hail Mary one of us blurted out, "Oh, you know what happened in school the other day?" The conversation transgressed, sometimes for hours, as our thoughts rolled out upon one another, eager to be heard, perhaps afraid of silence.

Mom held tightly to her reasons for praying the daily Rosary: the conversion of Russia and the end of Communism, the secrets of Fatima, and the end of abortion. The devil took control of America, she'd say, the day Roe v. Wade passed. The evils of communism and the complexities of world politics meant little to me; the sun falling from the sky in midday as thousands prayed at Fatima I thought intriguing; but the pain of a child not being loved or wanted – I completely understood.

Saints and sinners, angels and devils, heaven and hell became the paradigm through which I viewed the world. Rich or poor, white or black, and saint or sinner became the dichotomies by which all my experiences were judged. And I stood, straddled between the two, uncertain of where I fit in; ashamed of one, or the other, depending on the time of day and who surrounded me. Kissing my boyfriend during a game of truth or dare or laughing at a dirty joke as we sat in the backyard holding hands, created turmoil each night as I begged God's forgiveness for my sins. I longed to reconcile the dichotomy of God's love and the promise of heaven with my persistent fear of the devil and all things evil – but, at the same time wanted to simply be accepted and loved.

Amidst this confusion, around the age of ten, I somehow convinced myself that God had a special purpose for my life. I grabbed a folder and a stack of lined binder paper from the hall closet, climbed into my top bunk, and started writing my life story:

> *I was born two months premature on, October 31, 1963, the seventh child of Loyed and Mary Arnold. My family is sort of divided into two: Regina and the boys, they're the older kids; and the girls: Karen, Tina, me and my little sister Carol. I was born in San Diego 'cause my dad was in the Navy. We moved to Concord, California when he was discharged and to Rodeo when I was about three. He left when I was seven.*

Summing up my childhood in minutes, I headed down the stairs to Mom's favorite spot at the end of the couch where coffee mug, rosary and prayer book lay within arms' reach, on a fact-finding mission. "Can you tell me stuff from before Dad left?" I tried to sound casual and without purpose.

"When you were about two I took you for ice cream. We sat under one of those outside umbrellas and you looked up at the sky and said, 'I don't know why I have to go to heaven. I guess Daddy'll have to take me to heaven.' Then a year or so later when I gave you girls a bath, I asked what you'd be when you grew up. Karen announced she'd be a mommy, Tina said she wanted to be just like Regina, and before you said anything, Karen chimed in, 'Janet's going to heaven.' A five-year-old even thinking something like that gave me the creeps. Don't you remember? Then a couple years ago, when you got mad you'd yell, 'You make fun of me 'cause I gotta go to heaven and you don't; or you said stuff like, 'I don't know why I have to go to heaven.'"

I remembered yelling at my siblings about going to heaven, but the words 'Daddy'll have to take me to heaven' tossed and turned in my mind. *I can't be going to heaven, not if Dad has to take me. He can't take me anywhere. He abandoned me.*

According to Mom, and the incessant teasing of my siblings, Dad went crazy and stopped going to church right after I came along. With a sixth grade education and almost fifteen years in the Navy, my Dad completely revamped the Naval radar system manual but when he got no credit for his work, grew despondent and depressed, refusing to follow orders or even get out of bed even after being hospitalized for Manic-Depression.

After being discharged, with seven children in tow, they moved to the San Francisco East Bay where Dad sunk his entire pension into a restaurant which quickly failed, leaving them with nothing. Working at the US Post Office and a used car dealership, he wasn't home much and became increasingly distant. After twenty-one years, Dad decided he wanted no part of Mom or his eight kids and didn't come home. Investigators searched until the car he'd stolen from work turned up at the Las Vegas airport.

Mom burned his pictures, gave his clothes to the local thrift store, informed us he wouldn't be back, and packed away his memory. Case closed. No television cameras flooded our front lawn, no manhunt ensued, and no teacher or counselor ever asked me how I felt about it. Three pieces of furniture he built remained: the telephone stand, the bookcase built out of Carol's old crib, and the crucifix.

Memories of the man became legend. The older kids told of all out brawls, screams and threats, with shoes and books flying when Dad gambled away a paycheck or took off for weeks at a time. We laughed, sometimes hysterically, at the stories: Loyed getting kicked down a hill at a family picnic; Daniel backhanded for swearing; Karen knocked across the room for not setting the table quickly enough or yelled to stop crying when she slipped on the stairs and cracked open her eyebrow bone, needing several stitches; and me slapped on Thanksgiving for asking someone to pass the Kool-Aid minutes after he told us to wait quietly for dishes to be passed around.

We wondered, from time to time, if he might ever come back, or teasingly sang the tune of a popular television show, insisting we would complete our chores but we needed to "wait 'til our daddy gets home." Mom never shed a tear. She changed the bills and credit cards to her name, applied for welfare, and enrolled in the local community college to get an education. She tried to super-glue the pieces of her life back together, sending me on my way as if nothing happened, a bandage on a skinned knee, and sending a ripple through my soul with repercussions I am still attempting to comprehend.

I tried to be more loveable. Each morning I greeted my third grade teacher at her car in the school parking lot to carry her guitar, bigger and heavier than me, to the classroom, happy for the attention I got for being such a helper. I never again walked home with my mouth taped shut for talking too much like in first and second grade; and every Saturday morning, I crawled on my hands and knees across the rusty-gold shag rug covering our living room floor, to pick out all of the hair with my fingers because we didn't own a vacuum. I remember beaming with pride each time Mom exclaimed, "Who's the angel who cleaned the house?"

In third grade I began making outrageous claims about myself. Although all tests proved otherwise, I insisted I didn't see well and needed reading classes. I walked into school one-day announcing I spelled my name incorrectly all these years; I was not Janet, but Janette. Ms. Lowell never scolded me or made me feel bad. She promptly purchased a pair of magnifying glasses from the local drugstore and spelled my name the way I wanted. Every few weeks, as I changed my mind, she changed the spelling. I also passed out during my standardized tests. Pencil in hand, I began filling in the dots, eager to prove my knowledge, only to awaken in the nurse's office with Mom hovering over me, frightened.

I obeyed every commandment and every rule, wondering which I'd broken to deserve the punishment of being abandoned, and struggled to make sense of a God who loves the poor, allows pain and suffering so it can be offered up, and demands perfection for anyone to get to heaven.

In sixth grade I entered the public school classroom looking confident and unafraid, praying no one knew my insides felt like soft-serve ice cream melting in the hot sun. I needed all my friends from The Projects to be proud of me. Sitting at my desk, reaching into my most private relationship with God, begging for some trick to survive, I made an instantaneous, conscious decision and quietly said, "Shit." With my first cuss word came the determination to be every bit a girl from The Projects. By recess, I decided to cuss at every chance, as long as Mom never heard me. On our trips to the grocery store for bread, or milk, or Mom's cigarettes, I joined in the contests to see who could stick the most candy up a shirt or down pants or in socks without getting caught, walking away with a stash of Boston Baked Beans, Lemonheads and Hot Tamales to last the afternoon. Foul language and shoplifting quickly devolved into back-talking, cheating, and drinking.

I acted indifferent towards Dad, like Mom when she stated simply that he had problems and did what he thought best. I claimed apathy through it all, never realizing the fabulous webs of deceit and anger I created in an attempt to grapple with the silent pain in my soul. Each night, under the safety and security of my blankets, in a bedroom lit only by the flare of the smoke stacks from the oil refinery just behind The Projects, I'd roll into the fetal position and beg God to forgive me. No specific sins came to mind, no list of faults; but nights turned into weeks and months, my unworthiness permeating my soul.

I took my first drink at thirteen. I drank just enough to get a buzz, and not enough to get caught, whenever possible. I swore I'd never lose control or be carried in, unable to walk, like my brothers; I'd drink just enough to fit in with my new friends from high school. Mom caught me once and grounded me; within days I began sneaking into my brother's dresser drawer or my neighbor's kitchen cupboard for a sip or a swig of something, anything.

Four days before my sixteenth birthday, I drank enough to kill me. On an empty stomach so my clothes would fit just right, I started with Michelob. Just two. While everyone else drank Bacardi and Coke, I downed Bacardi straight because I'd sworn off carbonated sodas to clear my acne. After Bacardi came Tequila Sunrise, and my first glass of gin turned into a fifth of both gin and vodka.

I stepped out of the car, walked into the Homecoming game perfectly straight, and headed off to search for friends. From the top of the large stone bleachers making up the stadium, I spotted someone I knew. "Hey!" I shouted, waving my hat in the air, completely oblivious to the fact that I'd fallen into a tumble down the stairs. At the bottom, I picked up my hat and my clog and limped down the remaining three steps. Distracted by someone's parents, I stopped briefly to greet them. Confused by the gasping and the guffaws surrounding me, I rose from the lap of the woman suddenly sitting beneath me. Feeling dizzy, I welcomed the firm grip of the uniformed men surrounding me. "Hello, officers. Thank you so much. You are so helpful." Two police escorted me from the bleachers, through the main gates, and towards their parked car. "Oh, man. Sister Christopher. Oh, no. Please, don't tell my mother. Whatever you do, don't tell my mom." Sister Christopher, the principal, found my sister Tina to get me home.

Rolling over on the living room floor surrounded by newspaper, I noticed my unbuttoned shirt and unzipped pants. What happened to my dress? Had I gone to the dance? How did I get home? A feeling of absolute terror invaded me as I wondered what I'd done and, even more frightening, what may have been done to me. I tried to stand up, but couldn't. If I could just get past Mom, asleep on the couch, it would be just feet to reach the stairs. I crawled on my hands and knees and rested my head on the cool, plastic coating of the small wooden stairs. On the third attempt to get on my feet, I collapsed, dropped my head to the fold of my elbow and whispered to God, who I hoped would listen: "I'm not gonna live like this anymore. I want to give my life back to you." I said nothing the next day to my family about my private conversion as I endured the panic of Mom's interrogations and the snide remarks of my older siblings. From now on, as an alcoholic and a drunk, I'd never be trusted or forgiven.

"I know my punishment, but can I tell you something," I blurted when Sr. Christopher finally called me into her office Monday afternoon.

"What?" she asked with slight impatience.

"The other night, when I woke up," I stuttered, "I promised God I wouldn't live like this anymore. I'm done drinking. Really. I'm giving my life back to God."

Sister Christopher, stared for a moment and with her usual firmness replied, "I believe you."

Weeks later when a friend handed me a bottle of Jack Daniel's, Sister Christopher's words, "I believe you," flashed in my mind. I clung to the message on the T-shirt Mom gave me for Christmas: *I'm worth all the trouble I cause.* I wore it proudly, but I had so abandoned my personal beliefs and values, looking constantly to others for a sense of identity, that my promise to give my life back to God left me desperately looking for companionship and affirmation. My late night rendezvous with God returned in full force as I begged for strength to become who God wanted me to be, even if no one loved me.

Living and Dying class during senior year required a field trip to a funeral parlor. The smell of lilies and carnations flooded my nasal cavity as I walked into the barren chapel-like gathering hall. Gray padded folding chairs stood in perfect rows facing a huge stained-glass window. Directed to head down the corridor but afraid to be first, I fell to the back of the crowd with Sister Jane behind me. Death didn't frighten me. I'd attended funerals of neighbors and friends in grade school. Craig got hit by a train. Dave overdosed. A classmate's father shot himself while cleaning his shotgun. Mom called them all suicide and we prayed for their souls because suicide was a sin.

Regina's husband Tom died of cancer at twenty-one, after just six months of marriage. I missed him, wiped the tears from my eyes, and concluded: old people die. Pictures disappeared, hours of laughter we'd shared dissipated and we rarely spoken of Tom again, never in Regina's company. News of my new sister-in-law Judi's brain tumors interrupted my life briefly, but at eleven, I only thought of how to get rid of my pimples, who my next boyfriend might be, and the best way to wear my hair. We asked Mary to protect us every time we prayed a Hail Mary, now and at the hour of our death; I concluded death was a part of life, not something to be feared. Someone had determined years before that I would be going to Heaven, but I had no idea how or when it might happen.

My classmates 'wooed' and 'awed' as we entered the casket room. As my vision rested on row upon row of gray, brown, bronze, gold and silver empty caskets, I leaned towards the door, my hand slippery with sweat, barely able to grasp the handle. I stumbled across the hallway to a simple, benign parlor and slumped into the nearest armchair. Sister Jane followed me, instructing me to return to the casket room. I clutched my notebook, forcing my visions of death, of Tom, Craig, Davy, and others out of my mind. I maintained my composure until a classmate enthusiastically asked if she could climb in a casket.

Feeling every ounce of my breath being squeezed from my lungs, like a child might suck the last drop from an icy pop on a hot summer day, I crashed through the door and stumbled back into the parlor. Sister Jane pressed me to explain myself. Unburdening my soul for the first time since I'd listened to Mom's story of Karen's prophecy, feeling the weight of the secret lifted from my chest, I told Sr. Jane I thought I was dying; clarifying I was not suicidal, but certain I would die soon, perhaps from a brain tumor. I wanted to swallow my words, press rewind, and take it all back; but as I shared my deepest fears, she convinced me to tell my mother about my headaches.

"They'll lock me in a crazy house if I take you to the doctor demanding tests for no reason. You don't even have symptoms. Is Sister Jane a doctor now, too?" Mom settled the whole thing.

Crouched in the corner of a small darkened chapel, surrounded by those I scarcely knew, I wept. I wept for the soft freckled redhead child standing, front and center, head held high, stretching my neck muscles to stand just a bit taller; who first tried to be perfect hiding under the darkness of my covers with knees clutched under my chin, praying simply: please just let somebody – anybody – love me; who tried so desperately to be perfectly rebellious. I wept for the commandments I'd broken and the pain that I'd caused my mother, my teachers, and my father. Accompanied by the gentle strum of a guitar and with virtual strangers gathered round me singing, *"Long have I waited for your coming home to me and living deeply our new life…,"* I finally understood. God waited with outstretched arms for me, watching as I twisted my way through relationships, searching in pain, longing for a father who never abandons. Rocking to and fro, gripping my arms across my chest, fingernails ripping at the flesh near my shoulders, the refrain echoed in my soul, *"Come back to me with all your heart, don't let fear keep us apart."* I understood with full clarity that *'Janet going to heaven'* had nothing to do with physical death. I needed to die to myself to live in God. Tears of joy, rapidly replacing those of remorse, rattled me.

Dad left so that I could call God my Father; that's how Daddy would take me to heaven. I made another instant, adamant decision to mend my sinful ways and return to God. By the end of the Teens Encounter Christ (TEC) weekend, and just over a year after the Homecoming game, I stacked obligation upon obligation: no cutting class, no talking back, and no tough and careless attitude. I'd stopped drinking on Homecoming night, a token gesture, but to be truly Christian, to belong to God, I needed to surrender completely.

At the closing prayer service, I wrapped my arms around Mom as she stood stiffly in the circle. With tears in my eyes, I apologized for all the trouble I caused, promised to never disrespect her again, and declared that I loved her. After five or six years of lies, one weekend couldn't convince her of my conversion. "Yeah, I've heard that before."

I poured over the letters of Paul and the gospels searching for the best way to be a Christian. I mapped out how much of the Bible to read each night to complete both Old and New Testament in a year. Called to rejoice and be thankful, I released the apathy and boredom controlling me. I insisted we no longer cut class to grab breakfast and told friends I wouldn't lie about being late. Positive remarks countered the backstabbing gossip of our lunchtime conversation and I joyfully picked up the garbage in school and public restrooms, a simple witness to how a Christian can make the world a better place. I attended weekly prayer meetings, listening to others' attempts to perfect Christianity. Convinced God loved me, I wanted only to be a good Christian worthy of God's love.

Hearing vague rumors toward the end of high school that the government might consider drafting women, I feigned indifference and pronounced I would simply get pregnant or join a convent. I figured pregnant women and nuns wouldn't be drafted; my ludicrous hypocrisy laid buried beneath layers of my righteous indignation of being a good Christian. God couldn't want me to go to war, killing was a sin. Instead, I'd have Vernon's baby. Vernon: the buck-toothed boy everyone called Rabbit, whose name I'd shouted at Red Rover games and chased during touch football in the front yard; the drum major with a black-belt in karate; my backup date throughout high school. Vernon and I spent hours together in the backyard, he pontificating on the necessity and excitement of sex; I countering with religion, God and marriage. Scribbling love poems, praying for the salvation of his soul, I agonized over Vernon. Certain he should leave Marie, who'd been living with him since being kicked out of her house for dating a black boy, I never doubted by ability to rid him of his obsession with sex and marijuana. I could save him.

Vernon, the only boy who ever took me beyond first base, so dominated my heart and so captivated my compassion, I determined to give him everything he needed. When he took a job in Arizona the winter of my senior year in high school, I seriously contemplated running away with him. In the early pre-dawn hours of a sleepover with a friend, I hashed out my plan to tell him I wanted to go with him to Arizona and to satisfy his sexual desire at the neighborhood party the next evening.

I justified sacrificing my no-sex-before-marriage conviction for the salvation of Vernon's soul. The loss of my virginity would be a small price to make him truly happy and share with him my joy in knowing Jesus. The hypocrisy escaped me at the time as my own sexual curiosity grew. I prepared eagerly for the party and kept Vernon close by me as we talked and danced in the crowded apartment living room. Just as I took his hand to lead him, wide eyed and grinning, up the stairs, someone came running in the front door shouting, "They here. Come on." The guys charged out the door and down the street. By night's end, Buford had been arrested, Vernon nursed a stab wound to the thigh, and I regained my sanity, reclaiming my belief that sex is best reserved for marriage.

Talk of the draft dissipated as did my fail-proof plan for avoiding it, but thoughts of entering a convent lingered. I weighed the pros and cons of my childhood plan of marrying and having a dozen children, against the ability I might have as a Sister to influence hearts. I wanted desperately to share the joy I found in Jesus. How many teenagers, victims of divorce and abuse, just needed to know someone loved them? How many searched for comfort in drinking and drugs? Without my own family, I might help many more.

The few trusted teachers I spoke with listened with skepticism, insisting I should attend college and work in the real world before making such a decision. I'd worked from the time I turned thirteen and witnessed more in my neighborhood than most did in a lifetime; I knew enough about the world, I insisted, to leave it behind. God called me, why should I wait?

Mom, who had no idea how seriously I'd taken my conversion, sat stunned in her spot on the couch, a few days before my eighteenth birthday, when I announced I'd be entering the convent. A commitment to the convent shouldn't be based on the buddy system like choosing a college or joining the Army; this would be a commitment to God. Once I explained my desire to serve God, not my intention to follow my classmate Leslie who'd entered a few months earlier, she not only calmed down, but began to support my efforts to become a Sister, the life she once dreamed of.

Everyone seemed surprised, and almost shocked, by my decision to sacrifice my spontaneity and curtail my mischievous nature for the sake of saving others. I convinced them I could bring my joyful, carefree attitude to those who suffered; asking them to imagine the teenagers who needed the message I received: No matter what your situation, no matter how you hurt, God loves you. God will never leave you, never abandon you. As a Sister, I could bring that message anywhere. God called me. I needed to follow.

I scoured the vocation brochure looking for just the right congregation. Hundreds of advertisements calling anyone interested in following the footsteps of this saint or that, offering a lifetime of dedication and service, filled the pages of the magazines Sr. Thomas gave me. Mom explained some basics: Dominicans were academic. Franciscans, joyful. Carmelites, cloistered. Maryknoll's, missionary. She concluded I seemed more Franciscan than Dominican; too outgoing, loud, and carefree to consider the cloister. I wrote to six congregations for information. When I visited Leslie again in November, Sr. Thomas gave me all of the application forms and paperwork to complete. God must be calling me to join them, because a month passed without word from any other congregation. God couldn't want me to wait too long to serve Him.

Coworkers at the Social Security Administration bombarded me with every imaginable question. Could I really give up marriage and children? Did I really want to wear a black dress all my life? I'd been accepted at two local universities; why would I give that up? Two lunch-time Bible Study companions challenged the entire idea of forsaking marriage. God wanted woman to marry man, not to live in chastity forever. I needed to fast and pray, they said, to ask God for clarity. Although I'd never taken such drastic measures to listen to God, I liked the idea. Fasting would allow me to listen.

When I mentioned their idea to Sr. Thomas, she insisted Jesus set the example for living in chastity and God approved the vows through His

14

Church. I needed to keep oxygen going to my brain, not listen to fundamentalist Christians' criticism of Church traditions. She expected me to continue trusting that since she and the council had accepted my application, God must want me to enter.

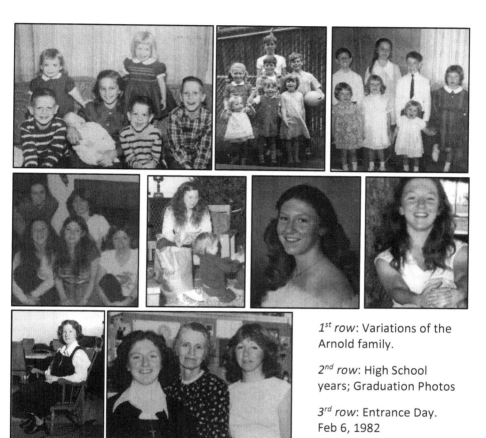

1st row: Variations of the Arnold family.

2nd row: High School years; Graduation Photos

3rd row: Entrance Day. Feb 6, 1982

Meditation Point, St. Clare's Retreat House, Soquel CA

Burnt Offerings

An oversized cowbell hanging above the carport driveway rang through the Santa Cruz Mountains, summoning me to the first of many regulated meals: split pea soup, cold cuts and canned pears. I smiled, spooned the creamy green liquid into my mouth methodically and prayed I wouldn't hate every meal as much as I hated this first one. Glancing around the small dining room overflowing with women in black habits, veiled versions of the grandmother I'd come to know and despise during high school, I clung to my polite smile to appear interested in the ramblings of these senior citizens, praying for patience to endure.

After lunch I stood in the wide, white-washed, sterile corridor of the convent I would call home, greeting the other postulants and novices. I'd met them all during my previous visits, but had never been allowed to go upstairs, to their dorm area, considered the cloister. As each welcomed me with open arms and a tight squeeze on the shoulder, my excitement melted into comfort.

"Didn't you have time to alter the jumpers I sent you?"

"Yeah, but I like my clothes this baggy. It's comfortable." I thought little of Sr. Thomas's question as I glanced down at the black smock hanging off my shoulders.

Turning to Leslie, she said, "Go get a jumper. These are unacceptable."

16

"Those are mine." Sr. Elaine Marie squealed with her customary excitement and belly chuckle. "And I'm three times your size."

Without missing a beat, Sr. Thomas turned to me adding, "You can't wear jewelry. Send it home with your mother."

A thousand responses ran through my head. My mother, and any of my high school teachers, would have been bombarded with backtalk. I'd only worn three pieces. My class ring, which I could do without, such a clear sign of worldly ways; the graduation ring from Regina, one of the people I admired most, not only my eldest sister, but a surrogate mother and friend; and my TEC cross, a constant reminder of God's unconditional love. All Sisters wore crucifixes, couldn't I?

After returning the jumpers to the laundry room down the hall as instructed, I quietly returned to my room placing twelve pair of nylons, twelve handkerchiefs, ten white cotton t-shirts, ten white cotton underwear and six bras neatly in the closet drawer. I hung my hand towel and washcloth on the rack above the sink and placed the soap, toothpaste and toothbrush on the sink board. My world: a closet, a bed, a nightstand, a sink and a community bathroom down the hall with four shower stalls, four toilets and a bathtub; ten bedrooms, a chapel, recreation room, library, laundry room and a dining room with a small kitchenette. Back home, nine people shared four bedrooms, a small living room and dining, kitchen combination with one bathroom. I'd adjust to the space and looked forward to giving my life in service.

"We watch national news every night and we have community recreation twice a week. Other nights, if you don't have homework, you're free to socialize in here until nine. Lights out at ten." Sr. Thomas explained as I entered the community room that evening, plopping myself unto the couch and resting my outstretched feet on the coffee table. "And we don't put our feet on the table."

"Okay, Mo…" I caught myself mid-word with a chuckle. "Sister."

"I am not your mother."

Except for the anchorman's droll voice, the room fell eerily silent. Commercials allowed for brief conversations regarding the newsbytes, but otherwise everyone sat knitting, mending, or creating hook rugs until sign off, when Sr. Thomas turned towards me, "From now on, make sure you have something to do with your hands while we're watching the news. Idle hands are the devil's workshop."

Turning to the others, she asked, "Anyone up for Canasta." Committing the rules of Canasta to memory proved easy compared to navigating the customs surrounding recreation and community socializing. We played cards in a cut throat, all's-fair-in-love-and-cards manner. With each go around someone needed to remind me to stop talking and to play the game; jokes could be told and stories shared, as long as no one interrupted the game. I wanted to get to know my new family; they wanted to win the game.

I soon learned Sr. Thomas didn't tolerate informality in the convent. I should not correspond with boys, except brothers, and all envelopes should be addressed with Mr. and Mrs., not first names. I should fill my glass only two-thirds full and slice my banana before eating it, with a fork; I needed to use a soup spoon, not a teaspoon, for my breakfast cereal; and to prove my vocation, I must maintain a good appetite. I went back for seconds that day and most days afterward. I should not fold my legs in chapel, always hold my book with two hands and never pray the rosary too loudly or read the Psalms too quickly. As we stood in the buffet lines waiting to dish our food, she told me to avoid the weak spots in the hallway floor so they didn't squeak. She described how to hold the door handles just right as the doors shut to avoid the snap of the latch. She suggested, with her superior's tone of voice, my shower time be shortened a few minutes, I leave the main bathroom light off and use only the light inside the shower stall, and that I turn the water off while soaping up, to conserve water. She monitored when I laughed too heartily or spoke too loudly, correcting my double negatives and insisting I respond to her with "Yes, Sister" rather than "yeah." Eager to become not only a good religious, but a saint, I listened intently to every suggestion, correction and admonition.

My first individual assignment: keep the three dogs properly groomed. Sr. Thomas didn't know that dogs not only scared me, but that I didn't like them. And I couldn't tell her. Sr. Thomas discouraged emotion and insisted on obedience. So, I gathered the large metal tub, the dog shampoo and the scrub brush to tackle, not only the dogs, but my fear. Tom, a large but mellow German Shepherd, stepped directly into the tub, stood very still as the water ran over his back and I held my breath to avoid the smell and to keep my hands from shaking, finished up as quickly as possible.

Jacoba, the neurotic Collie, refused to come out of her house. No matter how I tugged on the leash or spoke compassionately, Jacoba curled up, whining and shivering more than me. I finally had to yank her out of the house, pick her up and drop her into the tub full of soapy water. Jacoba wriggled free, running from the tub and down the driveway too quickly for me to do anything but spray her tail with the hose. Turning to Pepper, I picked up the small black mutt and placed him gently in the water. Pepper had little to no control of his bowels and couldn't keep himself clean. I pulled on the yellow latex gloves, picked up the haircutting scissors and began snipping beneath Pepper's tail. Frightened and disgusted, staring into the dog's butt, I knew I had to be obedient and clean the stupid dogs.

18

St. Clare's Retreat House, originally an old dude ranch set on fifty-two acres nestled among the Redwoods in the Santa Cruz Mountains, had been donated to the Sisters upon their arrival in the US in the early fifties. Over the years, horse trails became prayer paths and the mountains were littered with shrines, Stations of the Cross, Rosary Walks and various other paths for meditation and prayer.

Eighty to one hundred women arrived in carload after carload each Friday evening, escaping into the quiet solitude of prayer and reflection. The postulants and novices carried luggage and opened doors, served meals and washed dishes. After each meal, we straightened place settings in the dining room: chairs pushed in just right with the outer leg of each meeting the outer foot of the table leg; the placemat lined up with the edges of each chair. From left to right, napkin with open end facing out, salad and dinner fork on top, space for the plate, knife with sharp edge turned inward, soup spoon and teaspoon. The bottom of each utensil aligned perfectly straight just above the edge of the placemat; the water glass placed at the tip of the knife. Coffee cup and saucer, handle facing four o'clock, sat just at the tip of the teaspoon.

After the women returned to the world of work and family, novitiate members cleaned ninety-two dormitory rooms preparing for the next group of holy pilgrims. Beds attacked first: hospital corners tucked tightly into the space between mattress and box spring. Top sheet placed wrong side up, "St. Clare's Retreat House" beautifully embroidered on the top right corner of each sheet then folded over. Wall side tugged in, the outer edge of blankets and bedspread should not touch the floor. On the bottom center of each bed we placed a paper bath and shower mat, bath towel, hand towel, wash cloth, two soaps and a Dixie cup. Clean sheets in the dresser drawer. We scrubbed toilets, sprayed showers, and vacuumed. We gathered all of the soiled sheets and towels at the end of the hallway, waiting patiently to be separated for washing. Everything looked perfect for the next occupant.

We gladly performed services: bell-hop, waitress, bus boy, dishwasher, janitor and launderer. The routine became so familiar we sang, discussed Scripture, prayed the Rosary or simply chatted while we worked. We encouraged one another to complete even the smallest job as if we preparing for Jesus. We tried to perfect the age old attempt of all Christians to become Mary while not forgetting the work of Martha. While other girls our age experimented with new clothes, new make-up and different lifestyles, while they fought with college roommates and the girlfriends of their ex-boyfriends, we discussed, and even argued over, the placement of chairs, the fold of a bed sheet and the proper placement of books in the chapel.

I felt strong and confident with my new persona as I walked unto the small, hillside campus of the local junior college just blocks from one of Northern California's top surfing spots in Santa Cruz that first Wednesday morning. The nylons, white blouse and black polyester jumper, such an obvious breech of local social norms, clarified for me and all my classmates and teachers, I was somehow different.

Some asked outright, "What is your uniform for? What are you?" Others were more discreet, whispering to their friends or attempting a sideways glance. I hadn't been prepared for the attention or the questions. I proudly explained to anyone listening what it meant to be a Sister-in-training. Not a nun. Nuns were cloistered. They didn't leave the convent, they prayed several times during the day and night, and they only spoke for brief periods during the day, like the Poor Clare's right down the street from the college. We were missionary, with houses in California, Oregon, New Mexico, Arizona, Taiwan and Hong Kong. We ran retreat houses, schools, and group homes. I attempted to explain the beauty of a vocation; to share the gift of grace and the strength of my decisions.

But our work and our vows of poverty and obedience didn't interest them; celibacy did. Didn't I like men? And sex? Had I ever had it? Could I give it up? What about children? Didn't I want children? I explained how God called me to be Sister to all people, to give my life in service to others. They couldn't fathom giving up sex forever. I thought little of it.

Sr. Thomas warned me about establishing relationships outside of community. I discussed class material as necessary and tried never to be rude, but didn't allow myself to be drawn back into the secular world or the desire to be accepted and loved. Certain that any attempt to exist in both convent life and the secular world would be a constant threat to my vocation, I left the world behind quickly and swiftly, completely unaware how systematically my free spirited, spontaneous personality would be siphoned from my soul.

Each evening, balanced atop the stationery bike on the novitiate balcony, staring into the redwoods, I rode two miles as I imagined pedaling home; sure to reach my destination in less than six months. I pedaled desperately, hoping my simplistic exercise might silence the persistent voices inside telling me I didn't belong. I pedaled, rhythmically, praying I hadn't made a mistake and I didn't actually need to go home.

"People from broken homes never make it in religious life," Sr. Thomas said, conceding my parents had never really divorced, but still questioning my father's mental stability, and therefore, mine. She hoped my mother's strong faith would override my father's inability to commit and his manic depression. My vocation, in other words, was shaky at best. I wanted more than anything to be the perfect Sister, to do God's will, to die to myself in reparation for all I'd done as a teenager. If I didn't accept her authority, I would never survive. Sr. Thomas's voice quickly became the voice of God.

Seven years of not eating chocolate vanished the day Sister urged me to eat a brownie, one of many occasions in which she reminded me a good appetite indicated a true vocation. Sr. Thomas overturned my decision to live the gospel faithfully, rather than register to vote, insisting that, as a good Catholic, I had a responsibility to vote Republican. She forbade me to live frugally, by the example of St. Francis, because God rewarded us with luxuries for leaving mother, brothers and sisters to follow Christ. I tried to convince others of my perspective, certain that if only they knew how I knew poverty or the joys of complete dependence on God, they'd agree with me. Sr. Thomas interrupted my explanations with a lecture on the importance of obedience above all things and a reminder that my intelligence didn't negate my need to be obedient; which God valued more than brains.

Sr. Thomas's snub at my intelligence had become familiar. I'd always maintained an A-/B average, but I never fathomed I possessed higher than average intelligence until Sr. Thomas's sister Nancy administered IQ tests for all the postulants and novices in preparation for her own clinical exams. I scored 139, which Sr. Thomas explained made me even more susceptible to the temptations of the devil. My intelligence would be my downfall; pride, my greatest sin.

Surrounded by young women, many of whom had difficulty with the classes we took at the junior college, others who'd lived such sheltered lives they had very little knowledge of what I considered to be the real world, I heeded Sr. Thomas's warning. I thought too much, she said. I needed to keep busy so I didn't have time to think. She added chores, above and beyond the duties of the others, to my study and work schedule. Regardless of which assignment Sr. Thomas handed me or how much extra work she piled on to curb my pride or forget about those I loved, I rose to the challenge. I weeded the gardens surrounding the swimming pool, cleaned toilets in the priests' house, swept driveways, organized closets, and painted various parts of the building. I picked and peeled so many apples for pies and apple sauce each week that I developed carpal tunnel syndrome. I filled any free time with odd jobs. I kept busy and did the work assigned to me without question, caught, as I'd always believed I'd been, in a tug-of-war with the devil.

Replacing the college parking sticker on the station wagon window, I followed each detail precisely, certain that doing my best at even the smallest task would lead to salvation. As I wiped off the last of my finger smudges, packed up my utensils, slammed the door and walked away, the crash of the glass against the car frame startled me. I turned around to see the window in millions of pea size chunks of glass, my sanctity shattered at my feet. I cried and giggled simultaneously. My stomach muscles tightened and my arms and legs snapped like a tightly rung dish rag only to fall lifeless beneath me as I dropped to the ground where those who heard the crash and came running, found me.

When I failed at even the most minor detail, I requested penance immediately. We had no Chapter of Faults, the practice of admitting sins in public had been discarded with Church reforms in the late 1960's, but Sr. Thomas believed humility required postulants and novices to reveal their faults to her to receive an appropriate penance. She did not hear confessions, which the Church reserved for the priesthood; she simply expected to be told of minor infractions. We reserved our sins for the Confessional.

One night as the clock struck ten, I held the tip of the page tightly between two fingers. Two quick pages left to finish the chapter. Ten minutes, tops. I finished, marked my place with a holy card of the Blessed Mother, and reached to turn out the light. Immediately following morning Mass, I approached Sr. Thomas to request a penance. The penance, simple: recite one Hail Mary. The lecture, much longer: obedience is more important than anything. She assigned me to read Saint Therese of Lisieux to learn how following the most minor detail of the rule is the quickest path to sanctity. The Little Way she espoused meant she lived simply, tolerating obnoxious companions, sacrificing for the sake of others, and practicing humility. I needed to curb my pride, let go of my personal preferences, and listen to the will of God as expressed in the rules. Spiritual reading should not replace obedience.

As my mishaps multiplied, penances increased. Three Hail Mary's, Ten Hail Mary's, Litanies of Humility, and sometimes an entire rosary. Determined to become meek under Sr. Thomas's tutelage, I prayed for the grace to shut my mouth and offer up little sacrifices throughout each day.

On the afternoon of the benefactors' luncheon, responsible for dishing up one hundred twenty small servings of Easy Lemon Pie into short stemmed ice cream dishes and adding a mint sprig to the rim of each glass, I carefully placed each dish on the three-tiered dessert cart to store in the walk-in refrigerator until serving time. As I rolled the carts down the slight incline into the main kitchen, I reached around to close the latch on the heavy metal door, turning around with just enough time to witness the two carts filled with perfectly chilled dessert, tip over, spewing the Easy Lemon Pie and the delicately placed mint leaves across the kitchen floor.

I slumped down, pulled my knees to my chest, and tucked my head in my crossed arms, unable to even cry. This would be the end of it. Sr. Thomas would not have any penance for me; she would never forgive this. I may as well go pack my bags. She put up with the huge tub of coleslaw we threw out because I pushed the tip of my finger into the blade of the food processor. She'd been patient when I cracked a measuring cup into a batch of cookie dough, and she replaced the blouses I burned with the iron. She remained relatively calm the morning I fell off the step stool dumping five pounds of coffee grounds over my head and across the floor, and the time the pilot light from the urn flared into my nose and burned my eyebrows, eyelashes, and the inside of my nostrils.

One hundred twenty dishes and the dessert destroyed with them, at serving time, could not be fixed. One hundred twenty women, our wealthiest benefactors, waited to be served. The others worked around me to pick up the glass, mop up the pie and clear the mess, gathering every available dish for a scoop of ice cream and a cookie. The women needed refreshment. I needed redemption.

As the line between mistake and sin blurred, I became brutally honest with Sr. Thomas about my faults, not only in deed but in thought as well. I examined every thought that entered my mind and each feeling as it surfaced. I relied on Sr. Thomas to tell me what to confess and what not to; I no longer trusted myself and relied on Sr. Thomas to clarify right and wrong for me. Under her tutelage black became black and white, white with no room for discussion or areas of grey.

I attempted desperately to ignore the nagging voice inside that kept whispering, "You're not meant to be here." I could not admit that maybe I'd entered too quickly. I kept thinking maybe I should have entered a cloister to live a life of prayer and silence or I needed to find a way to live stricter poverty. Gathering courage, I explained myself to Sr. Thomas: I need to write to cloistered communities to follow God's call. Can I write from the convent or did I need to go home to pursue my true vocation?

"You shouldn't write," Sr. Thomas spoke in her typical matter-of-fact voice: We accepted you, didn't we? You know God's will. You are so presumptuous. A call to the cloister is a special vocation. Most people from broken homes don't make it in religious life. You should be grateful. Your vocation is a gift. Stop questioning.

"I wanted to know if I should go home to write to the cloister, or if I might stay here to write, not whether or not I should write." I tried to explain, stunned by the confidence in my voice.

"Don't write. If we feel it is God's will for you to be somewhere else, we will let you know. You have too much time to think. Just keep busy." Sr. Thomas stood

23

up and with her hand near my shoulder, led me toward the office door, ending the discussion.

Attempting no response, I returned to my room on automatic pilot. The superior is the voice of God. I had to believe. Life made no sense if I didn't. Don't write. Stop questioning. Biting my pillow in an attempt to muffle my sobs, I prayed to believe. I longed for the lumps and bumps of the rags packed tightly into the stained, smelly mattress back home and my light blue pillow, drenched many nights in tears, that heard my prayers and petitions to be loved, forgiven and understood.

I couldn't ignore Sr. Thomas or let her hear me cry. She hated crying. Crying is childish, she said, a lack of faith. I wanted to talk to someone, but I couldn't. Sr. Thomas made it very clear from the first day that community business stayed in community. I just needed to believe. I convinced myself Sr. Thomas knew best. Why would God call me to the cloister? I needed to be grateful for my calling, sinner that I was. I needed to bloom where God planted me, like Sister always told me to do. God would give me everything else, if I just kept busy and did the work assigned to me without question.

"Ricky has a tumor on his chest; the doctor thinks its cancer." The first words out of my mother's mouth after our superficial greeting during one of her monthly visits felt as if she'd backhanded me. They found the tumor on his chest. It took weeks to determine his type of tumor, but most common children's cancers had eight percent survival rates with chemo. His odds seemed good.

How will Karen, twenty-year-old mother of two, deal with the constant fear and confusion that certainly consumed her? I knew she would survive. I knew, because that's what Arnold's did. We survived. We survived our father leaving, Regina's husband dying, and Loyed's wife battling brain tumors. Cancer had become a familiar foe. Four-month-old Ricky would survive.

With Mom's weekly phone calls and monthly visits, I heard bits and pieces of Ricky's life. Karen's intermittent calls left my knees weak and my shoulders shaking. Ricky's rising white cell count, fevers and infections, overnight stays in the hospital, chemotherapy, hair loss, and pale skin. The hospital became her world. Surrounded by dying children, they faced death early and often. I promised prayers, offered words of encouragement and hope as best I could, and hung up in tears. Could I not be of greater support at home to baby sit Scott, clean her house, or cook a meal?

Sr. Thomas assured me Karen needed spiritual support more than a housekeeper. Ricky's birthday being on the Feast of Our Lady of Fatima, Our

Lady would keep him safe. My daily rosary tripled instantly; I added the Seven Joys and the Seven Sorrows chaplets; litanies and chaplets occupied my thoughts constantly. During a pilgrimage to Our Lady of Peace Church, for the novena to Our Lady of Fatima, I knelt devoutly behind the very last pew in the overcrowded church, praying for Ricky and for salvation: my own, my family's, the world's. Head bowed, eyes closed, I pleaded with the Blessed Mother to hear my prayers and take them to Jesus. Feeling someone's foot hit the side of my leg, I opened my eyes to witness a petite, gray haired woman lying behind my back. As others scrambled to help her to her feet, I shook with shame. That evening I approached Sr. Thomas to receive an appropriate penance.

"You try to be too pious. Do you think you're holier than everyone else?" Sr. Thomas assured me that my attempt to be over pious, to be holier than those around me, had led to injury. My pride had tripped the woman, not my feet. My feet, apparently, would be much easier to reign in than my pride. She instructed me to recite the Litany of Humility twice a day, to beg God for the grace to put others before me. *"From the desire of being loved, honored, praised, preferred to others, deliver me O Lord… That others be loved more than I… others be chosen and I set aside … others may be preferred to me in everything…Jesus grant me the grace to desire it."* I prayed fervently, quickly committing the prayer to memory, relying on the litany to carry me through each time someone commended or reprimanded me.

Keeping a journal kept me sane. No longer just a diary to secretly write about my latest crush, I wrote of my spiritual desires, begged forgiveness for my failings, prayed for strength to love. I could be myself before God with no pretense or falsehood.

I explained it simply as a prayer journal the afternoon Sr. Thomas approached to ask why I had an extra book at my place in chapel. I wrote for me and for my vocation: a place to vent, to dream, to be alone with God. She accused me of pride, reminding me St. Therese's superiors had commanded her, under obedience, to keep a journal; but that she had never told me to keep a journal. By the end of Sr. Thomas's interrogation, I recognized I'd been duped by the devil again; fooled by my pride. Teeming with guilt, I fired accusations of arrogance and stupidity inward as my shoulders slumped and the vulgar taste of depression lined my gums. Sr. Thomas assured me keeping any journals I brought from home would only weaken my resolve but burning all my diaries, journals, and poetry immediately was the quickest step to secure my vocation.

Sitting alone on the edge of the warm hearth near her office, I tore page after page from my notebooks and binders, gazing as flames curled the edges and devoured the years of reflection about my life, my dad, those I loved; burning the

25

poems of anguish, love and confusion so common to young girls, slowly consumed first the paper, next my soul. A virgin, offered here in sacrifice, burned at the altar to appease the gods.

As I walked away from the fireplace, Sr. Thomas patted me on the shoulder with the weight of her long sturdy fingers, squint her eyes with a grimace, and closed the door behind me.

I picked up a basketball, headed toward the makeshift court at the far end of the dorm buildings and pounded the ball on the pavement. Dressed in habit, I dribbled, dodging imaginary opponents and going in for a layup. I allowed the rush of movement and the rhythmic echo of the ball to force the tension from my body and soul. Each time the ball smashed against the backboard, my memories slammed one against another and my gut told me not to let go. I had no choice if I wanted to succeed as a Sister. Sr. Thomas, much wiser and more experienced, had seen too many young women try to hold memories of family and friends, even boyfriends. She had seen too many young women lose their vocations; she wanted to help me preserve mine.

Saint Jude quickly became my greatest friend. I had so much to overcome: my pride, my intelligence, my broken home, my father's mental illness and my own emotional attitudes. Sr. Thomas had laid it out so clearly, so often; few were more impossible than me.

When the time came to request a religious name before I officially entered the novitiate and received the habit, I remained indecisive until the afternoon Tina called, making me promise not to say anything to Mom. Jude was Dad's confirmation name. "That's what she said," Tina added. "And the time she left Dad, she came back on the ninth day of a novena to St. Jude 'cause she was pregnant with you. Mom thought you might not take the name if you knew." St. Jude had been my dad's patron and brought my parents back together.

During prayer that afternoon, I realized the night I crawled up the stairs with a hangover, stopping to offer my life to God, and the day I decided to enter the convent, both happened on October 28, the feast of St. Jude. St. Jude had been my protector and patron all along. I tried to stop crying, afraid that Sr. Thomas might walk in. But not even my fear of getting caught crying so close to my official entrance day, stifled my sobs. God and St. Jude had been with me throughout my journey.

The elderly Sisters gathered in the recreation room for the simple twenty-minute service welcoming my classmate and me into the novitiate. Sr. Thomas placed the black habit and white veil on my outstretched arms with the Rule and Constitutions on top, admonishing us to enter into an intense year of prayer and study in the ways of religious life. As she introduced us as Sister Mary Jude of the Holy Face and Sr. Nathaniel of the Holy Cross, everyone rose to offer the Sign of Peace with hugs and handshakes.

Moving to the library to sign the official papers promising we would never expect a monetary return for any services rendered if we did not persevere, I picked up the pen to sign my name in the official enrollment book. Speaking aloud as I began, "Sr. Nathaniel of the Holy Cross."

"No," someone shouted. "You're not Sr. Nathaniel; you're Sr. Mary Jude."

Everyone chuckled but for the next three days, each time someone called Sr. Nathaniel's name, I turned around. If someone called mine, I never responded. Others took my confusion lightly, thinking it almost cute. I shuttered, wondering if my confusion could be a subconscious sign that I wasn't meant to be Sister Mary Jude. Not that I had chosen the wrong name, but that I had chosen the wrong life. I attempted to giggle with the others. But just as my siblings' accusations that Dad went crazy because of me seeped into my soul, so did my inability to remember my own name. I tried to ignore the thoughts as superstitious and nonsensical, certain that the devil tempted me because he hated those who followed God faithfully.

The Rules and Constitutions and the Bible, became my spiritual guide, material for meditation, and bedtime leisure reading. I scoured prayer books, the lives of the Saints, and the life of St. Francis. I recited chaplets to Our Lady and the Sacred Heart, made the Stations of the Cross daily, and prayed incessantly that God break me to make me a saint.

At nineteen, just a year after entering, Sr. Thomas put me in charge of the retreat house kitchen, an assignment typically reserved for professed Sisters. As a postulant, I became responsible for the entire operation: menu planning, shopping and ordering, cooking and cleaning for twenty-five women on a daily basis and close to one hundred people each weekend, I managed the budget and directed the workings of the kitchen, dining room, and dishwashing station. I baked thirty dozen cookies every Tuesday, shopped on Wednesday after school, processed orders on Thursday, peeled twenty pounds of fresh carrots and potatoes, breaded 150 pieces of fish, and made 150-200 homemade crescent rolls each Friday.

Moving from one task to another quickly and efficiently, I slept quickly and soundly each night and had a purpose for each day. I created recipes, introduced new foods, improved the nutrition for our elderly Sisters, and stayed within the original budget they'd been working with for years. I savored each opportunity to serve appetizing, delicious, life-enhancing meals to those I'd grown to love just as I'd prepared chicken enchiladas, fresh cinnamon rolls, and zucchini bread for my family back home. I invited God into the kitchen with me each morning and felt

His presence, almost tangible, throughout the day. I created meals incorporating all I'd read about prayerful attentiveness to detail and serving God by serving others.

This continued until I became a first year novice and could not officially be in charge of the kitchen. Instead my time and attention turned completely to learning more about religious life. Called the canonical year, novices cut all ties with the outside. We could no longer have visits from the family, did not run errands, and stopped studying outside the walls of the convent. As the Canonical year came to a close, Sr. Thomas called me to the Hill just before Evening Prayer. "We need you to take charge of the kitchen again. Sr. Jean Ann's being transferred."

"I'm not going back to Cabrillo?"

"I registered you for a nutrition class and Cabrillo's Culinary program. You'll be at school three days a week. You've done the kitchen before, and you won't have retreat house cleaning this time, so I'm sure you can handle both."

Despite the grueling schedule balancing kitchen management with culinary arts and nutrition classes at the junior college, and on-going religious classes, prayer and community schedules, I suddenly felt completely alive. I balanced the infirmed Sisters' diets using computer programs at the school, calculated the exact price per serving for each meal served for the retreats, introduced quiches, chef salads, and lasagnas to replace the twenty-year-old menus, and established rules and practices that aligned our kitchen with the standards of safety set by the local health codes. For the month before Christmas, I rose an hour before Morning Prayer to start the yeast rising for 220 loaves of cinnaomon bread we distributed to our benefactors. I poured over pot after pot of marshmallows, melting them quickly, adding green food coloring, tossing in Corn Flakes, and shaping them into Christmas wreathes for others.

Definitely busy, I felt none of the usual bitterness towards others who didn't do their own jobs – unless their jobs directly influenced the rules I established for the kitchen. Arguments with other novices became rare, and my frustration levels dropped drastically. Leftovers became scarce and presentation became central. My school portfolio of recipes, budgets and menus overflowed with letters of thanks and appreciation from women who noticed differences in the food after years of attending retreats.

As my finals in Food Science approached, I felt confident that my kitchen ministry would continue to improve even without more advanced classes. I'd received the basics; I didn't need hotel management skills and other requirements like my classmates. The morning of my cooking final, Sr. Thomas called me into her office just after Mass.

"Yes Sister." I said, completely unaware of any misconduct or misunderstanding with any Sisters that might make for a confrontational meeting.

"Sit down. I need to speak with you." Sister's monotone voice betrayed no emotion. "Beginning tomorrow, you will no longer be in charge of the kitchen. You have become proud and arrogant. Humility is your priority if you ever hope to make first vows."

A blender on full speed would have caused less damage to my soul than the words spoken. I sat stunned. Questions cascaded through my brain. What had I done wrong? Who had I harmed? What did I miss? Why? Is it a sin to enjoy an assignment? Is it a sin to be good, very good, at what you do? Feeling like a boulder lodged in the pit of my stomach, I wanted to vomit, but barely mustered enough muscle to make my legs move. I wobbled out in silence. I'd finally found a reason to be proud of myself and my pride had destroyed me. As my jaws clenched, I fought my anger. If being good at what I do is wrong, and being proud of myself is evil, being angry at my superior could never be right. Besides, I had no time to brood, I had a final to prepare: chicken breast on a bed of wild rice, served with homemade mushroom sauce and a side of asparagus.

Sr. Thomas seemed to be the only person bothered by my success in the kitchen; everyone else sought my advice and continued to look to me for leadership. I returned to other tasks, desperately convincing myself Sr. Thomas knew best and that I needed humility, but nothing filled the void created by my loss, but I convinced myself that I wanted only to do God's will and I could find that only in Sr. Thomas's decisions.

One of the Sisters stopped me on the walkway to the kitchen as I carried in the week's groceries. "Your mom called. She asked me to tell you Vernon died. He committed suicide. His brother found him hanging in the shower." I stood, frozen, informed very matter-of-factly, and in passing, that a friend since preschool and my most significant relationship in high school had committed suicide. Completely incapable of knowing how to handle the news, I headed to the chapel, my knees trembling and my soul crumbling. I knelt at the back, staring beyond the tongues of fire representing the Holy Spirit in the stain glass before me. Memories stampeded over mountaintops, from beyond the evergreens, shouting about Vernon.

When I decided to enter the convent, I broke the news as he passed the porch. Good luck, he'd said. No emotion. No discussion. I instantly understood that the intensity, so excruciating and painful just months earlier, had been completely one-sided. He only wanted to win the argument and get me to have sex, nothing more.

His advances, although never genuine, did not erase our history. One of my oldest childhood friends had committed suicide. Nothing erased that.

Kneeling at the back of the chapel, I held my breath. Like a soda bottle cap, foaming as the seams split, I tried to keep from bursting. Sr. Thomas would be angry if I cried. When Uncle Pete, my mentor from TEC died months earlier, she'd tolerated my tears for about an hour when she finally said they showed a lack of faith and my friend wouldn't want me to cry. To her, God protected me from Vernon's evil advances and preserved me to be the Bride of Christ.

My purity no longer in question, I burst. As my shoulders shook and sobs invaded the secluded chapel, I wanted only to run to my room, flop on my bed, pull out my journals and weep. Fire had consumed the journals filled with his memory. I knew that the faster I stifled my emotion, the stronger my faith.

I looked down at my watch, swallowed my tears, and convinced myself faith would sustain me. I stood up, walked to the nearest bathroom to wash my face, and returned with jaw tightened, for Rosary and Office. Karen and Tina both called that night to ask about me but I assured them his family had my prayers and I would not be attending the funeral. Prayer became my solution for everything. I had no other recourse to deal with the pain that surrounded me. I relied completely on the faithful intercession of St. Jude, Patron of Impossible Cases.

"Sister Jude, I need to speak with you in my office." Sr. Thomas appeared to be suffering from one of her frequent headaches. Tammy had been in tears all morning and Sr. Elaine Marie hadn't left her room. Sr. Ignatius, made her first vows Saturday and had left for her home visit. I understood they might miss her, but didn't comprehend why anyone who cared for her would be crying? I walked into Sr. Thomas's office grateful for the admonition against particular friendship.

"I need to ask you some questions. I expect our conversation to remain completely confidential." Sr. Thomas's matter-of-fact warning for confidentiality seemed completely unnecessary since I saw Nancy sitting beside her desk. Whenever Nancy appeared unannounced, something significant had happened. She'd appeared when Sr. Paul sleep-walked onto the driveway overhang, when Sr. Wendy Francis dreamt of saints and angels appearing to her, and when Sr. Elaine Marie punched a hole in the wall in a fit of anger. My mind turned circles and flips trying to discover some mistake, something I'd done, some reason Nancy would show up wanting to talk to me.

"Did you ever join Sr. Ignatius for hot chocolate after lights out?"

"No, never."

Sr. Ignatius broke ten o'clock curfew, but she just made vows, they couldn't be that mad.

"Did you know others did?"

"Yes, I heard."

"Did Sr. Ignatius ever make a pass at you?"

"A what?" I asked, trying to shake the shock from my ears.

"A pass. Did she ever show interest in you beyond friendship?"

"Are you kidding?" Realizing the severity of the moment, I straightened up in my chair and answered directly, "No. We were nothing more than friends. Ever."

"We need to know if anything ever happened. Did you ever kiss?"

My stomach turned. I'd moved beyond boyfriends and they were asking me about homosexuality, forbidden by the church, and unthinkable for someone vowing chastity.

"No," I said simply.

"You knew Leslie before she entered. Did she ever indicate to you that she is lesbian?" Nancy continued to show little emotion, just the empathetic slant of her chin as she spoke. I noted her switch from Sr. Ignatius's religious name.

"No." My throat began to close, suffocated by my thoughts. Leslie'd shared many escapades but they'd all been with boys. She never, ever hinted anything.

"Thank you for your time. Do not speak to anyone about this." Nancy spoke as my superior. "Tammy will be flying home this afternoon. Pray for her; she will not be returning."

I prayed, immediately and desperately, uncertain what to do with the revelation that Leslie and Tammy had been caught making out on the night of her vows. I thanked God I never got enmeshed in their love affair or fell prey to the debauchery and their tangled web of deceit. I prayed for the grace to persevere.

Sifting through the photos Sr. Thomas asked me to throw out, the disappointment, anger and emptiness in my soul mystically transferred to the images in front of me, pain dissipating as the photos of all who had left, disappeared. Each time I reached for the white handkerchief stuffed in my pocket to wipe a tear from my eye, I mourned for the unspoken goodbye to my Sisters, to Vernon and to my dad.

On any given day Sr. Thomas told us to be packed and ready to switch rooms with others in the novitiate within the hour. She required a constant rotation of work assignments and seats in the chapel and dining room, reminding us of our missionary status, encouraging us to remain detached from even the slightest comfort or familiarity. Detachment fit comfortably in the "doesn't matter to me" attitude I so carefully crafted throughout my teens. I relished the opportunity to remain unattached and completely at the whim of my superior, and consequently, the will of God. I never thought much about the future or my life in five or ten years. I simply wanted to do God's will, as directed by my superiors.

Sr. Thomas spoke of each assignment as a mission and of every task being of equal importance, but no matter how often we rotated places in chapel or exchanged rooms in the convent to remind us we were missionaries, never attached to place or situation, everyone knew Sr. Thomas's heart longed for China. Watching Sr. Nathaniel prepare her passport and hearing the admiration in Sr. Thomas's voice each time she spoke, left me longing for Taiwan. I approached Sr. Thomas to suggest, in support of her cause, that I be sent to Taiwan after first vows.

"You are the last person on earth I would send overseas," she began. "You're far too immature and emotionally unstable. You'd never handle the adjustments. You're not like Sr. Nathaniel."

"You told me I'm mature. You said my upbringing made me more responsible, that I needed to be patient, that they lived cushy lives. You said it all the time." The words spilled from my mouth emptying the knot in the pit of my stomach with an uncontrollable flow, splattering about, leaving residue everywhere.

"Look at you. You get too emotional. Over your nephew, your dead friends, your father. You need humility. You're going to Oregon to be Sr. Cecilia's assistant in the kitchen. Sr. Ruth can monitor your progress. Forget Taiwan."

Sr. Thomas stood up and walked towards the office door, putting an end to the discussion. Rejection, once again, took up residence in the center of my soul – convincing me to cling viciously to my desire to go overseas.

Three days after my arrival in Oregon, Sr. Thomas sent word that Sr. Cecilia would be leaving in two days for a three-month home visit to China. Sr. Thomas made a point to clarify that Sr. Cecilia remained in charge, not me; but until she returned, I would be responsible for the kitchen.

A three-month home visit to China had to be planned, not determined on the spur of the moment. Visas, passports, physical exams took time. Sr. Thomas had known for months. I couldn't formulate the words that had to be true – or admit, even to myself, that Sr. Thomas used me.

Instead I kept telling myself that Sr. Thomas spoke for God; God did not want me in Taiwan. Sr. Thomas knew best. I would learn humility, Sr. Cecilia or not. Like Jacob who wrestled with the angel of God, I spent hours each night, in the darkened chapel, fighting against the will of God. Sr. Thomas's words, "too immature ... emotionally unstable ... last person on earth ..." swirled through my mind, interrupting my prayer and crushing my soul.

The more I questioned, the more frustrated I became. I reread Story of a Soul, the life of St. Therese of Lisieux, trying to grasp how one who never left her cloister, became the patron saint of missionaries. In the small, meaningless tasks of daily life she became holy. She desired missionary life yet remained faithful to God by offering her life as a gift of love, to be love to others as God loved her. I'd read it all before, but after seven months of longing and inner turmoil, I opened a prayer book and incidentally turned to my profession card: "Christ learned obedience from what he suffered and when perfected became the source of salvation for all who believe." With a sudden burst of enlightenment, I fell to my knees. Bent to the floor, I offered my life as a gift of obedience. If Therese offered love, I promised obedience. My desire to go to Taiwan disappeared. Content to serve God stateside, with no external sign of the cosmic movement that had taken place within, peace permeated my daily activities.

A week later, just seven months after my arrival in Oregon, Sr. Thomas visited.

"Sr. Cecilia has nothing but good things to say about how you ran things in her absence and how you're such a good assistant. You don't argue or try to get your own way like so many other young Sisters have in the past."

I wondered the purpose of this little speech until Sr. Thomas finally made her point: "Sr. Nathaniel is having a hard time. She's really hot tempered and keeps clashing with Sr. Ann. I don't want her to be alone anymore. She needs another American, someone who can deal with the elderly Sisters. You've done a good job here. We need you to help Sr. Nathaniel in Taiwan. You leave in August."

Working on the books in the accounting office, like I did every Tuesday and Thursday morning, I heard Br. Pete's footsteps as he passed through the dining room from the back door. Br. Pete, a young Franciscan friar who worked around the retreat house several days a week, a handyman of sorts, was my companion in projects involving heavy lifting and moving furniture. We chatted about St. Francis, enjoyed cool afternoon refreshment together, and encouraged one another in our pursuit of sanctity.

His footsteps stopped behind me. "Good morning," he said as he placed his hands on my shoulders. The gentle squeeze as he backed up sent a chill down my spine. "Have a good day." He left, but my legs were shaking, leaving me unable to focus on the books in front of me.

I closed the books, locked the office and headed straight into the pantry, rolled out the flour and sugar bins and began measuring ingredients for cookies. Twenty-five people on retreat this weekend, ten men. Oatmeal or peanut butter? Chocolate chip. Men like chocolate chip. Peanut butter could be just as filling. I'd bake both. Apples had to be peeled, too. Sr. Cecilia would be making pies. I'd peel the apples. Men meant more pies, six pieces per pie instead of eight; and many more sold on Sunday. Men always bought more pies.

By eleven I'd finished the cookies and apples. I'd have plenty of time to sweep, mop and wax the floors. Sweep and mop every week, wax and buff every other week. The dining room, comfortably fitting about twelve tables for six, wasn't too big, and rarely filled up, but I still cleaned the whole thing.

As I turned the chairs over like a child at the end of a school day, I sang: "*Oh, Lord, you are the center of my life. I will always love you, I will always serve you, I will always keep you in my life…*" grateful for the opportunity to keep busy on a day that began so oddly.

Turning around to grab a chair, I noticed Br. Pete walking towards me.

"Hey," he said, "Can I give you a hug?"

"Sure, is everything okay?" He'd never asked for a hug before but I opened my arms to embrace him, nervously.

"You've been working hard. I thought you could use a hug."

"Thanks," I said awkwardly.

As he turned to go to his car, I walked straight to the office and shut the door behind me, falling into the chair, baffled. Br. Pete and I had certainly become friendly with one another, but his physical advances unnerved me. Was he challenging my vows? Did he question his own?

"Sr. Ruth, may I speak with you?"

"Sure, what's up?"

"Brother Pete just asked me for a hug."

"He what?"

"And this morning he squeezed my shoulders."

"What'd you do?"

"I hugged him. What should I have done?"

"I'll take care of it."

When Sr. Thomas heard of the incident, she flew me to California a month ahead of schedule and confronted Br. Pete, who said he wanted to boost my spirits because I seemed to lack confidence. She reprimanded him for trying to seduce one of her Sisters and explained that he obviously did not know me very well because I had always been proud and arrogant and had no problem with my self-esteem. I never saw Br. Pete again.

34

ASSISTANT DIRECTORESS NAMED . . . Fran- ciscan Sister Jude Arnold has been named assistant food service directoress at Our Lady of Peace Retreat House, Beaverton.

She is a 1981 graduate of St. Vincent Ferrer High School, Vallejo, Calif. She joined the Franciscan Missionary Sisters in 1982.

SISTER
MARY JUDE
ARNOLD

35

"Christ learned obedience from what he suffered; and when perfected, he became the source of eternal salvation for all who obey him."

Hebrews 5:8

✠

In Remembrance of Profession of First Vows

Sister Mary Jude
of the Holy Face
O.S.F.

Sister Mary Matthew
of the Holy Cross
O.S.F.

✠

August 6, 1985

Sister
M.
Jude
Arnold

Franciscan Missionary Sister M. Jude Arnold, daughter of Mrs. Harry Arnold of Rodeo and a graduate of St. Vincent Ferrer High School in Vallejo, is off to the Orient for her first assignment: working in the Sisters' community at a hostel for students near FuJen Catholic University at Taipei.

Growing Up Asian
August 1986 – March 1993

Blinking to remove sleep from my burning eyes, I struggled to free myself from the mosquito net strangling my legs, and reminded myself I had landed in Taiwan just twelve hours earlier. Garbled words of childhood Christmas carols whistled outside the window as the thick, sticky air enveloped me and I struggled to understand why the ice cream truck playing songs about Santa, drove through the streets of Taiwan at 5:30 in the morning in late August. I learned later, the garbage truck played music to alert everyone to run out and toss their bags in the back as the truck drove by. Walking outside, I felt the air hanging around me like a wet rag, almost visible. Puffs of gray smoke poured from the cars and most who passed on foot or wheels, wore surgical masks. For the past four years I spent at least an hour in prayer before the day officially began and often went days seeing no one from the outside world. Honking horns, screeching buses and intermittent shouting sounded as foreign as the language spoken and the foods put before me.

Little old men on bicycles shouted towards open windows. Residents from all sides opened doors. Women in pajamas and slippers surrounded the salesmen purchasing their daily supplies of toilet paper, pork sausage, and chickens dangling precariously from a wire rack perched on the backs of the bikes. One cyclist after another rode by with slabs of raw beef, sausages, pork chops, chicken and duck dangling precariously from a wire rack perched on the back tire of the bike. My eyes were drawn to the flies and bees swarming closely behind. This had to break every sanitation code I ever memorized. I didn't have to imagine the germs growing on the meat; I leaned over and whispered, "That's disgusting; don't people die eating stuff like that?"

Without looking at me, Sr. Nathaniel said sharply, "They've been doing it for centuries. Don't be so quick to judge, it'll kill you."

Sitting in the chapel during the Mass I did not comprehend, I had plenty of time to think about Sr. Nathaniel's words. "Don't be so quick to judge…" Sr. Nathaniel and I often spent hours during novitiate judging. We judged those who didn't work as hard, those who ignored the rules, and those who lost their vocation. Why had she so sharply warned me not to judge?

"We sit in order of entrance," Sr. Nathaniel leaned in to whisper at the breakfast table, "all the time; and we eat breakfast in silence." Feeling caught in a blip in the time and space continuum, I glanced at Sr. Ann, the local superior who'd entered religious community fifty years earlier at the age of fifteen and kept rules that had disappeared in the sixties. Her stubbornness allowed her to survive the Japanese occupation, the Communist takeover, and a severe stroke; Sr. Ann should be admired and respected. One of the few living who personally knew our founder, she should be beloved and revered, not resisted. Grateful for the lessons in humility I'd encountered working with Sr. Cecilia, I silently determined to practice submission and compliance.

Each Sister dished up her own portion before we began eating. After finishing off her own meal by shoveling the entire bowl of porridge into her mouth and then slowly swallowing, Sr. Ann looked directly at me, stuck her finger on the edge of the lazy Susan and slowly inched the leftovers around until they parked in front of me. She pointed at the food and then at me, nodding her head the entire time. Seeing her sagging sorrowful eyes and her devilish grin, and desperate to curry favor, I picked up my chopsticks and continued to eat until everything was gone, ignoring the fact that I had already lost my appetite.

After our prayer of thanksgiving to end the meal (another strange custom), Sr. Ann, with a slurred Hunan accent, announced the end of grand silence. "You need to get to school. Sr. Nathaniel already signed you up for Chinese classes. She'll take you and show you around. I will talk to you more after lunch."

"May we take the bus, since it's Sister Jude's first day?"

With a frown Sr. Ann shook her head, clicked her tongue against the back of her teeth like a mother shaming her child, "Thw, thw, thw. Buses cost money, that's why you have bicycles."

"Fine." Sr. Nathaniel stomped out of the room with her jaw jutting tightly to the side. Following quickly behind her, I tried to wrap my brain around what I'd just witnessed; I'd never seen Sr. Nathaniel respond to a superior so curtly.

"Why're you so angry? We can ride bikes; no big deal."

"Everything's about money. Every single penny counts. It's ridiculous. Just wait, you'll see." Sr. Nathaniel turned abruptly and hopped on her bike.

I hadn't ridden a bike in five years and never in a dress. Mimicking Sr. Nathaniel, I stuffed my scapular into my waist belt to avoid it getting caught in the chain and climbed on, swimming upstream, one of the hundreds of bicycles that clogged the streets, dodging cars, mopeds, motorcycles, and sometimes ducks or turkeys. Engulfed by chaos, I looked up to see four cars in the middle of the intersection, each heading a different direction and honking at me. As I rolled my way to the curb to catch my breath, my nasal passages were assaulted.

Sr. Nathaniel pointed left and shouted, "Pig farm." Two oversized sheds housed massive cauldrons for brewing a concoction of slop to feed pigs. Attempting to hold my breath, I pedaled as fast as possible. The stench almost sickening, I refused to succumb. If I couldn't handle pig stew, I'd never be a good missionary. I couldn't let Sr. Thomas's original assumption that I be the last person on earth sent to the mission come true. I had to prove my worth.

Arriving on campus alone one morning, I heard music blasting from a loud speaker, and noticed everyone, including other bike riders, freeze instantly, all facing the same direction. Screeching to a halt, I imagined an air raid like I'd seen in movies. I'd seen soldiers with huge guns walking the streets and enforcing a strict curfew. Every citizen, male or female, had to join the army for two years. Maybe we were under attack. The music stopped abruptly and everyone resumed their activities, as if nothing had happened.

The flag pole in the center of the campus, according to my language teacher, stood as the focal point to which everyone turned during the playing of their National Anthem. I vaguely remembered reciting the Pledge of Allegiance in grade school; but never imagined college students freezing for the Star Spangled Banner each morning. Standing before a movie in the theatre, as practiced in Taiwan, seemed absolutely out of the question. Judgments raced to my aid helping me confront the onslaught of the unfamiliar until I remembered Americans stand before ballgames without complaint. Over the next several weeks, as my survival skills kicked in, things began to register. I had travelled to a different country, but landed in a completely other world.

"No spitting" signs hung everywhere, but "No smoking" signs hung nowhere. Men and women openly blew their noses onto the sidewalk; parents held children over gutters to pee; seatbelt laws and child safety seats were non-existent. Entire families rode on one mo-ped. Dad usually drove, with Mom's arms clasped casually around his waist, sporting a makeshift baby-carrier on her back and tucking a child in front of her. Dad had one between his knees and another sitting staunchly on the handle bars with sunglasses and a surgical mask to protect the face. Helmets were unheard of. My American concept of safety, and convenience, slowly began to crumble.

Convent customs were equally foreign. No industrialized dishwasher with just the right mix of detergents and the perfect water temperature stood waiting to devour and sanitize our dishes. Instead we scrubbed each dish in cold soapy water, rinsed in cold and quickly ran through a wok full of boiling hot water on the two burner hot plate that constituted the stove. Instead of baking forty dozen cookies on a Tuesday afternoon, I occasionally received permission to mix up a batch of cookies to bake, three at a time, in a small stove-top Dutch oven.

Manners I had meticulously mastered as a postulant were completely useless. We peeled and ate bananas without a fork, set corn-on-the-cob on the table, with no need for a special plate and tiny forks stuck in each end. Watermelon, not only did not have to be cut with a fork and knife, but was bitten off in chunks and the rind then rubbed on the face for a cool, cleansing rinse. We wore slippers around the house, scapulars only in public and veils came off in the community room in the heat of the evening. Rules that had become sacrosanct in the novitiate, and enforced by threats of penance, were yanked from beneath me.

I decided, from day one, to eat everything offered to me in this strange land: pickled vegetables, shredded dried pork, small dried fish, sweet bean soup, translucent black preserved eggs with wet rice porridge, sautéed chicken liver with gravy over rice, bitter squash and can after can of fried spam.

The morning I looked down to see worms swimming in my sweet green bean soup, I had to break the breakfast silence. "Sr. Ann, there are worms in the soup."

"They're cooked. They won't hurt you." Sr. Ann did not look up again. Sr. Nathaniel pushed her bowl away, and sat with arms crossed waiting for prayer. I took a deep breath and continued eating.

Inconvenience, I argued for years, is part of poverty. Sr. Ann and I understood poverty, or so I thought. Hesitations crept in when she began searching my garbage cans for abandoned threads, counting my toilet paper sheets, and stowing away the most delicious chocolates and cherished treats from the care package Sr. Nathaniel's mother sent. She hid away anything she thought could be later given as a gift to someone else. We had perfectly good food and should save the best for guests, Sr. Ann insisted.

"You're just stingy." Sr. Nathaniel blurted in anger, her eyes filling with tears. Stomping out of the room she shouted, "If your guests are so important, why don't you buy something for them."

With each retort, with every harsh word, and now with this outburst, I knew without a doubt, that something had to be done to save Sr. Nathaniel's vocation as Sr. Thomas indicated. Sr. Nathaniel had been thrown into an unfamiliar world. Language lessons at the community college could never have prepared her for the differences she encountered, completely alone. I had the advantage: her to warn me, to explain things, and to talk to, in English, on a daily basis. Sr. Nathaniel, had been preparing for the missions from the beginning: taking Mandarin Chinese at college, chopping vegetables with the

Chinese Sisters and being showcased as the first American Sister in thirty years to go to the missions. She fulfilled, by proxy, Sr. Thomas's personal dream of becoming a missionary.

Uncertain as to what I should or could do, I simply tried to be the mediator between Sr. Nathaniel and Sr. Ann despite how difficult it could be at times.

"Which box of chocolates does she like best?" Sr. Ann turned to me, shaking. "She can keep them. I just thought it would be nice to share with others. I didn't know she'd get so upset. She's so emotional." Noticeably upset by Sr. Nathaniel's tears, the parsimonious and miserly Sr. Ann still confiscated the most scrumptious bits and pieces each time a package arrived. Leaving me longing, as I had in America, for the poverty of St. Francis.

Sr. Ann's old fashion ideas were not limited to poverty. Desperate for physical exercise and relaxation, I asked permission to shoot hoops at the Dominican rectory down the street, only to be told I couldn't because I would lose my vow of chastity. A man would watch me, I would talk to him and then I would lose my vocation.

In utter disbelief, I forced myself not to explode with laughter at the simplicity. "If a man speaking to me makes me break my vow of chastity, then it's pretty weak already, don't you think." I offered the rhetorical question, knowing the discussion had ended.

My exercise consisted of walking through the Confucian temple and bamboo forest behind the house. Always asking permission and never leaving alone, we climbed through the long, whistling sticks of bamboo allowing a sense of sanctuary to engulf us. For a few minutes we imagined we weren't surrounded by noisy streets and factories spewing pollution into our lungs. Our second escape: the rooftop and our laundry. Each Saturday, despite the suffocating heat, I scrubbed grimy sleeves and a greasy hemline with a huge yellow bar of soap that crumbled like a chunk of cheese being grated as I rubbed it along the metal washboard. As the clothes hung lifelessly in the dank, musty air to drip dry, they scarcely kept from molding and the white slowly turned gray.

Glancing at rice paddies, I witnessed a barefoot farmer wading through ankle deep water cultivating his rice; not weeks later I stood fascinated by the apartment building growing in its stead. Scaffolds built of bamboo poles and plastic packaging ties shrouded in nets surrounded the taller buildings. No hard hats, no cranes or lifts to carry heavy objects; just simple, elderly men and women who looked as if the next wind could carry them away, harnessing bamboo poles across their shoulders with buckets of plaster and brick hanging on either end.

Learning Chinese fascinated and absolutely absorbed me. Relying on memorized Psalms and familiar Biblical stories, I deciphered the Chinese characters piece by piece, my Chinese prayer book and Bible becoming supplemental textbooks. I listened to every conversation on the street, the bus or the television. I made flash cards, kept a notebook in my purse, and carried a dictionary with me everywhere. I studied everything, from street signs to newspapers. My mind never rested and I felt absolutely exhausted.

Anyone who claims to be learning a new language without utter, absolute exhaustion is lying. Surrounded by chaotic noises of a foreign language, deciphering each word said and attempting to communicate, is not only a mental task, every muscle in your body is taxed. Despite the exhaustion, language study offered continual fodder for a good laugh around the dinner table.

With red hair, blue eyes and a foreigner's nose, I would not be mistaken for Chinese and, therefore, decided no one expected perfection. I spoke freely, accepting others' corrections and laughter as opportunity to do better next time. Monosyllabic characters, numerous homophones and many words made up of two characters left room for lots of confusion. One wrong sound or misuse of a basic tone might change the entire meaning of a sentence.

Mistaking "pibow" for "bowpi" I once explained that the skin removed at circumcision (not my purse) hit a man in the head on the bus. Sr. Nathaniel once said her 'pigu' (butt), instead of her 'pifu' (skin) easily got sunburned. A student at school yelled across the open air quad to a classmate, "You look great today with no 'kudza' (pants) when she meant to say 'hudza' (beard).

I said everything possible, whenever I could, mistakes or not. In five months, I had a reading and writing vocabulary of 3000 words. Simple words like 'excuse me' and 'thank you' still sounded stiff and unnatural and to this day, my Mandarin remains obviously American. Still, throwing myself completely into the culture allowed me to make connections and enter into a world outside of America that left me forever changed.

Much more than correct tones and proper pronunciation, I began to think Chinese. Instead of saying "Good Morning" or "How are you?" when encountering another person in public, Chinese greet one another with "Have you eaten?" When you return home, others announce, "You're home," a greeting acknowledging your absence left emptiness they are glad is now filled.

"You home. You home now." Sr. Daphne or Sr. John had announced from the sidewalk every afternoon when we had arrived home from school or from running errands during our training in California. "Yes, we're home."

One of us would answer curtly, mumbling amongst ourselves about stating the obvious and being nosey.

"You haven't eaten. Eat. Eat," they always insisted.

Missing an occasional meal, a rare taste of independence, we cherished; being greeted as children, by two Chinese Sisters who spoke very little English, led only to resentment. "I know I haven't eaten. I will. Don't worry."

Sr. Daphne and Sr. John demonstrated quirks foreign to most Americans. Jello and ice cream were placed on the griddle, just over the pilot light, to warm up before eating; See's Chocolates they'd received as gifts were packed into moth balls to be saved for feast days; their mattresses were propped up with red bricks to reduce occurrences of acid reflux; meals of special ingredients, prepared in private, were stored in microwave containers in a separate refrigerator; and extravagant dishes were offered to priests and any visiting guests, as if the meals we prepared were not good enough. We all complained about their idiosyncrasies but no one in America had ever attempted to understand.

The Chinese Sisters' simple statements haunted my novitiate days took on new meaning after moving to Taiwan. Forced to flee their homeland in their teens and early twenties, expected to cherish the opportunity to live in America, they acquired English with no formal lessons. Living on convent property, tucked away in the mountains of Santa Cruz and in the woods of Oregon for thirty-five years, they spoke all they knew of concern for those around them: a simple welcome home; a reminder to take care and to get some food.

The residents of Taiwan were awed by Americans, noticeably different from the black haired, dark eyed children who hid behind cars and bushes to point and shout names like, 'foreign devil', 'big nose' or 'American' as we walked down the street. I don't know if it was awe borne of reverence or of pure curiosity, but I do know the locals treated me with great hospitality and respect – a respect I slowly learned to return. The hospitality ingrained in the language spilled into everyday existence, slowly becoming my own.

Strolling the foggy cliffs of Keelung, salt lining my lips and dampness invading my bones, I listened to the waves crashing beneath me and breathed in the fresh coastal air. Local Coca-Cola Company workers, having a picnic nearby, ran to greet us, offered hotdogs and sausages, free goodie bags, and of course, Coca-Cola. As I stood among them, I marveled at the hospitality.

We walked by open door after open door on our journey home, admiring the various tile patterns decorating the floors in most of the small huts. As we slowed to examine one especially gorgeous tiling, a woman walked towards the door, opened it as widely as possible, and said, "Come in, please. Please, please come in. Have some coffee. Americans like coffee." The conversation continued with offers of milk, Coke and cheese, the woman desperate to offer something an American might want. We sipped the tea she set before us, thanked her and headed home.

As we headed to one of the coastal villages on another trip, the bus came to a standstill. A young man hopped off the bus and ran ahead to discover the problem. Within minutes he returned to inform everyone about a serious injury to four people involved in a car accident about a quarter mile up the road. "Let's let this bus take our injured brothers and sisters to the hospital," he suggested. Everyone quietly and quickly filed off the bus, opened their sun umbrellas and waited in the heat until the bus returned almost an hour and a half later. No one complained. I stood in awe thinking, "Never in America."

The people surrounding me were not Christian; only two percent of Taiwan was, but they lived the gospel better than many of the Christians I knew. It made no sense to me. It crushed me. On Easter Sunday, as we walked through the street market, bartering with the vendors over the price of slippers and a basketball, my heart ached for those who'd never heard the message of Jesus. What message could I bring these people? Cecilia, one of the young girls from the University, had said, "Buddhists can be good people too. If you want to bring the Christian message to us, you have to learn about us first. Don't be too quick to judge." I sat judging, and so far, the people of Taiwan were ahead.

By the time University let out for summer, Sr. Nathaniel decided to return to the States to regain perspective and perhaps return to work on her Bachelors'. Finished with my assignment to save Sr. Nathaniel's vocation, I applied to the University of Hong Kong to obtain my Bachelors' and a teacher's certification to make me eligible to teach at our mission, Immaculate Heart of Mary College, as Sr. Thomas directed.

Awaiting word from the University over the summer, I accompanied one of the students from the hostel to her home in southern Taiwan before meeting up with two of my own classmates from language school.

"You can take a shower in the bathroom before you go to bed. Let me show you." Phyllis led me to a small wooden door at the back of the house. Next to the toilet stood a huge metal tub like I'd seen in old movies. The faucet extended about six inches above the edge of the tub with no shower or curtain. "You can use this to rinse your body." Phyllis said, handing me a small aluminum saucepan, similar to the one Mom had always used to boil water for tea back home. I carefully doused my body with the cool water running from the faucet at my knees, grateful for the hospitality.

44

The poverty I knew as a child, and that which we attempted to profess in the convent, paled in comparison to the simplicity that surrounded me. As I prayed my *Night Litany for the World* before falling asleep I wondered how many suffered poverty far greater than I.

The next morning, I visited a long term care facility with Franca and Catherine. The beautiful surroundings of the green hills and majestic trees awed me; the lush tree at the center of the entry way, gorgeous. Frightened a dog might be at the other end of the heavy leash extending from the bottom of the tree, I slowed my pace until I could lay eyes on it. As the chain rattled, I watched in horror as a clearly uncontrollable woman wrangled with the leash. The enraged woman kicked and screamed, flailing almost in mid-air; the stench rising from her body, matched only by her matted hair and shredded clothing. The reality for me, almost unbearable. I gagged. Why treat any human being with such disregard? I wanted to reach out, wanted to grab her hand, to hug her brittle skin and boney frame, to let her know someone loved her. But instead, I offered prayer.

As we went inside the building, a courtyard opened before us. Many of the patients roaming the yard approached as one of the Sisters set up a stool for cutting hair. They had a routine: haircut, shave, toenail and fingernail clipping. Picking up the clippers and nail file, I knelt at the feet of these unkempt men and women, praying only for the blessings the Apostles received as Jesus washed their feet the night before he died. Could I not do what Jesus did? I'd reenacted the washing of the feet in ceremonial ritual but never amongst such filth. With no water for washing, I kissed each foot as I finished my job.

Moving through the compound, I realized the people we helped to tidy up were the only patients allowed the freedom to move beyond the walls of their cells. We changed the bedding and adult diapers of those confined to a hospital style ward, but many were locked behind bars as if they were criminals in prison. The further down the corridor we walked, the darker it got, and for me, the more despicable. I stepped passed cell after cell of naked women, sitting next to piles of their own feces, crawling in their own urine, reaching out to make contact with someone, something other than themselves.

I managed to choke back the tears until we walked beyond the main entrance and past the woman chained to the tree. We'd served for three and a half hours, clipping, cutting, brushing teeth and wiping the bottoms of more than forty men and women. We exchanged hugs, kissed feet and said goodbye, leaving them with just a temporary fix to the pain and humiliation they suffered.

"Why doesn't somebody do something about those conditions?" I gulped for air between my sobs.

"We do what we can; what they allow. If we try to change everything, they won't let us back and things will be worse. At least they get shelter and sustenance here." Sr. Franca spoke as a true servant. She had no tears left, but clearly understood mine.

Because I had just finished nine months of individualized Mandarin lessons when I arrived in Hong Kong, the Sisters expected me to pick up Cantonese on my own. Some words, similar to their Mandarin counterparts, came with the simple twist of an accent while others remained a mysterious mix of ancient literal Chinese and the influence of British English. I never knew which might influence a word most; I just had to guess.

One afternoon, unable to find an elevator, I attempted a direct translation of the Mandarin term electric stairs. I twisted "dian ti" into "din toi", certain of my Cantonese. I approached a woman with my request, only to be stared at. Panicking because I needed the elevator, I concocted a mix of English, Mandarin and Cantonese to describe a box with doors that open and close and goes up and down inside a building. "Oh," she exclaimed, "a lip." Apparently the word for elevator had been translated from the British term 'lift' rather than from the American word, elevator. I had to learn British along with Cantonese, discovering that potato chips are called crisps; cookies are biscuits, cigarettes fags, and napkins serviettes. My 'next Tuesday' became 'Tuesday week' and 'two weeks', 'a fortnight.'

A young red-haired American in a habit and veil, shuffling quickly through the train stations, I stood alone in a crowd. On early morning trips, the shopping malls that housed the train stations teemed with millions of commuters. In the silence of the rush, I only heard the rhythmic, steady footsteps, like tap dancers on stage, of commuters marching towards their goals. Caught in the shuffle and crammed into the aisle of a subway train car, I absorbed every word spoken around me, every word on every sign and billboard. I learned the bus routes, trains, subways and ferries quickly. We lived in the New Territories, in Shatin, which sat just miles from the border of mainland China, and Communism. I attended the university at the top of Hong Kong Island, about an hour away by public transportation although just miles as the bird flies. I had to pass through Kowloon to get to the island every day. Lion Rock Tunnel and Kowloon Tong became as familiar as the Golden Gate and Bay Bridge I'd traveled all my life. I turned from staring at the mirrored walls of the skyscrapers downtown, or the dingy, eight story public housing developments of the old parts of Kowloon, to marvel at the rice paddies and banana trees lining the hillsides and surrounding the thatched roof shacks scattered throughout the countryside.

Wiping water drops from my forehead, I no longer looked up, knowing someone must have just hung out the laundry. Each apartment building window had four or five bamboo poles hanging perpendicularly from the ledge, Hong Kong's version of a backyard clothesline. Dodging umbrellas in ninety-five-degree sunshine became almost second nature, although I never got used to using one myself. I learned not to expect sanitary toilet seat covers, toilet paper, or soap and after the initial awkwardness of maneuvering panty-hose and three layers of my habit to squat over the toilet bowls sunk into the ground, I rarely forgot to carry toilet paper for the public restrooms.

Hong Kong brought back the familiar, so rare in Taiwan: Western influence. Buddhist temples were scattered throughout the territory but easily situated within yards of a Burger King or the Golden Arches. MacDonald's sat just blocks from one another and western style department stores and markets littered the train station malls. I could purchase Skippy or Corn Flakes as easily as I bought my choice of live chicken from the cages in the marketplace.

Each day when I got off the bus from Kowloon, I walked through the temporary housing complex where thousands of mainland Chinese had been herded into these metal boxes; large extended families, with grandma and grandpa, husband, wife and three or four, even five, children sharing two hundred fifty or three hundred square feet of living space. Row upon row of these homes, surrounded by open sewers, above which were single faucets for washing vegetables and cleaning pots and pans. Residents showered, washed clothes and used the toilet in what they called the water sheds, community bathrooms between each block of six or eight rows of houses.

Intended to be transitional shelter for those who fled Mainland China during the communist takeover in the 1940's, the temporary housing housed several generations. Many of my students had been born and raised in these tin huts, freezing in the forty-degree weather of the winter months and roasting from May through September, when temperatures rarely, if ever, dropped below ninety degrees with ninety percent humidity. I loved the wrinkled smiles of the grandmas and grandpas, balanced on their haunches, watching the toddlers play on the hot cement as I took a shortcut through the compound. I smiled, through the guilt, as I returned to the comfort of my convent lifestyle.

Traveling to and from school alone, not expected to account for every minute of my time like at home, in the novitiate or in Taiwan, as long as I met convent obligations for meals, prayer, and community activities, no one questioned how long it took to get to school or home. Initially I left as late as possible and returned home by the quickest route, but without conscious awareness on my part, I began to walk – which kept me out and away from the convent longer each day. First I walked from University downhill to the ferry, then from the subway uphill to the University; from the ferry terminal to the train, from one train station to the next. I'd pass boxes and baskets overflowing with strange and intriguing fruits and vegetables; dried seaweed, shrimp, fish, shredded pork and beef – all lined up in boxes outside the markets, for people to look at, smell, touch and even taste. As a New Yorker might buy a hotdog or a San Francisco tourist may get a bite of crab on Fishermen's Wharf, people rushing to and from work stopped for a quick bite from vendors selling small purple sweet potatoes, corn on the cob, roasted chestnuts, smelly tofu, fish balls, or rice noodles smothered in peanut sauce. The stench of Shrimp Paste and Stinky Tofu from side shops became, not only familiar, but even appetizing.

Whether on bus, train, ferry, or foot, I observed the wrinkled, tattered faces of the elderly laborers rubbing elbows against the expensive suits of the young, vibrant business men and women heading to the downtown high-rises. I listened in the silence of the morning commute and the chaos of the market place as the guttural sounds, like shouts of anger, echoed off the buildings. In this silence and in these crowds, Hong Kong became a part of me.

With eight lectures a week and one small group meeting the British called a tutorial once a week at University, I occasionally missed a meal or prayers causing the Sisters to complain adamantly and leaving me feeling guilty each time I walked out the door. Towards the end of first semester the Sisters were vindicated as I arrived home each Friday exhausted and suffering with a swollen, sore throat. Anna, our devoted cook, greeted me at the door with a huge cup of Leung Cha – cold tea – to balance the hot air that engulfed me. When I began waking from sleep unable to breathe, I was admitted to the hospital for tests and a strict humidifier regiment. I sat for five days, face in the steam, three times a day with my patience alone being tested. With mounting fear that Karen's prophecy might finally come to pass and I would go to heaven before I graduated from university, I prayed for the gift of resignation and asked permission to return to the convent for Chinese New Year. My Friday routine continued, except with my cup of tea came increased, persistent complaints I did too much homework, stayed out too much, and took my studies too seriously.

Sr. Veronica approached in early May, handed me a plane ticket to see a doctor in the States and offered a warning that if my body couldn't adjust to the missions then I simply needed to remain in the United States. I returned to the States uncertain of my future but more uncertain about how easily Sister dismissed me because of a sore throat. Sr. Veronica only wanted me in Hong Kong if I caused no trouble and worked at school. I wracked my brain to justify the community's position: a sick Sister in the mission couldn't pronounce the gospel to others, would drain the energies of others, and needed proper medical attention. All such thoughts dissipated when a simple throat culture uncovered a severe allergic reaction to smoke allergies – easily curable with antibiotics. Confused by how I survived eighteen years in a house with Mom, a habitual smoker, without a single infection, it took weeks to realize my Friday morning Shakespeare professor chain smoked long, thin, brown cigarettes. Angry that I'd suffered so needlessly for an entire year, I returned to Hong Kong grateful for the simple solution: no more Shakespeare tutorials.

On my return, Sr. Veronica sent me to attend the English language liturgy at Chinese University in Shatin, making it necessary to balance my full course load at university with helping a Jesuit chaplain with the English speaking expatriate community. The workaholic nature I'd so carefully nurtured throughout novitiate blossomed. Sunday morning instruction extended to Saturday afternoons and eventually led to evening classes for the volunteer teachers, afternoon luncheons with the ladies, picnics, retreats and Christmas sing-a-longs. Working with expats from Australia, Britain, South Africa and America exposed me to a world beyond Asia. Different vocabulary accompanied different manners, humor and customs than I'd been raised with in my small, suburban ghetto. As I shared my faith with the children, I encountered a world of boarding schools, horse owners, chemical and mechanical engineers, and vegemite.

In a crowded train heading to the race track for lunch, a greasy little man who'd gotten off work early to place a bet asked why I was heading to the race track. Shouldn't I be doing something more constructive? I attempted to explain I taught their children about God, and didn't bet on horses; he marveled at how rich the horse owners must be.

I socialized with the wealthy as I battled the persistent and gnawing whispers, like a gnat circling in my brain, trying to convince myself that I did everything for the glory of God and that I would spend more time in prayer, not get distracted during meditation, wake up on time for Morning Prayer, and not get so angry with those I lived with when Confirmation classes were over, when I graduated, when I finished student teaching. I always had an excuse for why I didn't become what I believed I should be.

Desperate to eradicate the guilt and doubt ravaging my soul, I found solace in reaching out to the less fortunate. I sat to talk with the beggars on the street; with the blind and crippled. Ah-Kei, the one I visited the most, sat at the cross-section of the overpass outside the Central MTR station on Hong Kong Island. Without legs he moved about everywhere on his hands, his torso resting on a wooden flatbed dolly. When I first saw him, I wanted to avoid him. His gentle, childlike face drew a simple hello from me. As I passed each day on my way to and from the university, I began to search for him. Why didn't he get government help? What did he need? I started giving him spare change and packing a lunch for him most days. But mostly, I'd tell him a little about my day and ask about his. I missed the days I didn't see him. If he disappeared for too many days, I began to worry. His round, childlike face and large dark eyes were etched in my mind's eye. I didn't care that people stared; some even swore. One spat at me. I would never completely feel Ah-Kei's pain or embarrassment, but I treated him with the respect he deserved.

Once a week, during the summer months, I accompanied the mothers and fathers of sick Vietnamese children to the hospital. The Vietnamese refugees were locked behind chain-link fences and living in old metal converted plane hangars. Entire families shared the space of a bed-bunk. Food was brought around in a bucket, rice and vegetables were the stable meals twice a day. Children ran around barefoot with old hand-me-downs that never saw more than a bucket of cold water to get the dirt out. We brought them old paper and books, pencils and pens whenever possible. Treated like prisoners, they were not allowed to visit their children in the hospital. I watched the tears of the parents as they ran to the bedside of their suffering children and I held the babies whose parents couldn't come.

One afternoon trying to comfort a little crying girl about eighteen months old, I approached the bed of another about the same age. The child stretched her arm out and very gently, ever so slightly, rubbed the outer edge of the crying child's ear until she fell silent. The compassion of the patients to one another offered a sharp contrast to the indifference of so many of the hospital staff who often refused to learn the names of the children and only tended to their needs when it became impossible to ignore them anymore.

I graduated with so many merit-based scholarships that my entire university education had been paid for, but I celebrated alone. No one attended the graduation ceremony; no one remembered; no one said a word until we were all heading upstairs after Night Prayer. A group picture in front of a statue of Mary, the only celebration of my accomplishment, left me holding back tears that boiled just beneath the surface all afternoon as I'd suffered in silence.

My college professors asked if I could become a teachers' assistant, make presentations to classes, and supervise their teachers in training. Sr. Veronica would not allow it for fear I might become proud. Every job, each assignment for nine years had been designed to curb my pride. I accepted Sr. Veronica's decisions as I'd accepted all of Sr. Thomas's, but the complete lack of recognition for all I did crushed my spirit. I accepted being spat on for befriending a crippled man, but found being completely forgotten by those meant to be my family, almost unbearable.

Standing among those I called my Sisters, in cap and gown, trying to smile, I let go of three years of university and looked towards my final step in formation: Perpetual Vows. To prepare spiritually, I needed time to focus. I suggested waiting until after I'd worked a year but Sr. Thomas insisted she and the council made the decision and I didn't need time.

The expatriate families graciously donated enough money for Mom and one companion to travel to Hong Kong for the ceremony. Eager to offer the true flavor of a city where East meets West, I dragged my brother Dan, Mom, and my niece Anna through the streets and alleyways, introducing them to temples where 10,000 little Buddha statues gazed upon an old guru who remained cross-legged and plated in gold, years after his death; to the tram that crawled, almost vertically, up the side of Victoria Peak to overlook Victoria Harbor; and to the junks which carried us out to the floating Jumbo restaurant for a scrumptious nine course banquet. Pig carcasses hidden under market tables, buckets of dried shrimp and fish heads, the chaos of guttural shouts from the sweaty throngs rubbing against us in hundred-degree heat, and small unadorned restaurants where we sat on stools next to locals who spit chicken bones unto the floor as they ate, offered my family a side to Hong Kong most visitors never saw. Walking hours each day, I completely ignored the voice inside telling me, "Be still and know that I am God."

I stood gazing at the procession of white robed priests, honored by the presence of Cardinal Wu who presided at the ceremony despite suffering a fever of 104°. I commanded the undivided attention of hundreds of parishioners, students and classmates who gathered to pray with me. The Jesuit provincial gave the homily, reminding me that as Jesus promised Peter he would one day be led where he did not want to follow, so obedience would carry me. The words of the only English song during the ceremony: *"What do you want of me Lord? Where do you want me to serve you?"* drained my soul as I begged God for guidance and answers to questions persistently haunting my prayer.

As I lay exhausted on Anna's bed in the guestroom that evening I twisted the ring now adorning my right ring finger, symbolizing my marriage to Christ, wondering at my sense of disappointment. Mom insisted I simply needed a good night's sleep. Anna, suffering severe homesickness, collapsed in my arms in tears. Struggling to help Anna get through her pain, I began to sing *'My Favorite Things'* from the Sound of Music. Rather than listing the many blessings we had, I began rattling off the misery she'd experienced in Hong Kong: walking miles in the burning hot sun, seeing a dead pig under the table at market, the smell of stinky tofu in the subway station. As we sang, Anna's misery slowly turned to joy and I thanked God for the gift of the Holy Spirit and for the sacrifice I made in not being a mother. The irony of staying awake with a suffering child on the day I offered my life in chastity did not escape me.

Cardinal Wu, Mom, Daniel, and Anna in Hong Kong for my final vows.

The three years that followed my final profession, were a continual stream of those moments of irony, crisis and epiphany life sometimes offers that leave us forever changed.

Sr. Kathleen, the principal, appointed me English Department Chair, because my Post-Graduate Certification in Education made me the only qualified English teacher at the school. She voiced her fears about me destroying the English Department of her school and micromanaged my every move; she questioned my lesson plans and teaching methods. Within two months, she made an appointment with the Department of Education inspector, a visit most principals avoided, and insisted I present all of my lesson plans, my plans for the department, and the changes I'd made to the curriculum.

"I've been trying to get my schools to do this for years." The inspector said, obviously impressed with my program. "Tell your principal that not only is everything fine, but that I wish you could offer workshops to get this kind of program started in other schools."

I spoke briefly to avoid choking back tears. I couldn't tell this stranger the pressure I felt to satisfy Sr. Kathleen. *'What happens in community stays in community.'* Sr. Thomas's words haunted me. I just hoped that someday Sr. Kathleen would trust me and get off my back.

My troubles with Sr. Kathleen were not limited to her questioning my work. Sr. Kathleen addressed the students each morning, preaching the importance of common courtesy and respect for others, Christian charity and kindness; yet she turned around, seconds later, to yell at a teacher for forgetting to fulfill some minor obligation or to complain about the incompetence of a maintenance worker. She marched down the stairs completely oblivious to those around her. Students smiled and said good morning, but Sr. Kathleen, with her jaw set, was too preoccupied with the business at hand to even notice.

I had no recourse for dealing with the constant barrage of questions thrown at me by students and faculty regarding Sr. Kathleen's domineering, arrogant, hypocritical attitudes. I vented my concerns to superiors who insisted that if I didn't like it, I could return to the States because they needed Sr. Kathleen to run the college. Stuck in the middle of her hypocrisy, I stood only as a buffer, making no excuses, explaining only that we all did our best to live the Christian lifestyle, none of us perfectly; my own hypocrisy sinking to settle in my gut like an anchor.

I originally attended the evening Psychology and Spirituality course, conducted primarily in Cantonese, as my ticket to the more formal theology I hoped to study at the seminary. I never fathomed a simple evening class could so drastically change the way I understood myself. The basic concept of the Enneagram is simply described as a circle with nine points, each point corresponding to particular personality traits. As I sat the first week, absorbed in the presentation of each number, I felt exposed, almost naked, as if Sr. Dominique, the presenter, somehow gained access to the confines of my soul and secrets of my heart.

Convinced I'd discovered the requisite tools to cure my psychological and spiritual ills, I sat incredulous, week after week, as Sr. Dominique described each successive number. Judging and compartmentalizing, I shoved every Sister into a little box with an Enneagram label attached. Targeting the unhealthy in those with whom I lived, I created litanies of change that, if only they followed, might save them. Facing my own illness did not come so easily. I epitomized everything unhealthy about each: the perfectionism of number one; number two's need to be needed; number four's assertion of being special. With every list of unhealthy character traits, I became more bewildered. I'd always considered myself introspective and honest, but this course made me question my motivation, and every decision I ever made.

I begged Sr. Veronica to allow me to see Sr. Dominique for spiritual direction, but I stood on shaky ground even asking. Sr. Thomas did not believe in spiritual direction. One young postulant just left after insisting Canon Law mandated that she be allowed to see her spiritual director and being told that if she did not like our community's rules, she should leave.

Sr. Veronica begrudgingly gave me her blessing to meet with Sr. Dominique and, with her, I continued to grapple with my essence and what brought me to vocation.

The events in the world, and my own life, that followed the Psychology and Spirituality course led me to answers, and questions, I never considered. Beginning theology courses at the seminary, being attentive to political change and the reality of war, facing my own temptation, and looking death in the eye, set in motion a conflagration that left my soul parched and longing for salvation.

July, 1991
Portland, Oregon

Tears tumbled, one upon another, across my cheeks, as credits rolled on the dark screen, all unnoticed by passers-by eager to continue their lives. I sat, not quite paralyzed, but unwilling to budge. I couldn't let go of the communion and the conversion I'd just experienced watching Lieutenant Dunbar become one with the Sioux Indians in *Dances with Wolves*. The language, the food, the customs initially completely foreign, drew him in, became a part of him, and taught him who he truly was. That moment when Dunbar, called Dances with Wolves by the Sioux, is handed the bleeding heart of a buffalo, his initiation into the community is complete.

Like Dunbar, I'd been given a name: *An Yan Yi* (An Xin Yi, in Mandarin) which means peaceful, happy, contented. I'd even acquired certain nicknames: *Wu Jo Mao* – dirty little cat, for my not so refined appearance; *Da Ben Jiang* – clumsy elephant, for my not so refined demeanor and my accident prone personality; *Siao Hai Tze*, simply: little child. Like Dunbar, I'd learned the language and the culture that came with it. I gradually let go of American habits and assumed the practices of those around me. My rite of passage perhaps more gradual, less dramatic than Dunbar's bite from the buffalo heart, but for me, just as poignant.

Separated by thousands of miles from the young men and women in Beijing who'd begun a hunger strike in support of democracy, the citizens of Hong Kong quickly rallied to show their support. Posters were made, buses boarded and the "We Shall Overcome" chant filled the streets surrounding the newly built Bank of China, the tallest building in Hong Kong, a symbol of things to come following the 1997 return of Hong Kong to Mainland China. One million people marched the crowded, noisy, suffocating streets of Hong Kong Island in support of the cause. I held hands with them, thinking of all I'd read about the civil rights movement in America, remembering the joy we'd experienced in The Projects when they declared Martin Luther King, Jr.'s birthday a holiday. The camaraderie and the hope in Hong Kong infused our souls, helping us forget that we'd walked miles, taking turns forming the chains that held the crowds in, hundreds of us stooping to pick up trash along the way, an unspoken hope that our efforts might convince the Chinese communist government to embrace democracy.

On the morning of June 4, 1989, as TV screens across the world gave witness to the tanks bulldozing through Tiananmen Square, as we watched the bravery of the young man standing before the tank willing to die for his freedom, the cheering and chanting turned to tears. Standing among our students for Morning Assembly, watching Sr. Kathleen attempt to help them make sense of the senseless, I knew I'd never understand. The stoic, somber Chinese faces that held so much in for the sake of saving face, washed in tears. Men, women and children looked on in horror as the news cameras rolled tape of the atrocities, the bloodshed.

The crowds, who for three days bustled with excitement, stood stolidly behind a coffin representing those killed in Beijing, and marched in absolute silence. As the funeral procession passed the businesses stacked atop one another in the mirrored high rises, men in suits and ties and women in professional attire, stood unaware of the quest for money and power that regularly consumed their lives. July 1, 1997, the day Communist China would regain control of Hong Kong loomed large. Their hopes that communism might crumble like the Berlin Wall were demolished when a tank rolled over hordes of peaceful protestors. If the Chinese government could so betray one of their innocent citizens, what might happen to them?

Committees were formed. Conferences called. Lines to apply for foreign visas grew longer each day. The day that seemed so far distant became the only topic of conversation. The Bishop encouraged faith. Catholic community leaders insisted on strength in unity. Behind it all crept an insidious fear, a panic that no one wanted to acknowledge.

I found it impossible to isolate exactly what shifted in my soul after *Lok-Sei*: 6-4, as the locals called the *Tian An Men* Square Massacre, until in the small movie theater just outside Portland, Oregon three years later an unexpected clarity struck me. I must defend the rights of my Sisters. Sisters Clare, Kathleen, and Allegro were absolutely right. How could we say, "Have faith. Trust God," to the millions of souls to whom we ministered, if we had a way out?

Hong Kong housed many who narrowly escaped the Japanese occupation of Mainland China and the Communist takeover. Many grew up envisioning the stories of brutality, rape and murder told by their parents and grandparents. Proud citizens began life over, struggling to rise from the ashes of destruction and desecration to transform Hong Kong. They constructed, with sweat and labor, an oasis where Chinese and western culture collided to create a unique universe in the shadow of Victoria Harbor.

How could we, who taught their children, comforted them in illness, answered their questions, and prayed with them continually, now stand before them, American green card or passport in hand, to pronounce, God will provide? The older Chinese Sisters who'd escaped the Mainland and lived in the States for years, eagerly agreed to obtain U.S. citizenship, but the younger Sisters cringed at the thought of betraying their country. Sr. Thomas insisted: security, certainty, options. All the Chinese Sisters should have green cards before her term ended in 1992.

I'd said nothing. Sr. Thomas represented the voice of God. But Sr. Thomas's fear could not destroy the credibility Sr. Clare had gained with those she nurtured in faith. Sr. Thomas's fear should not coerce the others to reject their conscience in the name of obedience. My fear of Sr. Thomas could no longer silence me.

I spoke that very afternoon. The young Sisters needed to be respected. They were Hong Kong born and raised. They'd never been to America, they couldn't speak English, except for the prayers they were forced to pray. They didn't like cold cereal, huge turkey dinners, or potato salad; they couldn't adjust to the American lifestyle just because they were told to. Forcing them to give up their citizenship, to renounce their roots, would be as criminal as the Cultural Revolution, as immoral as forced baptism, as horrendous as Tiananmen Square.

In the eyes of the students, parishioners and the people they served, the Chinese Sisters would be traitors and hypocrites. If what we preached meant anything, we should be willing to give up U.S. citizenship to demonstrate solidarity with the people, not force them to become one of us. What good would it do for the gospel? How would it profit their souls?

Sr. Thomas sat with her almost transparent knuckles folded tightly on the table top defending her position: their true citizenship resided in heaven whether they carried green cards or not; the older Sisters thought it best; the younger Sisters hadn't complained to her. Her decision made, God's will had been decided. Obedience would provide all necessary graces for the Sisters and those they served. Our lives were built on the cornerstone of obedience. I couldn't cause the entire structure to crumble because of a ridiculous movie.

July, 1991: Chicago, IL

Growing up, I'd heard often of the more than twenty cousins residing in Chicago and always dreamt of visiting. Given permission to use gift money I received for my vows, I decided to visit my little sister in Idaho, my mom's relatives in Chicago, and my dad's sister in Iowa. Sitting with my cousin on the north side of Chicago, I picked up the phone, dialed information and asked for Davenport, Iowa and any listing for Hamby or Arnold. After jotting down four numbers, my hands with a slight tremor, I began dialing, desperate to take advantage of this opportunity, certain I'd never be in Chicago again.

On the fourth call I spoke with a woman named Darlene, my uncle Edward's wife. I'd heard the names before, but we never met. Contact with this side of the family had been virtually severed long before my dad left home. We didn't talk long, but made plans to meet at a truck stop in Joliet. Being in my habit made me easy to spot. After awkward hugs we headed towards the Quad cities. Darlene did all of the talking. I sat on emotional overload (grateful I could fulfill my lifelong dream of finding my roots) and attempted to filter the nonsense of Darlene's ramblings. I'd met plenty of strangers and, therefore, felt little discomfort until I heard, "your Dad and his wife Jenny came over for a barbeque with the kids." With the sting, as acute as a fifty-below zero wind-chill, my universe came to a screeching halt. She'd said, "his wife Jenny," and "kids." Dad had kids, eight of us. And he never divorced Mom, how could he be married to someone named Jenny? My mind exploded as everything I'd ever imagined about my dad and his lifestyle disintegrated. I continued to listen, but heard nothing.

His sister Kitten, claimed she never saw him, how had they all barbequed together? Struggling to grasp the reality that my father was not miserable, I made the necessary small talk as if it all meant nothing. I could not help but wonder if Kitten's lies included what she said in her letter.

In 1984 when she phoned to say that Grandma Arnold died, my hidden hopes revived. These people might be my life line to the Dad I'd lost. The possibility seeped into my brain, nudging me to make contact. That night I sat in my room, lit by a desk lamp, pen twisting in my fingers, attempting to write.

Dear Aunt Kitten,
Peace! You don't know me, but I am one of your nieces. Your brother, Loyed, is my father. He left our family in 1972. If you know where he is please tell him that I forgive him, pray for him every day, and would love to see him someday soon.
In Christ,
Janet

I checked my box each day for mail with a return address from Iowa. Months passed before I darted immediately to the chapel, ripped through the edge of the envelope and pulled out the small sheet of stationery.

Dear Janet,
I'm sorry I didn't write back sooner but I waited to hear from your father. I don't know where he is, but every once in a great while he calls me to check in. I read your letter to him and he asked me to send you a message. He said, "There isn't a day that goes by that I don't think about each of my children. I love them very much, but I think it is best that we leave things the way they are."
I knew he meant what he said because he was crying when he said it.
Love,
Aunt Kitten

"*...There isn't a day that goes by that I don't think about each of my children. I love them very much...* " I read and reread these lines over and over again thinking,

"He was crying when he said it." My dad was crying, that means he loves me. He thinks about me every day. He thinks about me every day just like I think about him. He loves me. My dad loves me. As the tears trickled down my cheeks, salt depositing in the corners of my mouth, I knew I had to respect his wishes. I had my answer, he loved me. I needed nothing more, I thought. But I could not escape the nagging truth: Dad left me. I searched for consolation in the Psalms I read three times a day; I sought peace through my prayer.

Forgiveness provided a salve for my wounds, but the scars were far from healed. I struggled desperately to reclaim the love I thought he once showered upon me. Try as I might, I had no positive memories, no sign of his love. Sitting in the chapel, reading and rereading Aunt Kitten's letter, I turned seven all over again, wondering what I'd done to make him leave.

Now as I sat in the back seat listening to Darlene, I couldn't help but think: Did Dad really think about us every day? Did he really ever love me?

Trying not to get angry at the betrayal, I greeted Kitten with a hug, praying for the grace to be open, hoping to learn the truth.

"Kitten," Darlene said, "you gotta tell her."

"Tell me what?" I wondered what could possibly be left to tell.

"Your dad just showed up on my doorstep with a young woman, about twenty, by his side, and two young children."

"When was this?" I interrupted, frustrated by the slow southern drawl unraveling my world at a snail's pace.

"Way back in, I don't know, the early seventies maybe. He told me he worked for the CIA and they were his assignment. I didn't know what to think until a couple days later when I walked in on them sleeping in the same bed. I got angry, but couldn't do nothin'."

"Did you think to ask about us?" I tried not to sound too angry.

"He said ya'll'd been takin' care'a with his pension." She sounded apologetic. "I didn't know."

I tried not to judge listening to the deception and lies they perpetrated, wondering if this woman really believed the story.

"Why'd you lie when I wrote you after your mom died?" I wanted desperately to understand.

"He made me. He made me promise never to tell you. He's the one who told me to wait to write back to you. He told me what to write." I almost felt sympathetic.

"Is he here now?" My stomach muscles tightened as the lifelong dream of meeting my dad, quickly becoming a nightmare, became probable.

"They got a little house, had another baby and lived here until about four years ago. Your Dad worked at the local grocer for years," she said, her back straight with pride, "really part of the community." She made it sound so cozy and quaint, I could almost picture the white picket fence and the shade tree in the front yard.

"He'd come and go, disappear for a couple of days; never tell us where. I reckoned it had to do with the CIA."

Darlene interrupted. "Do you still have the book he made for Ma's eighty-second birthday?"

"Oh, yeah. Bobby, go get the folder off the shelf in my nightstand. Hurry." She spoke to her son as he scampered into the bedroom.

As Bobby handed the scrapbook to me, I could almost hear the do-do-do of Twilight Zone's theme song. This man who refused to ever discuss his family or talk to his siblings, abandoned eight children, and then organized a huge shindig for his mother's birthday. He invited all of his fourteen siblings, their spouses, their children, and relatives from around the country. Invitations, decorations, menus, presents; he did everything start to finish. More than one hundred people attended. Thumbing the pages of the scrapbook, I tried desperately to reconcile the truth before my eyes with the fiction I'd been raised with. Sitting now, thumbing the memory book he made, I couldn't resist: "Never once, anywhere, does he mention us, the eight children and wife he'd abandoned years before?" I tried to sound nonchalant. I couldn't allow my pain to be audible.

"Ya know; Jenny knew all about ya'll." Kitten offered, like a consolation prize. "She even insisted on gettin' a picture of Regina for herself, bein' her daughter and all."

"What? How's that? If he didn't claim us, how could she? She didn't even know us." My anger began to surface, but I grit my teeth and asked again, "So where are they now?"

"In Las Vegas somewhere. They left here couple years ago. Jenny's daughter, real trouble, accused your dad of molesting her, so the lawyer told them to disown her and leave."

I didn't know what to believe, and what to think. Molestation? And how could anyone believe my dad and disown her own daughter? I had little energy left to sift through all I'd heard; no energy to be angry and no idea what to do with my new found knowledge.

"What the hell? He has a wife and another kid." I couldn't tell Mom, but needed to tell someone. Daniel's anger, mixed with the cackle of disbelief, gave me permission to vent. As Daniel picked up the phone, dialing information and calling every listing for Arnold in Las Vegas, I knew I could let it go. Daniel swore, "I'm gonna find him."

The next day, my neighbor Mary Lee asked me to drive her to visit her youngest son Joe, almost thirty-five, who lay in the hospital, dying of AIDS. Joe had always been a chubby, jolly, happy-go-lucky and friendly face around the neighborhood. I couldn't believe my eyes as we entered the small, simple room in the county hospital to see Joey limp and almost lifeless, the huge boils on his sunken face and bony arms, made him almost unrecognizable. I understood the tears that rolled down my dear friend's cheeks as she stared at her baby, but my heart sank; Mary Lee couldn't touch her own son. Her fear of the disease, and the stigma that still surrounded AIDS in the eighties, kept the once undaunted single parent of eight from caressing her dying son.

I slowly reached out the hand I had always prayed would be like the hands of Christ, picked up his limp hands, and prayed silently. I wiped the sweat from his brow and set my palm against his clammy cheek. Leaning over, I kissed him on the forehead saying my last good-byes.

"I couldn't do it, Sister." Mary Lee, who once claimed I'd never be a real nun, controlled her sobs and thanked me sincerely for comforting her dying son. "I just can't. I can't touch him." Joey died a week later and we never spoke of him or that day again.

I returned to Hong Kong recognizing I lost still more of my naïveté, my innocence and my ignorance. The years during novitiate I spent visualizing my father, praying for a healing of memories and struggling to forgive, had been based on lies. Knowing my father was not a transient, not mentally ill, and didn't think of me every day (but ran off, married another woman, and had another son) somehow invalidated me and everything I stood for. I silently forgave my father because my faith and my vocation offered no other option.

Just after my return to Hong Kong I attended the diocesan vocation camp as a mentor to those considering religious life. I helped with these camps often and everyone expected me. I expected no different, but my lack of enthusiasm caused concern among those accustomed to my frivolity and my passion. I publicly excused my lethargy as jetlag, hoping the uncharacteristic apathy I encountered that weekend would dissipate with sleep. Privately, I knew I'd never be the same.

Experiences from the summer danced within my soul and as events presented themselves over the next few years, isolated moments mingled and singular events mounted, setting the stage for me to question myself, my God and everything I stood for.

The day after Christmas 1991, I joined a group of men and women from the Diocese of Hong Kong to bring food and clothing to those in Wuhan, China suffering the aftermath of a flood which ravaged the territory the previous July. We gathered at the Kowloon train station, headed for Guangzho and prepared to board a plane. Sitting in the airport waiting for delayed and cancelled flights all day, unsure of myself and nervous about my jeans and T-shirt, I saw the Chinese people surrounding me staring, commenting on my short red hair, on the foreigner, the American.

I sat, wondering if John, one of our companions, noticed me. Approximately the same age, we paired off because our language skills balanced one another's: I spoke both Cantonese and Mandarin, John only Cantonese. I could act as his translator in Wuhan. We would spend the next two weeks together, but my instant desire for attention and my virtually automatic flirtation the minute I wasn't wearing a habit frightened me. As I sat curled up in the airport chair, pretending to get some rest, my heart slowly retreated to the simple prayers of my childhood. So many nights, lying in the darkness of my bed, I'd prayed about each new crush, changing the names, the prayer remained the same, "God, please let him like me."

Attempting to ward off the childish desire to be loved, attractive, and noticed, my body quickly reacted. By midday, my throat swelled and every muscle in my body ached. I curled into the best fetal position I could manage in the plastic row of chairs and pretended to sleep, longing for someone to protect me from the thoughts inhabiting my mind.

Before we visited any villages, the many city and government officials who accompanied us along the way insisted we do some sightseeing. Angry that we couldn't begin our ministry, their keen awareness of the needs of those around them touched me, as they always kept one eye open to see if we lacked anything. I had difficulty finding fault with a ritual which surely planted seeds of respect and humility in the hearts of those who follow it.

As I stood before the grave of Bao Zheng, a famous hero in Chinese history, the Christian values practiced by those who never heard the name of Jesus struck me. Bao Zheng an upright and honest man, tried to spread the truth. Listening to the stories, I heard the life of a saint. A prayer came from my heart and I jotted in my journal:

> *I believe you are a saint. I thank God for your example of righteousness and honesty. I pray you help me learn and ask you to help the people of China. If*

you happen to not yet be in the full glory of God's presence, I pray that you
may soon experience this joy.

We were all preoccupied with adjusting to twenty degrees below zero temperatures and three feet of snow on the ground. When we needed a bathroom we were directed behind a wooden wall to a deep hole in the ground or a room with a trough running the length of it. We had no privacy the entire week. We were accompanied, everywhere, by a member of the local town government, as we presented our gifts to the victims of the destroyed homes and schools. We were treated like royalty and met with utter simplicity from village inhabitants.

As we were welcomed into one home we saw a simple wooden frame with a mat for sleeping, a table and stool in the corner and a two burner cook top at the back of the room. "Did you lose everything in the flood?" we asked, observing the elderly woman's sparse accommodations. "No," she replied, exposing crooked, rotting teeth, "I got lucky. My son told me and moved to higher ground. I saved everything."

At the village school, students huddled in a large army tent with a simple light bulb hanging from the center of the makeshift ceiling. At the front of the classroom hung a small chalkboard that looked to measure just over four square feet. The students sat on stacks of bricks behind planks of wood lying across yet more bricks, pencil stubs clasped by mitten covered fingers, eyes squinting to not only see, but understand the math problem presented them. Nothing could have kept these children from the opportunity to learn more, to advance their education, to move ahead.

As I entered each village I observed people living with the bare minimum; I encountered extreme deprivation polished with joy in the rough, ragged hands of the women who held my own. I longed to run my fingers along the wrinkles that devoured their eyes, to understand the pain and the hopes, to read between the lines and invite them into my hopes, dreams, and fears.

As I left the smiling faces of the villagers behind me, my heart filled with a sense of sorrow, not for these villagers, but for myself and for my own sinfulness. How greatly God has blessed me with abundance of goods, yet I am still unsatisfied. I complain about inconveniences, yet waste so much of what others may cherish as prize possessions. These poor children study under such conditions, yet we waste paper, water, electricity, and food, and damage the goods we have with little thought. Some may say that the way we live cannot really influence the lives of those in China, but I still ask myself whether or not being more careful would affect the way I look at life and at others, and allow me to show empathy for others less fortunate – hoping one day given a chance, I could act so as to make a difference. Over and over the beatitude, "Blessed are the poor in spirit; the kingdom of heaven is theirs" came to mind. The joy they radiated and the freedom they seemed to possess, overpowered me from the first day and became stronger with each passing day. They seemed to be already living in heaven, no material goods blinding them to the beauty of nature and life.

Marching through snow packs more than knee deep, agonizing over the emotions consuming me, I grew angry. How could I claim to bring the message of Christ's love to these children of God lost in a blanket of communism, when I secretly longed for the man standing next to me? As we traveled from village to village, I sat next to John. Tired and cold, I fell asleep leaning on his warm shoulder, knowing I could completely justify any unintentional contact if someone else noticed. John was married and he never acted inappropriately. I never saw him again after our return to Hong Kong but knew I faced serious soul searching to discover how not being in a habit and veil, I could so instantly let go of everything I stood for.

I rushed to visit my spiritual director and my confessor upon our return to Hong Kong, hoping they would tell me what to do as Sr. Thomas always had. Father Cabrini, my confessor, spoke of normal temptation and a choice to remain faithful to my vows. Together we prayed in gratitude for my perseverance and purity. Sr. Dominique, my spiritual director, forced me to question my motivation, to ask why. Why did the thoughts surface so quickly? Why did I desire attention and affection? Why did I refuse to face the reality of my own truth?

I listened to both, but I'd made my choice. I didn't make final vows lightly. I studied and prayed, offering my life in purity. I would not allow chastity to become an issue. I thanked God for the temptation and for reminding me of my dependence on Him; thanked Sr. Dominique for her efforts; and returned to the enclosure I'd built around my body and soul.

Spring, 1992

Sr. Allegro and her family left for dinner after hours of sitting at her father's bedside in the sweltering heat of the crowded county hospital. I held his hand as I prayed silently. Wiping the sweat from his brow, I whispered in his ear: "Be at peace. Go with God." Mr. Chan's throat rumbled momentarily, his head dropped further into the pillow, and he died. Holding his hand, I remained at his side until his family returned, knowing I stood on Holy Ground.

I'd thought so much about dying, so early and for so long, that death lost all mystery and wonder. Cancer become a familiar companion and death a simple fact, neither scary, nor sacred. Accompanying Mr. Chan at death filled me with an awe and respect for death that I'd never known, and left me pondering my own readiness. But none of my experiences and none of my ponderings prepared me for the spiritual upheaval that began when I accompanied Sr. Veronica to a simple doctor visit.

Sr. Veronica rested in the bed beside me waiting for what we assumed would be inconclusive results from the same tests doctors repeated for years: a colonoscopy, an upper and lower GI, blood tests and x-rays. A young doctor walked into the room and without any explanation or discussion calmly said, "We can try some new treatments. They are experimental, but they have worked well with others."

"What kind of treatments?" I asked, angry with his vague demeanor.

"Chemotherapy."

"So I have cancer?" Sr. Veronica's voice cracked and her face paled.

"Your liver and kidneys are very diseased. This is the only option."

We rode home on the bus in silence, holding hands, neither knowing what to say. As the weeks unfolded, concern for Sr. Veronica came second to my anger towards Sr. Fatima who refused to use the word cancer and forbade any Sister from speaking to Sr. Veronica about the possibility of dying. She insisted the Chinese didn't talk about death and it would only make Sr. Veronica worse.

"She is clearly dying." I argued as we stood in the middle of the kitchen after others headed upstairs for bed. "Shouldn't we be helping her to accept death, be at peace? Forget the Chinese way, what about the Christian way?"

I argued with Sr. Fatima but said nothing as I massaged Sr. Veronica's feet, rubbed her earlobes, and combed her hair. I fed her soup and served her tea. Still, any day Sr. Veronica felt worse, Sr. Fatima blamed me, claiming that I said something offensive. Desperate not to give up her lifeline, Sr. Fatima made the entire community hold Reiki sessions on a regular basis. Frantically, we laid hands on one another, believing somehow that the universal energies channeled through our finite, sinful hands would restore our beloved matriarch, our anchor, our obsession. Maybe the universe would give back her life and ours. Sr. Veronica, tried to smile, pointing out from her chair in the corner the missing butter on the table or asking with strained voice and eyes closed, "Oh, you go to school tonight?"

Sr. Veronica and I sat in the community room one evening watching a television program about a Buddhist nun who'd left her monastery. As the story unfolded it became clear the woman's choice to leave was viewed with as much admiration as her choice to join; each step on her journey, respected.

"The Church needs to respect people's journeys more like the Buddhists do." Sr. Veronica spoke softly but deliberately. "Some people would be better off if they had the courage to leave religious life, but everybody looks at it like a scandal."

Sr. Veronica's words pierced through my thoughts, a shooting pain straight to the heart. Did the reality of death change her so drastically? Could she really believe what she said? Should I tell her my thoughts?

By the end of April, I spent each day at school and each night in the hospital. In the wee hours of morning, Sr. Veronica would acknowledge her own death, envisioning her mother waiting on the other side for her and voicing her fears of being unacceptable for heaven because of her sins. I leaned beside her on the bed, brushing hair from her face, telling her of God's unending merciful love for her. I spoke of feeling called to work with people on the street, of my desire to give more, of my own thoughts of death. Sr. Veronica blessed me and assured me that God would show me what to do and that she would be with me.

"I want to die at home, not in the hospital." Sr. Veronica whispered late one night. The next morning, we asked for her discharge and prepared the guest room on the first floor of the convent. I insisted Sr. Thomas be called. "She is the Superior General. At least you should tell her how absolutely serious this is. We're near the end." Sr. Fatima refused. A letter at this point would take too long so one morning, while others slept, and without anyone's permission, I snuck to the phone to call Sr. Thomas. By the time Sr. Fatima found out, Sr. Thomas had boarded an airplane.

The next day, Sr. Joanne, frightened by Sr. Veronica's moaning, called an ambulance. The fifteen women who lived with and been touched by Sr. Veronica gathered in the small hospital room in prayer. The atmosphere, anything but peaceful: half of us angry that Sister called the ambulance, some wishing to numb her with painkillers, others anxious about Sr. Thomas's arrival. We each took moments to whisper a blessing in her ear and we all cried. Sr. Veronica never said another word. She held Sr. Thomas's hand when she arrived at 9:40 p.m., listened to her greeting and opened her eyes to see her. At 10:00 p.m. Sr. Veronica breathed her last.

Sad though I was, I held tight to the precious gift I'd been given being allowed to spend so many moments with Sr. Veronica as she lay dying. I would never forget her cute bucktoothed smile, her simple heartfelt concern for my well-being, and her ability to gently scold. I'd loved her as a mother, but knew in full confidence she remained with me, guiding me and loving me along my way.

Watching Sr. Fatima collapse atop the coffin being wheeled from the church, unable to follow the procession without supportive arms virtually carrying her, I saw her as never before. The admonitions we received to have no particular friendships, to find our companionship in Jesus, clearly went unheeded. Sr. Fatima lost her nearest, dearest friend and was inconsolable. The strong, tough, no nonsense woman I'd grown to love and admire became not only human, but almost pathetic.

Summer, 1992: Holy Land

Sr. Veronica's announcement months earlier that I would accompany Sr. Clare on a pilgrimage to the Holy Land surprised me but I hoped that praying on the very ground Jesus walked might squelch the frustrations swirling in my mind. As Sr. Clare and I walked the halls and lobbies of the airport in Rome, discussing community problems we hoped might be solved by the upcoming Chapter, she nonchalantly said, "Sr. Fatima told me to be careful about hanging around with you. She told me to keep an eye on you and to keep you away from Sr. Allegro."

A vacuum could have sucked the air from my lungs and left me with more life than her words. "You're a bad influence and she said I couldn't leave you and Allegro alone." Attempting to maintain some sense of composure, I shrugged it off with a flippant remark. The words 'bad influence' rolled around like a loose ball-bearing in my head. Each time the words shot through my mind, my heart cracked under their weight. My heart felt parched, shriveled. Sr. Fatima created my nicknames, chosen me as companion on all of her errands, and relied on me to do her dirty work. She'd treated me to MacDonald's and spent hours explaining the nuances of Chinese culture. We'd walked miles running errands; we'd laid cement, fixed Venetian blinds, and painted fences and playground equipment. I'd even accompanied her to China. I'd been her arms and legs when arthritis flared, her eyes when she couldn't see, her constant companion. She'd called me Shiao Hai Tze, little child. The sense of abandonment engulfing my soul would destroy me if I couldn't ignore and stoically offer it up as I'd always been taught.

As my companions on the pilgrimage gathered at each church, hill or holy spot to take pictures for scrap books, I knelt in prayer. Determined not to waste a moment of my time in the Holy Land, each prayer, each movement of my emotions became profound. The Church of the Nativity, constructed in such a way that one must kneel to enter the birthplace of Jesus', conjured a longing for the humility Sr. Thomas so desperately desired to instill in me. The Wailing Wall of the Temple where Jesus prayed and argued with the elders, the mount of the Transfiguration, the Upper Room of the Last Supper and Pentecost, kneeling under the tree which tradition says heard the cries of Jesus as He sweat blood in the garden of Gethsemane, all drew me into the mystery of Jesus' life and death, leaving me eager to imitate His sacrifice. At the Church of the Resurrection, Saint Peter invaded my prayer. Saint Peter, always rash, also realized quickly when he'd been wrong. Saint Peter, suddenly my hero. I prayed desperately that Jesus use my rashness and be gentle with me as He'd always been with Peter; I walked away with an acceptance of my own limitations and an assurance that God would continue to lead me.

Mary, Mother of Jesus, always somewhat distant, a bit too perfect for me, slowly became more approachable as I walked her stomping ground of Nazareth, Bethlehem, and Jerusalem. Meditating on her life wrapped up in the life of her son, I began to see that focusing on her virginity and her Immaculate Conception made it impossible for me to see that to all those around her, she was an unwed mother, misunderstood and scorned. Kneeling in the Church of the Annunciation, I struggled with my images. Her Fiat: "Behold the handmaid of the Lord, be it done unto me according to your word," stood as witness. Mary offered her acceptance before she knew exactly what it meant, just as I did when I pronounced my final vows.

Walking the Via Dolorosa, praying the Stations of the Cross, at sunrise in a silent, solemn procession moved me, but not until we joined the public devotion did the Way of the Cross become absolutely awe inspiring. Moving through the narrow streets, up hills and around corners of the regular marketplace, the crowds shouted as marketers sold their wares, women scolded children, people rushing to buy food for dinner pushed and shoved their way through the multitude. Dirt, dust, noise, sweat. The crucifixion wasn't sanitary and sanctimonious. Those who witnessed it never fathomed the incredible events taking place in their midst.

As I sat on the low branch of a tree at Caesarea Philippi, where Jesus invited his friends to 'come away and rest awhile', I could hear Jesus ask his disciples the question I attempted to answer for so many years: "Who do you say that I am?" The question penetrated my thoughts, accosting me. My life and my words needed to match. The words of the gospel, my Rule and Constitutions, everything I'd studied and read about the life of St. Francis jumped in and out of my consciousness as pages flashed through my thoughts. I simply wanted to become more Franciscan. With each reading of our Rules and Constitution, I lined and underlined the why of our existence. Idealism, others said, not reality. No one could answer my question about the purpose of our community's existence. Each offered her own answer, but most spoke simply of getting to heaven. My life in community made no sense. With no preferential option for the poor, we had no clear charism, no real purpose, no passion. A hole opened in the pit of my stomach and I knew nothing would change.

On August 4, the second anniversary of my final vows, the leader of our pilgrimage asked me to share my vocation story at liturgy. On the Diocesan Vocation Commission for three years and having given talks on religious life in parishes from California to Hong Kong, a vocation talk would be no problem, but in the shadow of Golgotha and the mountain of the Transfiguration, I stood speechless. Stumbling over my words, I spoke of hearing God's voice and answering His call, but my heart suffered absolute emptiness, leaving me absolutely confused and frightened at my new reality.

Mount Sinai

Our journey began at 1:30 in the morning, in the cold and dark. Knowing Sr. Clare feared heights and hated walking down stairs, but needed to appear strong in the eyes of the public, I asked four friends to help her walk up and down Mount Sinai leaving her dignity intact and helping her without being obvious. I stayed within fifty paces ahead or behind Sr. Clare and made sure that my cohorts stayed within arms' reach. When we finally reached bottom at midmorning, I knew I could take my eyes off of Sr. Clare.

We entered St. Katherine's Monastery at the foot of Mount Sinai, grateful for refuge from the scorching heat. Given a brief tour, we were invited to spend time in reflection before loading the bus. I found the back staircase that led directly to what our guide called the Meditation on Life and Death.

At twenty-eight, when many young women think of careers, marriage and children, I knelt in the basement of a monastery at the foot of Mount Sinai staring at a jail cell full of dried, hollow human skulls, meditating. So many of the dead came to mind; memories of several lingered.

I thought of Mrs. LaFrenz my next door neighbor from childhood. Handing over her daily paper and old National Geographic and Saturday Evening Post, she sat on the arm of the couch to share the neighborhood gossip she'd gathered visiting the elderly shut-ins, her Christian duty. She arrived each Christmas, bearing gifts of socks, pajamas, crayons and simple toys. To us more precious than gold, frankincense, myrrh, and a small envelop filled with McDonald's gift certificates, our yearly fast food treat.

Mrs. LaFrenz celebrated each set of braces coming off, every good grade, and all of our birthdays. She witnessed every first: bike ride, Communion, Confession, and date. The thew, thew, thew, of her clicking tongue each time I misbehaved echoed against the consistent praise and encouragement she lavished upon me. Mrs. LaFrenz replaced the grandmother, auntie, and father I never knew.

I remembered Sr. Dolores, a World War II veteran. Suffering with cancer resulting in a colostomy, she maintained a cheerful disposition and attempted to work until the end. I helped Sr. Dolores irrigate and clean the attached bag several times a week. The grunt work added one more sordid detail to my daily chores during novitiate, but sitting on the edge of the tub in the bathroom, wiping the tears from her cheeks, encouraging her to share her jokes and admiring her courage, I grew in admiration and gained strength to confront my fears and overcome the pride endangering my soul.

Kneeling on the cool stone floor, I stared at the jail cell filled with skulls of those who had died. I fixed my gaze on the hollowed faces of those who walked these holy halls and attempted to meditate on the Four Last Things: Death, Judgment, Heaven and Hell. My soul fixed on the final judgment scene of Matthew's gospel: "Whatsoever you do to the least of my brothers that you do unto me." Easily remembered from Matthew's gospel and one of my favorite childhood church songs, I conjured the images – when I was hungry, you gave me to eat; thirsty, you gave me to drink; naked, you gave me your coat; homeless, you opened your door. And I wept.

The last time I'd attempted to open our convent doors to someone in need, Sr. Fatima severely reprimanded me. Sr. Nathaniel and I sat correcting papers at the conference room table, as we did most nights of the week, when the gate bell rang. Looking at the clock, we froze. Almost midnight. We grabbed our shoes and headed out the door. Rushing to the gate, we found one of the students from our youth group in tears. She'd argued with her parents and hopped in a taxi to seek our advice. We brought her into the house to offer warmth and to calm her. Sr. Fatima came down within minutes, called the taxi, and sent her home. They sent Sr. Nathaniel and me to bed immediately, promising to talk in the morning. We attempt to explain she could be in danger and we should have listened before sending her home, but they were outraged. They made it very clear only superiors decided when to serve the needs of others, our convent was not a soup kitchen or a homeless shelter, and our apostolate was education, nothing more. As my eyes drifted from one skull to the next and I imagined my own among them, I begged Sr.

Veronica, from her place in heaven, to give me direction. I prayed for the grace to stand up for my convictions and to let go of my fears.

By the time we returned to the hotel to pack our things, Sr. Clare spoke furiously. "How could you just leave me stranded like that? You just want to make friends with everyone; those other people mean more to you than I do. I am your Sister, remember? We are community, family. They aren't. You know I'm afraid of heights. Where were you?" Her controlled barrage resembled calculated rage. Sr. Clare bombarded me with questions, but any attempt to answer would be futile. She would never believe I surrounded her with body guards and watched her every move. Just as she would never know that I sat awake most of the previous night, leaning against the hallway door to keep it from rattling in the night wind being funneled through the open window. We'd have suffocated with the windows shut, but Sr. Clare would never function if the rattling kept her awake. I sat, half awake, with my back against the door all night because Sr. Clare needed to sleep. Nothing I could say would change Sr. Clare's mind. I clung desperately to my truth and excused myself from the next days' excursions due to illness.

Holy Land

Dead Sea, Mount Tabor, Jordan River

74

I would have never categorized the events of my daily existence in novitiate as brain-washing, but by the time Sr. Thomas arrived in Hong Kong with a Vietnamese postulant, I realized Sr. Thomas treated those in training as a cult leader might the masses. While most communities insisted women wait until after college to enter the convent, Sr. Thomas preferred teenagers. More docile, she'd said. More easily manipulated, I realized.

My initial suspicion began with Sr. Philomena, a young woman from the Philippines, who had been a postulant in Oregon. Asked to leave because of an inability to follow basic instructions and a stubborn insistence about being right, Sr. Thomas invited her to reenter just after Sr. Veronica's death. Certain that cultural misunderstanding caused her initial failure, she sent Sister Philomena to Hong Kong for her second attempt.

Sr. Thomas asked me to rewrite lessons from the Vows and Virtues course taken by novices in America since the 1960's. She wanted me to simplify the language and find reading materials from the convent library in Hong Kong so Sr. Grace could teach the classes. I reworded, reworked, and rewrote the lessons, initially attempting to replicate them as closely as possible, but quickly questioning the reality before my eyes. Entering into the section on vows, I assumed I'd find several lessons on each of the three vows: poverty, chastity and obedience. I turned the pages of my notebooks over and over, thinking I missed a chapter or skipped a page. I found one lesson on poverty, one on chastity and eight on obedience.

Poverty had been reduced to nothing being called my own and never keeping money I received as gift or salary. Before making vows we were required to sign a release form agreeing that if we were to leave, we would never request funds from the Congregation for services rendered. We pinched pennies and kept a running record of every dime spent. Chastity focused on sinful, dirty thoughts and avoiding sexual activity. We avoided particular friendships, being friendly with men, and reading or watching anything that might lead to impure thoughts. Chastity meant distance and separation. The next eight lessons explained the vow of obedience in fine detail. Obedience outranked every other vow or virtue. If we were simply obedient in all matters our reward would be great in heaven, regardless of a lack of charity or any sin of omission.

I scoured the table of contents, the index, and every relevant chapter of any book that discussed anything remotely resembling a vow or a virtue. Poverty meant more than communal ownership and penny pinching. We couldn't continue to live comfortably, more comfortably than most we served, claiming poverty.

Poverty had to include simplicity, detachment, generosity. Chastity meant availability, not frigidity. We'd never discussed intimacy, how to handle our sexuality, what to do to remain whole. Sexual intimacy couldn't be avoided as a danger; chastity must be embraced positively. I needed something, anything, to support what my heart knew. I couldn't in good conscience, continue the blatant bias. I tried to point out the incongruence to Sr. Thomas, but she told me to hand the lessons over to Sr. Grace unaltered. Questions crowded my prayer and interrupted my sleep. Agitation invaded my soul.

Sitting at the dining room table one morning just after Sr. Thomas moved to Hong Kong, I listened to her telling Sr. James, a young novice she brought along, to put on a sweater because she was cold. My arguments about the eight lessons on obedience flooded my mind. As Sr. Thomas spoke, a decisive awareness shot through my existence as if a knife pierced my ribcage. My lungs twisted, sucking oxygen from my blood, my head spinning as thoughts collided with memories of my early convent training. In a life-flashing-before-my-eyes kind of moment, I witnessed the systematic dissemblance of my personhood. Sr. Thomas initiated my demise from day one. She chiseled away any modicum of self-confidence I possessed. She decided what I would wear, where I would sit in chapel, which room I would sleep in, and how I would spend my days; she told me who to vote for in public office, what to think and how to feel. She consistently destroyed my self-esteem, questioned my mental and emotional stability, and led me to question my intelligence and my integrity.

Under her tutelage I wrote an arrogant letter to my sister-in-law offering my understanding and acceptance of her, despite her practice of another faith; I refused to acknowledge my little sister's wedding because it wasn't in the Catholic Church and was told not to congratulate my older brother on his ordination to the Baptist ministry; I condemned the TEC movement that led me to my vocation as over emotional, leading participants to a homosexual lifestyle. I became a rigid and judgmental fundamentalist, offending family and friends, attempting to gain Sr. Thomas's approval.

As the weeks passed, I witnessed Sr. Thomas's presence directly influencing not only the postulants and novices, but the entire dynamic of the house. Sr. Fatima, who questioned and rejected most of Sr. Thomas's ideas for years, but still reeling from Sr. Veronica's death, latched onto Sr. Thomas like a bird to the morning worm and listened to every comment and suggestion as if it came directly from God. Sr. Thomas insisted my 5:00 am Tai Chi lessons with Anna, the cook, were unnecessary, so they stopped. Sr. Thomas said that Sr. Clare and Sr. Kathleen had too many responsibilities outside of community to be included in the Sunday cooking schedule, so they were left off and I took their place. Sr. Thomas felt the members of the Provincial Council shouldn't have to clear the table or dry dishes as they did for over twenty years, so they stopped. She systematically destroyed the confidence and camaraderie the Hong Kong house worked so carefully to preserve, as she had destroyed me.

Returning for seconds at dinner turned into thirds, and then late night binges. Two pound boxes of chocolates, a half-gallon of ice cream, or an entire pie became my bedtime snack. Minor headaches, burning eyes, taste of dirty dishwater at the back of my dry throat, sticky skin, continual heartburn accompanied by belching like a frat brother – symptoms slowly consumed my body. By late September I went six days without a bowel movement. Late at night, after everyone went to bed, I sat on the toilet for almost an hour, with wrenching pains in my abdomen, chills, shaky knees, and a smell that reminded me of the brewing slop from the pig farm in Taiwan. Feeling as if I'd just completed drug withdrawal, I wobbled to bed and collapse.

With Sr. Veronica's death still so fresh in our memories, I resisted saying anything. When I finally did, they sent me straight to St. Theresa's Hospital where Sr. Veronica died. Sr. Kathleen, usually too busy to bother with anyone else's problems, cancelled her afternoon to accompany me. The Western medicine doctors, finding no problems with my blood work, sent me home suggesting Metamucil and Pepto-Bismol just as they'd done with Sr. Veronica for years. No one said what we were all thinking, 'Sister Jude probably has cancer.' Eleven of the thirteen Sisters who ever died in our community died from cancer. Four others currently suffered through periods of remission and relapse. Memories of Sr. Dolores, Sr. Cecilia and others whirled in my thoughts. I sat for hours in the chapel, agonizing over what to do. Wanting to be resigned to God's will, for the first time in my life, I didn't want to die.

October, 1992

Sr. Nathaniel suggested I make an appointment with the natural medicine doctor she'd seen once. I took the train to North Point, just blocks from where I regularly met with my spiritual director, frightened by the possibilities lying in wait. Would I uncover secrets long repressed like Sr. Nathaniel said so many others had? Fearful of what I might find, I almost walked away to ingest fiber powder daily, accept the cross God gave me, and offer up my sufferings for the salvation of souls as Sr. Thomas insisted. Climbing the narrow staircase leading to the second story office, the smell of incense and the hum of classical music sent a chill down my spine. Beaded curtains marked the entrance to the office and I wondered if I'd been caught in a time warp, heading back to the sixties, with incense, black lights and psychedelic drugs. My muscles tightened and I began to shiver. A tall thin man in a white tunic top, jeans and flip-flops summoned me to enter through the parted beads. He introduced himself, looked at my eyes, rubbed the inside of my arm, turned my hands over and poked at my fingernails, and asked me to stick out my tongue. I never filled out any paper work listing my symptoms, never answered any questions, and never undressed. He asked me to sit, rummaged through his desk drawer and pulled out a book. Flipping through the pages, he folded the book opened, pointed at a picture and began to read. I listened as he listed each and every one of my symptoms; he even added conditions I never consider problematic.

"You are not sick," he said. "You are overworking your liver. Your body is under extreme stress. Outside elements, the air you breathe, the food, your lifestyle. You don't have any serious illness, but if you don't change the way you live right now, you will die of cancer in ten years. You must reduce your stress level."

I tried in vain to slam button after button in my brain, trying to find the code, to hit the right nerve to break the tidal wave I couldn't ignore but also couldn't listen to, a voice whispering: *You need to leave.* I could reduce stress. I argued with myself. No matter where you go, you take you with you. I learned this long ago. I could fix this. I would reduce stress; doctor's orders.

The doctor explained it very carefully: You have years of toxic build-up clinging to the walls of your intestine. You need a complete detoxification. As the treatment progresses, you'll see every color and shape coming out. Don't be alarmed. Be near a bathroom, especially in the morning. Afternoons are easier. You'll feel terrible at first, but get better as the days go on. As you clear your intestines, you clear your mind. As you clear your mind, you experience emotions that years of stress and abuse have blocked from your awareness. Expect to feel everything intensely. Spiritual enlightenment and sexual awareness come together. Day three and day seven, for some reason, tend to be the most difficult. Find someone to support you.

Sr. Thomas didn't care and Sr. Fatima ranted that no one gave me permission to follow this doctor, to not eat dinner, to stop eating desserts. He said nothing was wrong with me, so why all the fuss?

Sr. Nathaniel supported me, but it became the two of us against the rest. I'd already been called divisive. Sr. Clare already reprimanded me repeatedly for our friendship: we spoke English, we worked together, graded papers together, and we sat near each other at table. Because of Sr. Nathaniel's limited ability in Cantonese, Sr. Veronica often made me accompany her to events or to people's homes. I had no option but to spend time with her but I'd always spent time with others, too. I'd never refused to accompany any Sister anywhere. I never refused to help. Asking for her help would just cause more troubles, more criticism. I would do this alone.

Sr. Joanne said nothing in the beginning, but as my next doctor's appointment neared, her festering disgust could no longer be contained. I heard the click of her tongue along the ridge of her mouth each evening as I sipped my tea. I continually rejected her offers for just one piece of chocolate or just a small dish or two of ice cream, but she finally gained control when she forbade me from getting out of bed early to spend extra time in chapel.

Rules and restrictions kept me in bed, but nothing confined what happened within my soul. As I saw the toxins pushed from my body, like the cleansing flush of an unclogged drain, my eyes stopped burning, my skin became smooth, and the sour taste in my mouth vanished. Freed from the heavy load I'd been carrying in my gut, I began to feel, to desire, to dream, as if the toxins made it impossible to hear, not the voices around me, but the voice within.

Christmas, 1992

Maybe my research paper on the denial of self in Mark's Gospel or on the theology of suffering, maybe the trip to mainland China, or maybe the moment I knew my father was not mentally ill or homeless as I'd always imagined caused the shift. The idea wasn't new. From my first days in novitiate I struggled with how we lived poverty. I attempted to make my point, but obedience was most important and more precious in God's eyes. I can't say that I heard a voice or even a whisper telling me to work and live among the poor. I don't know exactly when the feeling began to gurgle up from my unconscious to fill my conscious awareness, but slowly I could not walk down the street without the face of each handicapped or mentally ill person and every beggar burning through my heart. I could scarcely leave the convent or sit within its walls without being convinced that I needed to be one with them. Each prayer I prayed, every Scripture I read, every song I heard at Mass, yelled that I needed to leave behind the comfort of the convent to become one with those on the street. I could no longer ignore the gnawing sensation, a longing for something more. I'd channeled it to working with youth, getting them fired up, excited, aware. I'd always convinced myself to let it go, to deny myself, to die to my own need to go beyond. Sr. Thomas called my desires pride, a desire for attention but I could not ignore the voices screaming in my heart to be Christ's hands and feet to the world; to be one with the poor, not to save them but to accompany them; to heal the suffering of the poor and marginalized. I did all I could to be obedient for ten years. I crushed every dream, swallowed every admonition and followed God's will. Now I questioned everything.

On Christmas Eve, just before Midnight Mass, I walked the malodorous halls of the government hospital singing "Silent Night" and "Joy to the World" with a longing to bring peace and joy to the suffering patients. I thought of my own nephew, Ricky; of Judi, still battling brain tumors after almost twenty years; of my brother-in-law Tom, who'd died so young. We sang in English and Chinese and I knew, with every word, only Jesus could bring true comfort. Walking from bed to bed in the children's ward, I watched the big brown eyes light up at the sight of the stockings and Santa's hats, the candy canes and jingle bells. As we gathered in the nursery, I glanced down at the child lying in the first bed.

"What's his name?" I asked the attendee.

"He has no name. He's waiting to die."

Pulling back the covers I noticed the child's severe deformities. His internal organs were growing, in a pouch, extending from his abdomen. He had no legs and only the stub of his left arm, a deformed skull, and a cleft palate with a hair lip. I lifted him gently in my arms and, in a whisper, sang "O come let us adore him" in the small, precious child's ear. How could anyone abandon this child? What pain must the mother be feeling, knowing her child is alone in this hospital? How could she give him up? Are my tears for the child or the mother? Who am I to pass judgment or lay blame? Am I here to offer pity or peace? I stood staring into the child's eyes as I rocked him in my folded arms. Tears streaming down my cheeks, I remained until we needed to head to Chinese University for Midnight Mass. Placing him gently on the bed, I headed toward the taxi line twisting through the medal poles, dozens of revelers enjoying holiday cheer.

"Can we get the next taxi?" I asked the person at the front of the line.

"You're a nun. You can't be doing bad things. You do good. Go. Go." The willing passenger stepped aside as he stumbled through his English.

The baby inhabited my mind as I sat in the taxi. Years of disappointing, empty Christmases dissolved. Years of praying at the feet of the plastic, artificial baby Jesus lying in the manger, praying to make room for Him in the inn of my heart were suddenly realized in this little abandoned child. This little child, with no name, no family, no one to love him, became for me Emmanuel, God-with-us. I longed to return to the hospital to cradle him in my arms, to hold him while he died, and to give him some dignity. Instead I headed to the University to help with Midnight Mass.

For Christmas, we could ask for one gift. For years I asked for money to have Mass prayed for my father. This time, I requested a retreat on Cheung Chau.

"Why do you want that for Christmas?" Sr. Joanne asked, looking dejected and disappointed.

"I need some personal prayer time. Some quiet, that's all. I usually used my Christmas gift to offer Mass for my Dad. But I know he's at peace; I need peace now."

"Can't you do that here? Why do you have to go away?" Sr. Joanne pleaded, and I knew she knew. I confided in Sr. Clare, asking for her prayers, seeking insight from someone I trusted as more level headed than I. Obviously she betrayed me. "I don't want you to be alone."

"Sr. Clare should go with you so you have someone to talk to."

Certain Sr. Clare betrayed my confidence, I didn't want her near me as I prayed. "I'll be on retreat. I won't need someone to talk to."

My patience wore thin as I imagined how their conversation must have gone. Sr. Clare, with clenched jaws, saying, 'She told me she needs time away. She is thinking of leaving. God wants her to live on the street.' If Sr. Joanne knew, so did Fatima, Grace and Thomas. They kept no secrets. The dam now cracked, the walls would burst any moment and the torrent would be unstoppable.

Sr. Clare and I didn't speak. Nothing could be said. She'd left home to enter the convent eighteen years ago, against her father's wishes. He swore that if she left home she would never be welcomed back. Sr. Clare had not seen nor talked to her father since that day. She'd abandoned her father as my father abandoned me. Now, we walked together towards the retreat house at the top of the hill in absolute silence.

I fell in love with the outer island of Cheung Chau years earlier at the moment the crowd pushed me forward without me moving my feet, on to the ferry that shuttled visitors to and from the small, simple island without cars. I loved passing the junks littering the harbor, wondering what brought the inhabitants of these houseboats to the docks of this small island. Most of them could not even step foot on dry land without being arrested as illegal immigrants. They relied on their children for sustenance, choosing to survive on this small wooden boat rather than return to Mainland China and the possibility of poverty and persecution. On my way to and from numerous retreats and workshops over the years, I'd walked the narrow, stone roads, twisting and turning by factory upon factory. Dark, poorly lit rooms with row after row of workers cranked out clothes, toys and household goods. The goods finally got stamped, "Made in Hong Kong," but they'd never be touched by the housewives and children of these streets; rather, they'd be shipped to the United States just as I would be soon, never able to tell of the journey.

On my first private retreat nearly five years earlier, struggling in prayer to know the will of God, I'd clearly heard the message, "Learn to love and I will lead you." The desire to love as Jesus loved became my goal. I spent hours, over months, meditating on the lines from the letter of St. Paul: "Love is faithful. Love is kind. Love is never rude." I replaced the word love with my name or the pronoun "I." I prayed to be love. I did all I could to convince myself that God willed for me to stay right in community. I would love the congregation to the end. I just needed to stand up for what I believed and work at changing things, not give up.

As we approached the building, I prayed that love might continue to be my guide. My thoughts were interrupted by Sr. Clare as she swung her body, full force around to look me straight in the eyes, "You planned to meet her here, didn't you?"

I looked up to see Sr. Dominique standing at the entrance.

"I had no idea she'd be here. I swear." I knew Sr. Clare would never believe me, just as she did not believe me in Egypt. She and the others blamed Sr. Dominique, for every word and idea I shared that they didn't like. Dominique listened to the movements of my soul and helped me clarify the desires of my heart, but she did not cause them. Greeting Dominique as we walked in the door, I silently said goodbye forever to Sr. Clare, my sister and friend.

Sisters Joanne, Fatima and Thomas insisted that I speak to one priest after another about my desire to live and work with people on the street. First, a Franciscan they trusted listened to my conviction that God called me to work with and live among the poor, and promptly agreed I must take the time and space necessary to discern God's will in my life. Next, they sent me to a Jesuit who recommended I take time away from community to get perspective. Finally, the Vicar for Religious encouraged me to remain in Hong Kong, but to physically remove myself from community for the psychological space I needed. The Sisters rejected one recommendation after another, becoming more and more hostile to my simple desire to discern God's will. We had schools to run. I could not disgrace the community by living and working with people on the street.

"You should have never taken theology. That's the problem." Sr. Fatima shouted during one of many evening sessions in the small parlor where most official meetings took place. "Too much brain takes you away from God. I told Sr. Veronica, God rest her soul. I never wanted you to study. Sr. Veronica was afraid you'd go back to the States if we didn't let you." Sr. Fatima's face flamed, beads of sweat streaming down her hair line and across her forehead as the words spewed from her mouth. "You never really belonged here anyway. We just needed someone to teach English."

"Sr. Veronica encouraged me, all the time." I felt tears welling in my eyes as my voice clogged my airways. "She said everyone has a different path and people need to respect other people's journeys. If she were here, she would respect me." My response sounded lame, but the wrenching pain in my gut when Sr. Fatima said I never really belonged felt as if it would rip me apart.

Don't talk like that about Sr. Veronica." Sr. Joanne wiped the tears from her own cheek as she spoke. "How do we know that anything you say is true? Don't lie about Sr. Veronica."

"I'm not a liar. She told me everyone's path is different. She did." I began to shriek. "How can you call me a liar?" Pushing my chair back, I lunged for the door and slammed it behind me.

The pain of Sr. Veronica's death, still too raw, stung as I sat on my bed, rocking, knees at my chest. I didn't belong in Hong Kong. I never really did. They'd let me stay, but I never fit in. The words rang through my brain.

Sr. Fatima and Sr. Joanne refused to speak to me from that moment on, except when absolutely necessary. Sitting directly in front of them at Mass, I turned to offer the sign of peace, only to be ignored as an outcast. The rejection felt worse than the abandonment I'd lived with my entire life.

Sr. Thomas, certain she could convince me my ideas were foolish, insisted that because she allowed me to make final vows, God willed for me to be in the congregation forever. They were the voice of God, that couldn't change.

"If you are so certain I should be here, then what about Sr. Francis Anne. She made final vows, remember?" The sharpness in my voice startled me. With each conversation that took place, discernment and discovery of God's will moved further and further from my reach as we engaged in a battle, me against them, no holds barred.

"Sr. Francis Anne was different." Sr. Thomas stuttered.

"Why? Because she's an alcoholic, like your broth….er." I couldn't catch the words as they left my mouth.

Sr. Francis Anne, a finally professed Sister, was quickly and secretively shuffled from house to house and job to job until she eventually asked for a dispensation, only to request re-admittance five years later. Granted a probationary acceptance and given a new name, Sr. Francis Anne tried to reintegrate with the community until they asked her to leave again because she relied too heavily on Alcoholics Anonymous meetings and support groups instead of on God and community.

"Sr. Francis Anne made final vows. Why did you kick her out? If final vows mean it's God's will, how can you decide later it was a big mistake? Maybe I'm a big mistake, too."

Sr. Thomas stood, dumbfounded. Stumbling for some answer, she said, "Sr. Francis Anne had problems." Neither of us mentioned my reference to her alcoholic brother.

"So final vows and council's decisions are valid if we don't develop a problem? As soon as we're troublesome, unable to contribute like you want, we can be thrown out. Then we're disposable?"

I argued my point with anyone who decided to approach me, but I desperately needed someone to make the decision for me. I didn't know how to trust my own judgment. More than anything, I wanted them all to understand I wanted to do God's will, not my own.

Five students across Hong Kong committed suicide within five days at the beginning of January 1993. The discrepancy between how I spent my days, what I thought I should be doing, and the headlines that greeted me each morning made my soul ache. As the weeks passed, suicides diminished, but the first month of the year totaled thirteen. I could not help but wonder if the instant jump of the child, slow death from alcohol and drug abuse, or the more socially acceptable, death by food or work, was more authentic.

Since my days in novitiate, I listened to Sr. Thomas's consistent message, "stop thinking and keep busy." The natural medicine doctor and my detoxification had been my first attempt to break my cycle of addiction to both food and work; the Sisters condemned me for my attempts to be healthy. From utter exhaustion, I'd returned to nightly binges, eating boxes of chocolates and any other sugar I could get my hands on. I began to sleep more and could no longer focus during prayer. Remaining in a situation wreaking havoc not only on my body, but my soul, the bravery of the students quickly convicted me. I began to judge every discussion and each idea in juxtaposition to the plight of the poor and suffering. Hearing one Sister proudly pronounce, "We'll find out who's right at the Last Judgment" when discussing Sisters who no longer wore the habit and veil, appalled me. Children jumped to their deaths around us, and we somehow reduced the Last Judgment to wearing a veil. I stood up and left the room.

Listening to the gospel proclaiming "people in darkness have seen a great light," I finally found the guts to articulate my own question: What light are we providing by insulating ourselves inside this convent? I wanted to become authentic and to reconcile what I believed at eighteen with what I'd come to know at twenty-nine. Wearing a habit and veil no longer meant total commitment if I could not serve the poor. I could no longer destroy my own soul in the name of following community rules. As I pushed for a leave of absence to move physically and spiritually more closely to the poor in Hong Kong, Sr. Ruth, the new Superior General, suggested I return to the United States for time and space to discern. With her words came my hope that maybe one day someone might say, "Go with our blessing. We realize God is calling you to another way of life."

I planned to return to the United States when school let out in July, but each day became more unbearable. I couldn't teach without breaking down in tears in front of the entire class. I couldn't mark papers or plan lessons. Teachers began to ask questions and students sat, watching their efficient, jovial yet demanding teacher, completely disintegrate before their eyes. Every book, magazine or article I picked up reminded me God called me to be vulnerable. I could no longer wait for the approval of others or for someone else to tell me what to do. I completed the students' exam preparation and left Hong Kong on March 6, 1993. The official announcement: I returned to the States on doctor's orders to recuperate from an ongoing illness and would return after a few months' rest and relaxation.

I'd been in Hong Kong five and a half years. Since leaving home, I'd never lived anywhere as long. What had once been so strange, so different and so new had become so comfortable, such a part of who I'd become. Not only did Cantonese become understandable, at times I forgot how to say things in English. I dreamt and thought in Cantonese, and followed the Cantonese rules of etiquette.

I gave my all to those I met. I answered the questions I could and questioned with them if I had no answer. I listened to their stories of pain and held them as they cried. I struggled with youngsters learning the limits of lying and stealing, friendship and dating. I prayed with the mother whose daughter had been gang raped. I comforted the daughter who found her mother half dead after a suicide attempt. I held the hand of a dying father and a bipolar parishioner. I prayed with them and for them all. In English and Chinese, kneeling, sitting, walking on the street or riding a train. I was available as their Sister. Never really preachy, I simply tried to be genuine. I wanted my life to be sermon enough for others to believe. I wanted to live the gospel in a way that would compel others to ask why I did what I did. Now I needed to leave behind everything and everyone I'd come to know and love.

Prodigal Sister

Returning to the United States
March, 1993

The tears of the Sisters who escorted me to the airport left me with little sensation. Neither happy nor sad, I dropped to sleep within minutes of take-off. The awkward pity on the faces of those who greeted me in the United States left me longing for solitude. I wanted nothing more than to sleep. I could muster no energy to explain or defend my process, but they gave me no choice. Sr. Thomas arranged for her sister Nancy, the clinical psychologist who performed the IQ tests years before, to meet with me the very next morning to evaluate my condition. She took down my family history starting with my grandparents and anything I knew about my parents' childhood. She asked about every crushed dream, each pain. I dredged up and waded through the saga of junior high and high school, becoming the tough girl, the class clown, and the sneak. I recounted my drinking, escapades of cutting class and forging signatures and of my sister Karen's near fatal car accident. I provided details of day to day life in novitiate through my time in Asia, retelling stories of frustration and personality conflict, exposing the desires of my heart and the movements of my prayer. I spoke articulately of my constant questioning, my call to work among the poor, to heal the sick and to be available to the outcast.

Finishing my biographical drudgery, I assumed I'd finally begin the process of discernment and discuss the point of the detailed family history. Instead, she simply thanked me for my honesty, promised to send her conclusions to the superiors and said goodbye. She scoured my soul and left me raw to pull the pieces together, isolated and alone. I anticipated the arrival of her report, certain that this would be the final catalyst necessary to propel me into mission with the poor. Sr. Ruth summoned me to her office, almost ten days later, to reveal forty-five pages of dictation; my life, the condensed version, written in pencil on a lined yellow notepad. A typed cover letter stated simply that I definitely had a vocation and should be allowed to do community service in my spare time. She said nothing of my childhood pain, my joys, or my dreams. I'd bared my soul for naught.

I walked through my days with little affectation but with an insistence that I would not simply return to cooking and cleaning at the retreat house. Unable to handle the pain of constant whispering and looks of disappointment from those around me, I begged for the opportunity to visit family. For the first time in eleven years I spoke honestly when my brothers and sisters asked how things were, retelling stories of manipulation and humiliation I should have told long ago. With each revelation I realized the motto I'd heard so frequently, 'what happens in community stays in community,' protected those in power but left me, and many others, crippled by silence. My family not only allowed me to vent, but challenged my convictions, reminded me of my commitments, and shot through each conversation with a strong dose of sarcasm and comedy, still leaving my dignity intact. As the days passed, perspective shifted, and I regained a sense of self and a modicum of sanity.

Summer, 1993

Certain that I needed to stop listening to others and spend time alone with God, I requested to make a 30-day silent retreat with the Spiritual Exercises of St. Ignatius program. With my Bible, prayer book, journal, colored pencils and walking shoes in hand, I wanted no secular music or reading materials to distract from my time with God. I entered easily into the imaginative prayer style, savoring the moments that allowed me to incorporate memories still vivid from my pilgrimage to the Holy Land. Thirty days of silence, four hours of structured prayer each day, this retreat provided that cave that St. Francis spoke of, where I could be myself with Jesus and he with me; where together, we could decide what I needed to do. Each hour of prayer left me with a peace my spiritual director described as consolation. He outlined the scripture passages for me to pray with each day, explained the movements of desolation and consolation, and questioned my emotions surrounding each prayer period. God would give me direction, he said, no need to search for answers elsewhere.

One of the few on retreat still wearing a habit, I felt courage mixed with defiance each time I walked barefoot in the grass or sat in the evening sun allowing my hair, which I'd begun to grow beyond an inch, to dry in the wind. Whether I walked for hours in the hills, picked buckets full of wild blackberries for the dinner table or sat cross-legged on the floor of my room, the question of my future with the congregation and my desire to work with the marginalized perched like a vulture on my shoulder.

A decisive moment came during my meditation on the Loss of Jesus in the Temple, a scene I'd considered each Sunday afternoon for years as the community prayed the Rosary of the Seven Sorrows of Mary. I watched, in Ignatian style, as Mary and Joseph hunted for their twelve-year-old son. I walked with Mary in her panic and felt her pain. I listened to Jesus as he argued with the elders in the temple and eavesdropped on the conversation between Jesus and Joseph just after they found Jesus.

"Did you not know I had to be about my father's business?" Jesus looked up at Joseph as they stood on the stairway leading out of the temple.

"It is not yet your time," Joseph said with his hand on Jesus' shoulder.

"But when will it be my time? How will I know?"

"When you are no longer agitated," Joseph answered quietly.

I stood watching the father and son exchange, knowing that Joseph's words were meant for me. I'd been too anxious to change my community, to change the world. My time would come when I no longer felt frustrated, anxious, or agitated. I knew in that instant that I could only act if I acted in peace.

Nearing the final days of retreat, as I picked blackberries, formulating what I might say to Sr. Ruth in the discussion she promised to have regarding my next assignment, Jesus gently reminded me He is the only one who needs to know the truth of my heart besides me. The Sisters may never understand my decisions. He gently reminded me, ""You have always prayed: 'Break me, if that's what it takes to make me a saint.' I have not neglected your prayer. I've heard your plea."

By the time Sr. Ruth phoned on the final day of the retreat, I had surrendered "all my freedom and my memories; my understanding and my will" according to the offering of St. Ignatius, and felt ready for anything.

"I am concerned about you. I want you to be in a safe, supportive environment so that you can continue discerning and processing everything that is happening in your life." Sr. Ruth spoke sincerely as we walked the circular path surrounding the Oregon retreat house. "You're so vulnerable right now; you need a place to be yourself and to have a lighter work load. I can make sure that happens if you are here."

Two days later, Sr. Ruth spoke tentatively. "I need to ask you something. Listen before you answer. Sr. Marianne and Sr. Gabrielle have both asked for leave to return to the Philippines to start their own community. We have no one to teach at Holy Angels so the Council and I would like you to go to teach sixth grade."

"Teach sixth grade? I'm not really trained to teach in the United States. I haven't been in this education system for ten years. I've never taught sixth grade…" Excuses rolled from my lips quickly and with little hesitation. Sr. Ruth encouraged me to take a little time, to think about it. "But, I'm supposed to be figuring out if God's calling me to work with the poor. That's why I'm here; you said it yourself. I taught in Hong Kong. I don't know if I'm emotionally or spiritually stable enough to take on a teaching job."

Even as I spoke, I knew I would concede to the will of the Council. I always had, especially in the big things. Until just weeks ago, I'd never refused even the simplest request.

"Oh, and while you're considering the Holy Angels thing, the Sisters are very upset you aren't wearing nylons. You aren't in Hong Kong anymore so heat isn't a concern. Why aren't you wearing nylons like you are supposed to?"

"Wearing nylons and shaving your legs is vain. Nylons represent the objectification of women. On retreat I knew in my heart, I had to be counter cultural. I have an obligation to follow my own conscience. We're buying into mainstream fashion and worldly opinion by the habit we wear. It's supposed to be a sign of poverty and simplicity, not conformity to societal norms."

"What about the rules? Did God tell you to stop following them, too?" Sr. Ruth sounded disgusted.

"If rules contradict my conscience, I cannot follow them. Since you're so concerned though, I'll pray about it." I spoke precisely and carefully. I'd never been so assertive. I didn't need anyone to tell me what to do anymore. I could trust myself. I spent hours in the chapel that night. When I could be certain I'd be alone, I lay prostrate in the aisle before the Blessed Sacrament. I'd given over my entire will to God during retreat, could I take it back now?

I knew what to do about Holy Angels when Sr. Ruth called me into her office the next morning, but she noticed I still didn't wear nylons.

"But you said you'd pray about it."

"Praying about it means I listen to God's will, not that I automatically do what you want. I am showing solidarity with the poor. If I can't work with them I can declare, in some small way, that women are not sex objects and that, as religious, we should not be supporting the objectification of women. My conscience will not allow me to wear them just so that other Sisters or people who see me aren't uncomfortable. People are uncomfortable at the sight of poverty too."

"You've never refused to follow a rule. What happened?"

"That's it. I've followed simplistic, ludicrous rules so long; I never stood up for the issues. I need to be one with the poor and oppressed, to be counter-cultural like Jesus."

"So, I suppose you'll refuse to go to Holy Angels."

"No. You've heard my reservations. I don't think I'm fit to go, but if the Council decides they need me, it must be God's will. I just don't understand why Sr. Joanne or Sr. Jean Ann or Sr. Paul can't go. They're all trained to teach grade school in the United States."

"They refuse to live with Sr. Simon."

"But our Constitution says we're called to work together in harmony, with loving respect. I can't be assigned to a community because of who I like."

Fall, 1993

I grew quickly to love my time in the classroom, opening the minds and the souls of the young people God gave me, but life in the convent remained almost unbearable. Sr. Clare expected me to ask permission to walk on the playground or have an evening snack. She cancelled appointments I'd made and became irate because I offered to help care for a brain injured teen in the parish one evening a week. She would approach at 7:45 as I prepped for class, "You know, if you can't handle this, I have someone lined up to take your place. You can quit if you want."

She left notes to say she would be out visiting family for the day or spending time with some parishioner, but if I did the same, she accused me of not caring about community and not being obedient. She expected me to be submissive and subservient. If we disagreed about something the night before, she sent a student into the classroom the next day with a note of apology and a long-stem rose. I felt as if I were in a twisted, destructive love affair.

Recognizing my struggles to live as an adult in an environment determined to treat me as a child, the spiritual director from my thirty-day retreat suggested I see a counselor to work through problems rather than run from them. Sr. Ruth refused to let me see a counselor because Sr. Thomas convinced her I needed lithium for manic-depression, like my father.

"Most people would have cracked long ago. It's impossible to live with Sr. Simon." I voiced my frustrations during a telephone conversation with Sr. Ruth one evening, "I'm practically under house arrest."

"I wouldn't have sent you there if you hadn't volunteered."

My heart almost stopped. "How could you say I volunteered? Forget it. If you think that, I can't talk to you." My knees snapped as I slammed the phone down. Volunteered, I thought, sitting on the bench in the enclosed phone booth. My words, twisted again to stab me, not in the back, but in the chest, cutting into the essence of my soul.

Stunned that the superiors presumed to assess my psychological state, my spiritual director located the names and numbers of several therapists. When I informed Sr. Ruth that I planned to begin therapy with or without the Council's permission, she reluctantly consented. She also gave me permission to keep any gift money I received to serve the needs of the poor, making a conscious decision to personally encounter those who begged from me. I handed out no money but offered food to anyone who asked.

As I walked from the subway station to the office of my therapist, I stopped to speak with a thin, haggard woman holding a sign that read, "Have children, need food." They had a place to stay, she said, but very little money for food. Glancing up the street I spotted a food mart on the next block.

"What would you like? What do your children eat?" I asked, as we walked the narrow aisles.

"Anything," she stammered. Together we loaded our basket with spaghetti noodles and Ragu, Macaroni 'n Cheese, Jif and Welch's grape jelly. Looking up from the pack of Oreos I added to the load, I noted the tear in her eye. "God bless you," she said as we parted. I knew He already had.

Handing out sandwiches to the guys begging in the 7-eleven parking lot, I looked them in the eyes and asked their names. I fed their bodies and they fed my soul, gifting me with the humility that Sr. Thomas so desperately tried to drill into me during the novitiate. Waiting for the bus one evening after a power outage forced hundreds of subway passengers to ground level, a parishioner I ran into and I were approached by a transient named Robert. Turning around, I saw a MacDonald's behind us and invited Robert to order whatever he liked. "May I have Chicken instead of a cheeseburger? I'm trying not avoid red meat."

The parishioner snickered as Robert walked away, glad to be free of his stench. "How can he have a preference when he is being offered a free meal?"

"Just because he's homeless and poor, you think he can't take care of his health?" I heard the indignation in my voice and knew I still needed to learn humility.

One afternoon I waited to cross the street when a young man with dirty blond hair and even dirtier clothing stood about fifteen feet away. He wore a rosary around his neck and a small Bible stuck out of his shirt pocket. As he approached, I stretched out my hand to shake his and to ask his name. He touched me briefly then knelt to the ground and kissed my feet.

"Praise God for giving us someone so holy and blessed to be with us. Bless me Sister. Please." He spoke loudly enough for all those near the intersection to hear. I stood, almost petrified, for just a second before grabbing his elbows, raising him to his feet and hugging him. Laying my hands on his head I asked God to bless him and grant him peace, saying to him, not quite as loudly, "Praise God for giving me someone so holy and blessed to be with me. Please pray for me."

I never saw nor spoke to that man again, but his face is still visible to me as I close my eyes. He appeared to be mentally ill, but I could only believe that he acted as God's angel, reminding me that my habit is a symbol of my call to holiness and I needed to serve Jesus in the poor.

Feeling oppressed by the constant watchful eye of Sr. Simon, I asked Sr. Ruth if I could spend our monthly day of prayer outside of the convent. I rose early to get in and out of the kitchen to fix my lunch before anyone else woke up. I tiptoed down the stairs only to see the light on in the community room.

"Where're you going?" Sr. Simon's voice didn't surprise, but annoyed me.

"St. Paul's for 6:30 Mass. I am spending the day there, remember?"

"St. Paul's doesn't have 6:30 Mass." The whine in her voice set me off.

"Are you calling me a liar?"

"No, but St. Paul's doesn't have a 6:30 Mass, I checked."

"So you're calling me a liar? You don't believe me. Where do you think I'm going?"

The conversation reminded me of fights I had with Mom at thirteen.

"What do you want to hear? That I'm running off with some man, to spend the day on the beach? What?"

"Where are you going?" Sister's redundancy fueled my rebellion and anger.

"I'm spending the day before the Blessed Sacrament at the chapel of the Missionaries of Charity at St. Paul's. Any problems with that? Thanks for helping me start my day in a prayerfully. Have a nice day, Sister."

"You're sneaky and conniving." I heard her voice behind me as I headed for the door. "You have no idea what community is."

"How have I been sneaky?" I flipped back to look at her. "Yesterday I told you exactly where I planned to spend the day. You do it whenever you want, can't I? Why is your way of praying the only right way?"

"I am the superior."

"So your spiritual life is more important than mine?"

"Just go ahead. Do whatever you want. You do not have my blessing."

"Be careful what you say." I reached for my coat and the keys. "I'm taking the car that's been acting up. Do you want it on your conscience if something happens?"

I wouldn't back down or give in. I would do what I needed to be healthy, to make good decisions, and to discover the will of God in my life.

The dank, cold December rain blanketing the cemeteries surrounding Colma turned torrential as I stood in the slow moving checkout line at the local grocer. I quickly snatched an umbrella from the rack strategically placed just beyond the counter, remembering I would need one for my trip to the therapist the next day. When Sr. Simon walked into the kitchen asking when dinner would be ready, I showed her the umbrella and a ninety-nine cent rubber spatula I'd purchased.

"You talk so much about poverty this and poverty that. You don't ever live it. You just buy whatever you want. You want poverty for everybody else but yourself."

I could feel the heat rising to my cheeks and the smell creeping from my chest. I'd followed every rule I'd learned about presuming permission. I'd done nothing wrong. "I'll take'em back if you want, but we really do need the spatula. I broke one yesterday." My voice cracked as I spoke, frustrated with my passivity.

"I have an umbrella in the garage. You never ask. You just do what you want. You talk about community; you don't know what community means."

I gripped the spatula handle as tightly as I could, fighting to maintain my composure as my seething anger began to boil. The spatula hit the floor with the full force of my rage, "You can tell me I shouldn't have bought the umbrella. You can tell me to return the stupid spatula. You can even tell me to never presume permission for anything again. But you cannot, you will not, ever judge my intention. You will not tell me what I think or feel or what I want. I am sick and tired of your constant judgment. I am an adult, not a child. I deserve just as much respect as you do."

The words spilled from my mouth. Her lip trembled as I exploded, slowly inching towards her until I stood six inches from her face, speaking directly into her frightened eyes. "I'm taking the car. I'll be back."

My knees rattled against the steering column as I sat in the dark garage waiting for the car to warm up. Squeezing the steering wheel in an attempt to stop trembling, I wondered where I could go. I drove to the end of the block, pulled to the side of the road, and put the car in park. I hadn't screamed and hollered like that since I'd left home. No one in the convent ever saw this fanatical, almost maniacal side of my personality. What did I just do? What would they do to me now? I couldn't turn around. I'd made my move; I couldn't back step. Gaining some composure, I drove six blocks to the home of the school secretary who knew Sr. Simon, heard of our arguments, and would understand.

"Who is it?" the surprised voice came from behind the door.

"Sister Jude. Please, I need to talk."

"What's the matter? Are you okay?" Betty's warm embrace when she saw me shaking, felt so safe, I burst into tears.

"I exploded." I managed to spit out between sobs. "I yelled at Sr. Simon, up in her face. I didn't hit her or anything, but I'm sure she thought I would. She looked scared."

"You what?" Betty asked with disbelief.

"I completely controlled myself but I couldn't take it anymore."

Betty lifted the tea kettle off the stove, took it to the sink and turned on the water. I leaned against the counter, my knees still shaky.

"What started it?" Betty asked.

"I bought an umbrella without getting permission first, and a rubber spatula." I almost chuckled. It seemed so silly already. A cup of tea and a bear hug from Betty sent me on my way, but instead of heading back to the convent, I turned left onto the on-ramp towards San Francisco and Sacramento. With a tight chest and my fingers gripping the steering wheel, I hit the gas pedal and sped straight to Suzanne's, knowing she'd still be awake.

Always the reasonable, controlled one, Suzanne, my high school counselor, listened warmly and offered questions. She offered no solutions; she did nothing to sway my opinions or decisions. She directed my reflection on what happened, how I'd gotten to this point in my journey, and what it meant for me. She hugged me and sent me on my way in the early morning hours.

I called Sr. Ruth before Mass the next morning, knowing Sr. Simon would have called already, but surprised to discover the Council already decided to fly in for a meeting.

"That's like me going up against the Inquisition. Why don't you just damn me now? You know the Council will take her side; she's the superior. We need an outside facilitator. I cannot attend a meeting without someone from outside moderating it."

The next day we sat in the community room with Sr. Ruth and a Franciscan Friar facilitating the meeting.

"Sister Jude's changed; she's rebellious and divisive."

"I haven't done anything. I'm an adult. Treat me like one."

"But I'm her superior. It's my job to take care of her. She doesn't even join our days of prayer."

"I can take care of myself. I can't pray surrounded by people who don't trust or respect me.

The aggressive volley continued with Sr. Simon refusing to address me, sounding like a child tattling on her sibling.

"Excuse me." Father interrupted. "I'm sure you've been down this road before. Can we take another angle? Huh? What do you need for this situation to work? I want you each to take some time tonight to list the three things you absolutely need for this situation to work for you. We'll work towards a way to co-exist. Tomorrow we'll start with that and see where we can go from there."

I spent the rest of the evening, and most of the night, in the chapel before the Blessed Sacrament. Jesus' willingness to be with us forever had been my driving force for years. As I stared at the Host with my eyes, I could only see a thin, round wafer. To my heart it spoke volumes. Whenever I wanted to renege, taking the easy way out, I turned to the Blessed Sacrament, repeating the Prayer of St. Ignatius: "Take all my freedom and my memory. My understanding and my will is yours. All that I have and cherish you have given me, Lord. Your grace and your love are enough for me."

I wanted to be trusted to seek counseling and spiritual direction as needed. I wanted to have the freedom to go for a walk, even on school grounds, without asking for permission. I wanted to be trusted to spend my free time as I saw fit just like Sr. Simon did. I wanted her to stop treating me like her lover, sending roses into my classroom to apologize for yelling at me the night before. I wanted to be a vital, contributing member of a loving, supportive community, not a child with an overprotective mother. I wanted to be available, present, and incarnate to the people with whom I worked. I wanted to be Emmanuel, God-with-us, for the poor, the outcast, the transient and the mentally ill. A vow of obedience did not mean I was immature and incapable of ordering my daily schedule. I loved living in community, serving my Sisters, and spending time with them. I just needed respect. I'd agreed to teach and had been doing a fine job; but that didn't mean I couldn't still minister to the poor. Sr. Simon thought it did. We disagreed on many things, but did that mean we couldn't still live in community and share a life of faith and prayer?

I prayed, I cried, I chanted familiar Taize songs in Cantonese. Trying to calm myself with prayer, I opened my Bible, attempting to meditate as I'd learned on my thirty-day retreat praying Jesus be with me in this. I didn't want to be rebellious but to follow my conscience. "Be still and know that I am God," I reminded myself. "Rejoice always."

As I prostrated before Jesus in Blessed Sacrament, I imagined his blood pouring over me, washing me clean from impurity. I lay prostrate, asking that the Holy Spirit fill me with wisdom and knowledge. I wanted only total obedience to the will of God, not to get my own way. I wanted plenty, but Father asked me to name only three things I needed. I needed to be respected as an adult, not treated like an incompetent child. I needed to be trusted in my spiritual, personal and professional life. I needed to be allowed to reach out in an apostolate to the poor and marginal as I felt called, as long as it didn't interfere with school schedules or scheduled community events. I read my list the next morning and waited with anticipation for what Sr. Simon might need.

"I need to speak with her spiritual director on a regular basis to make sure that what she wants to do is really in her best interest. I need to meet with her counselor, on a regular basis, to make sure that he is good for her and to make sure she is making healthy decisions. I need to be told by Sr. Ruth how much freedom I should give her, since it is my job to take care of her."

Sr. Simon could not see beyond her ingrained need to control and manipulate me. I sat, silently praying that Father and Sr. Ruth could see her sickness. Appearing as stunned as I, Sr. Ruth and Father sat in silence, staring at Sr. Simon. Father attempted to redirect questions and guide her to consider how she desired to be treated or how house rules might be changed to accommodate both of us living together. When Father suggested that maybe she needed to give me some psychological and spiritual freedom to follow the will of God, she jumped to her feet and stomped out of the room, her face red with fury.

"You may go Sister." Sr. Ruth spoke for the first time.

"Are you kidding? That's it. What am I supposed to do?"

"I'll let you know," Sr. Ruth said. She returned to Oregon that evening without a word. I gathered my stacks of papers to be graded, my lesson plans and all of my textbooks, loaded them in the trunk, and headed to my mother's house for the weekend.

Sr. Ruth called me the next morning. "I've spoken to the Council and we've made our decision. You will return to Oregon with Sr. Celestine on Friday, for Christmas break."

"You're transferring me?" I could scarcely say the words. "You're just letting her get away with it, just like that? She throws a tantrum and I get thrown out. What about my classroom, the students, the job I came to do?" I felt myself rambling, a desperate attempt to not swear. "She obviously needs help. You have a responsibility to help her."

"We also have a responsibility to keep a principal in the school. I had no choice." Sr. Ruth's voice strained as she spoke.

Red pen in hand, I kicked off my shoes, plopped on my mother's couch and began work. As my pen struck incorrect answers and calculated scores at the top of the page, my mind traveled through the three months I'd shared with my students. I decided to spend the week in review with trivia games, spelling bees and a comprehensive test. My replacement would know exactly where we left off and the students could begin fresh with the New Year. Monday morning, I explained that my superiors made an official decision to transfer me for the good of the community and it had nothing to do with them. I outlined the week for them and made plans for how each day would unfold in the classroom.

"Is it because you swam with us at Caritas Creek?"

"Was it because you let us drink water in class all the time?"

"You're the best teacher we've ever had; how can they do that?"

Unable to field the questions thrown at me, I redirected their attention to the task at hand, grateful that I had no more tears left to cry. When the bell rang for the first recess and the students strolled onto the playground, wiping tears and muttering disappointment, I headed to the office to collect papers from my box.

"Sr. Simon would like to see you in her office immediately." Betty's stern voice matched the frown across her forehead. I hadn't spoken to Sr. Simon since she'd stomped out of the room. I knocked on the door and entered with clenched jaw.

"I've called the Superintendent and she would like to speak with you." Sr. Simon handed the phone to me.

"Hello, this is Sister Jude. May I help you?"

"Sr. Simon explained you're being transferred, that you told your students this is your last week, and you wrote a note to the parents."

"Yes."

"She also explained you aren't stable enough to be in communication with parents and you had no permission to write the notice."

"She said I'm not stable? Are you kidding me?" I couldn't maintain the politeness I thought due this stranger.

"She mentioned your breakdown. I'm afraid you are a threat to the students and you shouldn't return to the classroom. Effective immediately."

I could no longer contain my anger. "I have not had a breakdown. I simply wrote a note ..."

"If you continue to raise your voice ..." Sr. Simon attempted to interrupt.

"What? You'll fire me? You've already arranged that?"

Nausea churned in my stomach and my entire body shook as I walked back to the classroom, accompanied by Sr. Simon. I picked up my keys, my cup, my statue of St. Jude and my Bible as I heard Sr. Clare' words swirling through my brain, 'Good morning children. Sister Jude has an emergency and will need to leave immediately. I will be substituting for the remainder of the day. Please sit down and take out your religion books.'

As the week progressed, Sr. Simon forbade all contact with students or their parents. I could not be seen on campus and could receive no phone calls or mail. Virtually under house arrest, I moved from room to room in a stupor and I slept. I slept through prayers, through meals, through Mass.

"Obviously you just wanted your way." Sr. Simon approached me as I sat in the cold, dark community room late one night. "If you were truly obedient and wanted to live in community, you would join us for prayer and wouldn't be missing Mass. What do you think God thinks of you now?"

I said nothing. On Friday, I woke early to get my luggage in the car while others were in Mass and I waited in the parking lot for Sr. Celestine.

"Can you believe she got up and tried to convince everyone to be happy? The Friday before Christmas they shouldn't need convincing. Everyone seemed so sad." Sr. Celestine said, visibly upset as she climbed into the passenger's side of the white Cavalier we'd be driving to Oregon.

I pressed my foot to the gas pedal, hovering at ninety miles an hour until the tank neared empty. Pulling into the gas station, I slammed the car into park. "I don't know why I'm in a hurry. I don't have anywhere to be."

When I stepped out of the car at Our Lady of Peace, Sr. Jean Ann grabbed me by the shoulders, threw her arms around me, tight bear-hug style, and whispered, "Welcome Home."

I spoke with clenched jaw, wrenching from her grip. "I have no home."

Winter, 1993 – 1994

I slept in each morning, skipping prayers, Mass and breakfast. I dragged myself out of bed around 10:30 or 11:00, grabbed a bite to eat and returned to my room before others came in for lunch. My eyes swollen from tears and my throat so dry I couldn't speak, even when I did join the community for Evening Prayer. I heard others whispering: she's giving up on her vocation, losing desire for prayer, childish, proud, giving in to the devil's temptations. Only Sr. Ruth knew the whole story but she said nothing in my defense. I finally turned to Sr. Teresa David, for solace and wisdom.

Sr. Teresa David transferred to our community immediately after Vatican II when women were leaving religious life by the hundreds. Disappointed in her community's attempt to modernize, she sought refuge in the traditional. Certain she would understand my confusion, I poured out my heart. She held my hand in her lap, nodding her head as I spoke of my desire to do God's will, of feeling called to work with the poor, and of giving my all to community and still being tossed aside.

"Do what love is telling you to do. Don't worry about what anyone else says. You live for God, not for them." She spoke with her eyes closed – as if at prayer.

I walked with the elderly Sisters, pushing those confined to a wheelchair, holding the hands of the bedridden. I fed them, bathed them and changed their diapers. I meditated often on the Incarnation. Just as Jesus became one with us in our pain and sin, so I would become one with the sisters who suffered. I slowly began to join the others for Mass, meals and community life.

I spent hours with Sr. Stephen who, crippled with arthritis and lupus for many years, sat continually with clenched jaw, refusing to eat or talk. She simply moaned. Several times each day she'd be force fed a can of liquid nutrition through a tube in her nose; occasionally her screams of anguish could be heard throughout the house and into the chapel. As I watched her pain, certain that, being Asian, she could not tolerate the dairy products, I convinced Doreen, the head nurse, to try something different. Together we developed a soy based nutrition drink and within a few weeks Sr. Stephen not only stopped moaning, but began smiling and eating semi-solid foods.

"You'd make such a good mom," Doreen said as we stood at the blender.

"If I wouldn't be a good mom, I couldn't be a good Sister." I spoke simply, refusing to question my true desire.

The first few sessions with the new therapist Sr. Ruth found for me, entailed my parroting every argument, discussion and the final explosion in Colma that led to my arrival in Oregon. I summarized my demise in Hong Kong, and capsulated my twelve years into compartmentalized stories. We met several times before I felt comfortable enough to speak about my issues.

"I convinced Sr. Samuel to take the Franciscan Girls' Club members to a Christian Rock concert last night. As we listened to the music calling us to live the gospel, I stood up, marched down the stairs to the foot of the altar and, by my actions, declared that I was not living the gospel as I should. Anyone wishing to renew their commitment to Jesus, the pastor said. So I got up. I followed hundreds of people into the side room as the preacher's helpers asked people to fill out cards with their name and address, to be contacted later. As I stood there, card in hand, others assumed I was one of the counselors and asked for my help.

"It hit me that, as a Sister, I needed to be of service, even in my own time of need. I needed to get my relationship with Jesus straight by myself, in private. No one believed I needed renewal and forgiveness.

"At breakfast Sr. Samuel told everybody how I embarrassed her when I answered the altar call. She couldn't believe I'd show weakness in front of the girls who might think of being Sisters one day.

"I need renewal. Don't we go to confession for renewal? Aren't we all sinners? I was just so frustrated."

"Why were you frustrated?"

"They called me a disgrace."

"Why does that bother you?"

"Because being true to the gospel should never be a disgrace. They're too concerned about appearances. What about the gospel? Besides, they're supposedly my Sisters – but they keep saying I'm a disgrace. Those were Sr. Paul's words anyway."

"When did she say that?"

I felt the saliva catch in my throat as I attempted to talk; it would have been easier to swallow silly putty. I wasn't ready.

"I can't talk about it now. Not yet." I felt vulnerable and couldn't expose myself with something so shameful. Holding back, unwilling to cry in front of Linda so soon, I answered quickly and simply. "It's nothing really."

Linda sat, notepad in hand, in the arm chair across from me, waiting. I stared at the apple scented candle flickering on the coffee table in front of me. "I'm sure you've noticed that sometimes I … mmm … have a problem. I kinda … stink."

Linda acted as if my revelation meant nothing to her. "What does that have to do with Sr. Paul?"

"When we were at the catechetical conference the other day I started to stink horribly all the sudden. By the time we got back on the bus, everyone could smell the unbearable stench. I tried to keep my arms down, but it rises from my chest."

Linda made no attempt to ask questions and barely jotted a note. "That night I overheard Sr. Paul telling Sr. Ruth I needed to learn personal hygiene and I shouldn't be allowed out of my room until I controlled my body odor. She said I didn't deserve to live in community."

Linda shifted in her seat, crossing her left leg over her right, with her pen finally resting on the top of the yellow notepad. She still said nothing, so I kept talking. My back muscles began to relax as I sat back in my chair.

"I don't remember having a problem before I entered the convent but Sr. Thomas constantly told me to take extra showers. I seemed okay in Hong Kong, until about the last year. Since I went to that Natural Medicine doctor I've been pretty open about it. But no one ever called me a disgrace or said I didn't deserve to live in community."

My voice cracked and I choked on my words. Tears dripped onto the knuckles of my twisted hands with the rhythm of a ticking clock, witnessing the moment of my rebirth.

"I went straight to the kitchen and started pigging out. I ate about twenty cookies, then half a cake."

"Do you do that often?"

"A lot. Once in Colma I ate six dozen cookies in about an hour. I shovel food in my mouth by the fork or fist full."

"Do you get sick? Do you vomit?" Linda hinted at an eating disorder.

"I'm not bulimic or anorexic. I just overeat."

"How do you feel after you do something like this?"

"At first I just feel satisfied. Satiated. Complete. Then guilt takes over. I play tug-a-war inside my head. I'm yanked back and forth, but neither end is strong enough to win. I know I'm trying to eat away my stress. It got better after I saw that Natural Medicine doctor, but since I left Hong Kong, and especially since Colma, I've been a mess."

"So what's the food for?" Linda poked at the core.

"What'ya mean?"

"Next time you're pigging out, try to slow down and talk to the food. Next time you grab a piece of cake or a bunch of cookies, ask why you are eating it, what emotion it's helping you hide, what you're afraid to face. Let the food speak to you. Listen. What emptiness are you attempting to fill?"

"I'd like you to take a look at this book." Linda handed it to me at our next meeting.

The emotional cause of body odor, it read, is fear of rejection; the inability to accept yourself and fear that others will never accept you. Positive affirmation would undo the old tapes of fear. *I love myself. I accept who I am with all of my faults and failings. I recognize my goodness.*

I felt my shoulders sink under the weight of the truth. Fear of rejection. For years I stank. I battled the sneers and covered noses of strangers and acquaintances alike. Sitting in Linda's office I realized that for twelve years, I showered, changed clothes, and tested every imaginable deodorant but around Sr. Thomas, I always smelled absolutely offensive. My body reacted like a skunk: sensing a predator, it would spew a repulsive odor to protect me from danger. I would rather turn people off than be turned away by them.

I could barely see through the puddles filling my eyes. Every conversation with Sr. Thomas, each time she told me to shower, played back in my head. I only wanted to be loved. I'd done everything I could to be accepted; I became obedient, submissive and productive. I allowed myself to be used, over and over again, to prove my worth.

I hadn't planned on collapsing in front of Linda. I'd intended not to cry, but as my entire body shook, I rocked back and forth attempting to calm myself. My breathing became rapid and shallow as I gasped for air. Linda allowed me to cry, offering tissue, and taking charge of the movements active in my soul.

"Do you think the body odor and the pigging out are connected?"

I couldn't answer, though I knew: I just wanted to be loved like the little girl trying to fit in, hoping to be picked for the kickball team. Reading my thoughts, Linda asked, "Are you afraid of not being loved or are you afraid of not being perfect enough to be loved?"

I didn't see the twist coming. Afraid of not being perfect? Afraid of failing? Better to die than to fail. I sat absolutely frozen in my seat.

"I never thought of it, but it makes perfect sense. That's why I've always been so preoccupied with death. If I die, I won't have to worry about failure or rejection; an easy out. But why do I have such an irrational fear of failure?"

"Has anyone ever given you a reason to believe you wouldn't fail?" Linda wouldn't let me stop.

"Whenever I did well in the convent, they accused me of being too proud or arrogant." I began in a matter-of-fact tone.

"And as a child?"

"I don't know."

"What about your father? Didn't he leave when you were just seven?"

"Yeah. So?"

"You grew up blaming yourself?"

"Yeah."

"So you failed your entire family then?"

I stiffened. I'd never been a good enough daughter. I failed at the one thing I shouldn't have had to be good at: being a daughter. I tried in vain to be a perfect teacher, missionary, and Sister. Sitting in the small office, facing this woman I'd known for just a few weeks, I articulated the reality of my own truth. I had to believe in myself or no one else ever would.

March, 1994

Rocking back and forth, with a handful of chocolate chip cookies I'd smuggled from the walk-in and an aching in the center of my gut, I longed desperately for someone to make my decision for me. Dropping into a fetal position, I attempted to ignore the voice whispering in my mind: Dad would understand. In my agony, I connected with the father I never really knew. He must have agonized before he left us. He must have loved me. A sudden longing to be wrapped in his arms, bathed me with the clarity I'd lacked. I sat up, certain I could offer my community nothing more and they had nothing to offer me. I would pursue my calling to work with the poor. Transferring to another community became my only option. Sr. Ruth promised to support me, certain God gave me a vocation, sorry it hadn't worked out.

I began corresponding and having lengthy phone conversations with several communities, from the east coast to the west. With no timetable or plan, I trusted the transfer process would unfold in God's time. I spoke most with a Franciscan missionary community with a clearly stated preferential option for the poor who managed government housing projects for low income families on their motherhouse property. They'd accepted several Sisters through a transfer process about ten years prior so they were familiar with the integration process. They invited me to a workshop and to start the process.

"Who will do your work while you're gone?" Sr. Ruth said when I approached her with the idea of visiting them for a weekend. My mind instantly flashed from the kitchen, to Hong Kong, to my last week at Colma when I'd been ripped, each time, from my work. Anger boiled in my chest as I sat on the edge of my bed, staring at the votive candle on my nightstand, praying for guidance. The next morning, I walked into Sr. Ruth's office and asked for a leave of absence. After phone calls to the Council and various priests, she told me I could not take a leave of absence; I would need to be exclaustrated. Exclaustration required me to live my vows, but the community had no fiscal responsibility towards me. I would be completely on my own.

In the midst of my packing, Sr. Ruth asked me to help her design a vocation brochure. She insisted I meet with the designer to offer my ideas and my designs for the brochure inviting others to join the community I just chose to leave. I found the entire situation ludicrous, but very quickly created a motto, *Where do you stand? Where will it take you?* With Mary and Francis at the foot of the cross, a globe highlighting the US and China in the background. The words of conviction that guided me for years now convicted me. I didn't really want to leave, but could stay no longer.

Becoming Invisible

I bolted into my bedroom slamming the door behind me. Knees shaking, I dropped, almost numb, onto the foot of the twin bed, staring ahead at the closet with the attached sink and mirror. No toothbrush on the sink board. No nylons hanging from the towel rack. I'd never again stand here to pray that I speak only kind and gentle words as I brushed my teeth; never again to ask God to keep me walking in His ways as I cleaned my nylons. This mirror will never again reflect my face praying to mirror the face of Christ. Two black habits and two white habits hung, listless, in the closet. My habits, no longer mine. My routine forever changed. Twelve years of life undone because of a simple desire.

In a room just like this, somewhere in the world, for twelve years now I'd let go, put my feet up, dared to dream; I took off my veil, slipped on pajamas, knelt to pray and crawled in bed. I read. I wrote. I cried. In this room now, I took off my habit and veil for the last time.

I reached down to pack the last few items lying on the bed next to me. A crucifix. A gift, hand-painted by Sr. Nathaniel, my classmate and friend. The cross read, "Sanctae Regulae: To stand by the Cross with Thee." The framed embroidery piece given by Sr. Celestine on my final vows, "Choose Thy Love; Love Thy Choice." The desire of my heart. Just three days ago I'd written simple words for the vocation brochure. "Where do you stand? And where will it take you?" The words of conviction that guided me for years now convicted me. I didn't really want to leave, but I could stay no longer.

Picking up the brown velour polo shirt I found at the local Good Will store snapped me into the moment. I grinned at the thought of obedience dragging me away from the familiar, the predictable, and the almost mundane. Just three weeks ago I pushed forward with my new understanding of obedience. I always asked for permission to take a walk, to purchase a needed item, to watch a T.V. program, or to make a phone call. I couldn't continue the childish, immature, incompetent obedience anymore. With a free Saturday afternoon, I had to do something. Finally, with some fear and trepidation, I'd checked the calendar for an available car and told the house superior I wanted to see a movie. Sr. Jean Ann, stunned, simply said, "Okay."

After the movie, unsure why, I stopped by the Good Will. I felt awkward, sneaky, almost dirty. I didn't know what to look for, I just knew I wanted brown.

105

Franciscans wear brown. I had no conscious intention of putting aside my habit; but walking from rack to rack, my soul knew that sooner, not later, I would.

I slowly slipped the brown shirt over my head, knowing a simple change of clothes would once again change my life forever. Each morning when putting on the habit and veil I'd prayed. "I clothe myself with this holy habit, O Lord. Grant me grace to increase daily in virtue and perfection." The words had become so automatic, such a part of my routine, I barely realized I prayed them. Which prayer accompanied the brown shirt and tan pants I now wore as I stepped into the hallway?

Heading down the stairs, I approached the infirmary. My silent goodbyes rose like prayers from a heart filled with admiration for the women who gave their lives to this community, to God. I fed them, bathed them, cut their hair; I'd massaged their feet and held their hands. Stopping in the chapel, as I always did on my way out the door, for a quick genuflection and a prayer for a safe journey, I lingered, thinking of so many. When I entered at eighteen, fresh out of high school, the apprehension of living with so many elderly Sisters scared me. I took it then, as an opportunity to make amends, to show remorse for the bad will between me and my late grandmother; but since then, I'd moved beyond reparation for past offenses to sincere admiration for the Sisters. I would do almost anything for these precious women. I'd laid some to rest, while others lay, clinging to life behind these very walls. They would all be sorely missed. They'd each touched me and taught me about life and love. Now I chose to leave, not to reject them but to love even more.

Walking out the main door of the new building, I noticed Sr. Jean Ann and Sr. Augustine standing in the hallway. I'd insisted, contrary to community custom, on being allowed to say good-bye and made a point of saying good-bye to everyone else, whether they wanted to or not. I knew Jean Ann and Augustine would find me.

Sr. Jean Ann and I entered together on February 6, 1982. Because Jean Ann, age 39, worked in the inner-city schools of L.A. and they considered her more mature, she entered the novitiate six months before me; but we always shared a certain bond, confided on a different level. Not like Sr. Nathaniel and I did, but we definitely supported one another.

Sr. Jean Ann held out her arms, tears in her eyes. "Good-bye," is all either of us could say. Sr. Augustine managed a "We'll miss ya, kid."

I'd never minded when Sr. Fatima, Sr. Veronica and Sr. Augustine called me kid. I'd always been one of the youngest. Even as people entered behind me, I remained the youngest for ten years. I seemed to have a grandma – grandchild relationship with each of them. Sr. Augustine, a divorcee in her sixties and a grandmother whose son and grandchildren came to visit often, had the mind of a forty-year-old and the bones and heart of a ninety-year-old. She lived in excruciating pain most of the time and feared being discarded. She possessed a sharp mind and she confidently gave her opinion and clarified facts for the less educated members of community; driving the younger Sisters crazy.

Sr. Augustine and I spent a great deal of time together, running errands, seeing doctors, visiting the cemetery, or stopping at the shoe store. I never pitied Sr. Augustine and I thoroughly enjoyed her company. With tears in her eyes, Sr. Augustine opened the door for me to head towards the car out front.

I climbed in, buckled up and prayed. *Bless, Oh Lord, this journey we are about to undertake for the honor and glory of God, for the honor of Our Blessed Mother and for the salvation of souls. May thy Holy Angels be with us now and on our last journey to eternity. Amen.*

I'd avoided this journey for years, ignored the signs, refusing to follow my heart. Recitation of the three Hail Mary's that followed didn't interrupt my thoughts. I had no doubt, no fear. I actually felt confident, even excited, for the first time in years. This journey would be "for the honor and glory of God."

"I'll miss you." I offered, looking at Sr. Ruth, not sure what I expected in return.

"Why?"

"Because I love you."

Her strange question and silence following my simple declaration of friendship didn't surprise me. I respected Sister's inability to respond.

"I appreciate what you said, but I'm not used to people showing appreciation of me." Sr. Ruth spoke softly.

"So you'll mail the two boxes next week?" I wasn't ready to see Sister cry.

"Yes."

"I gave you the address in Chicago, right?"

"Yes."

Seeing the tears in Sr. Ruth's eyes, I said no more.

At the airport a "thanks for everything" broke the silence and put an end to the prolonged hug between us.

"You're welcome."

I stepped off the plane uncertain who would meet me because I never bothered with the logistical details of my travel. I always just let at least one person know what time and where I would be arriving, and figured someone would meet me. Seeing an old friend from high school caught me off guard.

"Hi, how are you?" I suddenly felt totally insecure with my new role. "You can't be here to meet me; I haven't seen you since high school."

"Hi. Wow! Last time I saw you, you were entering a convent."

"Well, now I'm leaving. So, you've missed the same twelve years of my life as I have."

The biting sarcasm surprised me. Had I really missed twelve years of life? I never thought so, but subconsciously I must have felt it. I never regretted one moment of the past twelve and a half years, but I couldn't admit, even to myself, my giggle and the confidence I now felt in leaving, masked a good deal of pain.

I noticed my mother out of the corner of my eye.

"Hi." We nervously and awkwardly hugged each other as, behind Mom I spotted the shy grimace of my four-year-old niece, Sarah, perched on her daddy Randy's, arm.

"Hi, cutie." I tickled her tummy. Sarah withdrew, tucking her head into Randy's armpit.

"She's not sure who you are. She's never seen you in regular clothes."

"Oh, yeah, I forgot." I began to feel self-conscious.

"What should we call you anyway?" Karen asked.

I hadn't really thought about it. Except for the oldest few nephews and nieces, the rest knew of the grandkids knew me only as Sr. Mary Jude. They'd always called me Aunt Sister Jude. Even my mother and siblings. For the last ten years I'd been called nothing else. Officially still a Sister, I decided to take a year off to figure things out. I received Exclaustration, the official church term for living outside of the convent, but I remained a Sister. I needed time to figure things out, to decide what to do, but right then, I had to say something.

"You can call me Janet if you want, but I'm still Jude with other people. I'll just drop the Sister part. Call me Jude, or Janet, if you want."

My head, ears, and arms were bare in public for the first time in twelve years, except for the few trips into China and up Mt. Sinai. I suddenly felt naked, as if everyone in the airport knew I should be wearing a habit and veil. No one smiled with a nod of approval, no strangers greeted me. The usual inadvertent stares and sideways glances were missing. I had simply become invisible. Invisible felt worse than naked. With a simple change of clothes, I had become just another face in the crowd; absolutely no one special.

Hands clasped in front of me, clutching my carry-on bag, my left hand methodically turned the silver wedding band I wore on my right ring finger, softly caressing the twisted rope engraved down the center. The rope symbolized my devotion to St. Francis and my three vows.

"When you leave, just put everything neatly at the foot of your bed. I'll take care of it." Sr. Ruth said that morning.

"Can I keep my small crucifix and my ring?"

"No, why would you do that?"

"Because I'm still a Sister. I'm still the Bride of Christ. I'm still a vowed religious. And for now, I'm still a part of this congregation."

"We've never let anyone do it before. You're supposed to be completely on your own."

"But I'm still a Sister. You can't just cut me off completely."

"Well, I guess you can wear the ring, for now. When you make some decisions, we'll decide what to do next. Just don't tell anyone I'm letting you keep the ring."

No one special. For years I resisted being treated special because of my habit and veil. I refused seats on the bus. I insisted on people seeing me as a human being, with strengths and weaknesses. I didn't get preachy and I tried not to be too aggressive; but I had always been proud of being a Sister, a missionary, a Franciscan. Now, no one knew. I had become invisible. And I wondered, at that moment in time, walking through the Oakland Airport, if I'd ever survive.

I woke early the next morning and as my feet hit the floor, I prayed:

Benedicamus Domino. Deo gratias. Blessed be God. Blessed be His Holy Name. Blessed be Jesus Christ, true God and true man. Blessed be the name of Jesus. Blessed be His most sacred heart. Blessed be His most Precious Blood. Blessed be Jesus in the most holy Sacrament of the altar. Blessed be the Holy Spirit the Paraclete. Blessed be the great Mother of God, Mary most holy. Blessed be her holy and Immaculate Conception. Blessed be her glorious assumption. Blessed be the name of Mary, Virgin and Mother. Blessed be her most pure heart. Blessed be St. Joseph her most chaste spouse. Blessed be God in His angels and His saints."

The Divine Praises. I'd prayed them every morning; that didn't have to change. I made my morning offering. I offered my prayers, works, joys and suffering of this day for the intentions of the Sacred Heart, in union with the Holy Sacrifice of the Mass throughout the world, in reparation for my sins and the sins of the world.

I attended Mass at my parish church where I still knew most of the old timers. They'd been so proud of me when I entered. In the twenty-eight years we'd lived in Rodeo, they had one vocation to the priesthood and one to religious life. I had been that one religious. Would they understand if I just walked in with plain clothes? Should I at least wear the simple brown dress I'd bought? Maybe then I'd look like I just changed habits.

The daily communicants, those devote Catholics whom I prayed with so many mornings before I entered, were surprised to see me. Whispers and raised eyebrows, but no one asked. No one really spoke to me like they always did during my visits home. I wanted to stand up after Mass to shout, "I'm still a Sister. I'm just trying to discern God's will, to be faithful to the Gospel. I am not a failure." Instead, I knelt silently for a moment, not really praying but not knowing what to do. I finally stood up and walked out quietly.

Driving down Parker Avenue I noticed Suzanne in her rose garden. Pulling off the road I drove down the gravel driveway to park behind the house. Suzanne was my teacher and counselor in high school. She always drove an old green and white Volkswagen van, wore funky clothes and usually held her very thick, frizzy hair in two buns at the back sides of her head like Mickey Mouse ears. Some students called her weird and odd, but I admired her simple joy. I found her genuine, unique, natural. Everything I wanted to be. Suzanne had always been supportive. As she listened to the fears, the criticism, the dreams I held in my soul, it felt as if she held my dreams as her own.

Our friendship began when Suzanne offered me a job babysitting and cleaning her house. She put up with my antics throughout high school. She let me hang out when other teachers kicked me out of class; she didn't punish me even though I led the teepee crowd to her home Halloween night. She never called me ridiculous, immature, or crazy. She never condemned me.

Other teachers tried to convince me I shouldn't enter the convent prematurely, should go to college, work a while, do anything but make a commitment at eighteen. Suzanne encouraged me to apply for college and financial aid months earlier; she didn't bring it up again. Instead she listened, reminded me of my intelligence and encouraged me to make my own decisions. She remained loyal and supportive through every twist and turn of my convent days, listening and advising every time I needed to talk, cry, or just figure things out.

As I stepped out of the car, I wondered, for a moment, if she would judge me. Will I look good to her? Do I seem healthy? Will she say I've grown or will she think I gave up or gave in?

Suzanne rushed to meet me halfway down the long drive, arms spread wide in welcome. As her arms wrapped around, squeezing me to her bosom, I felt like the prodigal son returning home. Fear of judgment gone, I relaxed, grateful for someone who really understood.

"How are you? You look great." Suzanne held me at arms' length and gazed into my eyes.

"I feel good. Really!"

"What's your plan?"

"I'll be here for two weeks. Loyed's getting married next week. Then I head for Chicago."

"Oh?"

"I've been in contact with some groups back there. I want to take a closer look. I'm staying with my cousin Sue."

"So you are looking to transfer?"

"Yes. Definitely. I just want to find a group I'm more compatible with. I want to be true to the gospel."

"What's your official status then? A leave of absence or exclaustration?"

Without explanation, she understood the details of religious life, a transfer, and leaving. Suzanne had been a Sister who left years before she taught me in high school. She knew.

"Exclaustration. Sr. Ruth promised to support me. When I came back from Hong Kong, and when I did my thirty-day retreat. She said she'd wait to discuss my retreat before she sent me anywhere. Then she called me, on my last day of retreat, to tell me she assigned me to Oregon. Then within two weeks, she sent me down to Colma. When she yanked me out of Colma she told me to explore, to experiment, to discern. She knew I needed to go, but when it came down to it, she couldn't stand up to the rest of the council. They encouraged me to find a community that fit me better, but when I asked to go visit a community in Chicago, they worried about covering my work."

"That seems valid." She tried to bring a voice of reason to my emotions.

"I should have been in Colma teaching, not in Oregon, remember? They didn't care about my work when they kicked me out. In Oregon they just loaded the same stuff on me, cooking, shopping, and running errands. Someone did the work before I got there, they could do it again.

"I just wanted to go for a weekend workshop. I even offered to camouflage it by stopping at Loyed's wedding. Only the superiors would know. They just refused. Flat out."

"So they left you no choice."

"I am officially exclaustrated. I have a plane ticket and $3000 to my name. I'll stay with my cousin until I find a place to live and a job."

Visiting with Suzanne gave me the confidence I needed to face the upcoming days. In my head I needed no one's approval, no one's permission to figure out my life; I could be myself and follow the path God laid out for me, once I found it. But my heart longed to be understood, supported, admired.

Everyone I ran into wanted to know why I no longer wore my habit and veil but I still wore a ring. They didn't need to call me Sister, but I still went by Jude. I wanted to leave my congregation but join another. No one really understood. My family tried. But I didn't even know them. I'd had a two-week home visit every year until I went overseas and then saw them once every two years, but I had been so guarded. I had always been in my habit. Once in a while I took off my shoes before going to my room for the night, but my habit and veil stayed on. I had become a religious first and family member second.

In 1982, when I entered I had eight nephews and nieces, all under the age of ten. Now there were twenty-two. I knew their names and could figure out their ages if I tried hard enough, but I didn't know their favorite sports or songs or colors. I didn't buy gifts, take them to lunch or have slumber parties. I had never been the favorite aunt; just the nun aunt - great for show and tell. They'd invite me to school because I dressed funny and I lived in China. But now I was just the one that used to be.

The history I had with my family I'd almost forgotten. I never forgot big things, but the rest had been virtually lost for lack of being revisited. Occasionally, we'd laugh about old times, but not often. Instead, we discussed faith and philosophy, religion and life. We talked about the children, heard stories of their growth and laughed at their jokes. But for twelve years, I never let them in. I'd physically and emotionally left mother, brothers and sisters to follow Christ. I never told them of my questions, of my hopes and dreams, of my pain. My twelve years in the convent replaced, rooted out, and destroyed most of what had been. I wondered now if I'd ever get them back.

My first week home happened to coincide with Holy Week, the holiest, most important week in the Church year. In the convent we worked constantly. Washing and ironing altar clothes, arranging flowers, cleaning floors, oiling chapel pews, and attending extra chapel services. We kept vigilant watch on Holy Thursday remembering Jesus' agony in the garden and his arrest until midnight. I sang hymns, recited litanies, prayed in silence and allowed my spirit to rise like incense before the glory of God. In the convent, we spent Good Friday in complete silence. No one spoke, unless absolutely necessary, from the service on Holy Thursday night until Saturday morning. We fasted and we prayed. We suffered with Jesus as he walked the road to Calvary to save the world from sin. We remembered the crucifixion and the death with solemn somber faces.

I needed to call Sr. Ruth before the week's activities got into full swing or I'd have to wait until after Easter.

"Yes, Sr. Jude can I help you?" Sr. Ruth answered the phone professionally and in a very businesslike manner.

"Can you ask the Sisters in Hong Kong to send me a reference letter? If I try to get a job, I need something to say I held a job for the past few years. At least my teaching in Hong Kong counted as a real job, even if the other ten years didn't."

"I don't know if they'll do that. They're pretty upset."

"All they have to do is write a letter stating I worked at Immaculate Heart of Mary College as English teacher, department chairperson, and member of campus ministry for two and a half years; a simple letter. I actually wrote it for many teachers. It's common practice. They don't have to recommend me; they just need to say I held the position." As my voice cracked, I felt myself losing composure, appalled they would refuse to give me a simple letter.

"I did a great job. They never gave me any credit. I don't want praise, just a letter." In tears, my anger and disappointment were difficult to contain.

"I'll call and ask them." Sr. Ruth remained almost stoic.

On Spy Wednesday, the day Judas met with the leaders of the people to arrange handing Jesus over, deciding to betray his friend Jesus, I sat, betrayed.

Sr. Ruth called back on Holy Thursday.

"They say you're trying to control everything. They won't do anything to help. As far as they're concerned, God wants you to stay in the congregation."

I hung up the phone in tears, devastated by how small, disgusting, and unchristian they were being. I'd seen it when others left and before I left Hong Kong when they stopped offering me the Sign of Peace at Mass. My tears evaporated quickly, leaving behind apathy. I didn't care. They abandoned me. I felt stuck, isolated and uncertain; in limbo, or maybe even hell.

At Mass that night I heard Jesus speaking through the priest as he raised the bread and wine saying, "This is my Body – This is my Blood. . ." I gave almost thirteen years of my life to serve with and for these women. I'd sacrificed more than they would ever know. I'd given up so much in little, secret, hidden ways to be the servant. I'd washed their feet, both figuratively and literally. Listening as Judas kissed Jesus in the garden; I felt the sting on my own cheek. "What have I done to you to deserve this?"

I prayed for the grace to carry this burden, to bear this cross. I prayed for the grace to forgive. I wanted to experience the joy in persecution that St. Francis talked about; that I'd prayed for and preached about for so long.

More than anything, I wanted to punch someone.

On Good Friday I woke up feeling almost numb. Lying in bed until eleven, I finally picked up the phone and apologized for interrupting Sr. Ruth's day of recollection.

"What do you need?" Sr. Ruth spoke just above a whisper.

"Whether or not the Sisters are willing to give me the letter, I am going to get one. It's mine by right. I deserve it."

"How will you do that?"

"Call the office. The Vice-Principal will give me one."

"Why would you do that?"

"Because it is rightfully mine. I'm never going to get a job if I don't have any proof of experience. I'm gonna get it. But it won't be good for Sr. Kathleen or the others. Everyone knows people who leave get a letter. What kind of witness will it be to the teachers; they're sure to find out?"

No one except the few Sisters in charge, and Sr. Nathaniel, knew why I returned to the States. The teachers and students, even some of the Sisters, thought I needed to recover from stress related illness. If I called for the letter, everyone would know Sr. Kathleen refused to write a letter for one of the best English teachers the school ever had. I spoke clearly and logically of my disappointment at Sr. Ruth for giving in to the other Sisters' power to destroy. I spoke about justice and charity, rumors and reputation. I had these conversations with Sr. Ruth often during my last few months in community. I pushed every boundary and forced her to face the many hurtful, horrible ways the rules and customs of the community could be harmful.

That afternoon I went through the Good Friday motions, if not for myself, for Mom, for God. Maybe a half day of recollection would do me some good anyway. I got to the church just as the service started. As I walked through the parking lot on my way in, people looked at me with a 'you're vaguely familiar' look in their eyes. Then they'd recall, "That's an Arnold. The Sister. But what happened? She's not in her habit?" Some moved closer to say hello but others turned quickly to avoid eye contact. I didn't sit in the front; I couldn't even walk down the middle aisle. I needed to be in a corner, off to the side. Alone with God.

"Crucify him. Crucify him." As the community of believers joined in the traditional rendition of the passion of Christ, I felt the humiliation, the rejection, the betrayal like never before.

I thought of Sr. Thomas and Sr. Fatima. The minute I'd expressed confusion and concern almost three years earlier, they'd cut me off. They called me names, accused me of lying and refused to offer me the sign of peace at Mass. Did their refusal to write a letter really surprise me? They rejected me outright just for questioning.

Sr. Ruth called back on Holy Saturday to say they'd write the letters, to apologize for my pain, and to thank me for standing up for the sake of justice again. Short and to the point, she hung up quickly. We both knew they were only writing the letter because I threatened to get it on my own. Nothing more needed to be said.

Bag in hand, I turned around and headed down the boarding tunnel uncertain of exactly what I would do or how long I would be in Chicago, but excited about my new home and mission. I had a suitcase full of the clothes I bought at the second hand store and Sr. Ruth would mail two boxes: a wok, some simple dishes, spices and soy sauce, some prayer and reflection books, and the journals I'd kept from the destructive grip of Sr. Thomas's fears.

As I squeezed through the narrow aisle searching for Row 16, Seat B, my carry-on bumping first the side, then the back of seat after seat, the realization that I had no life or mission waiting for me sat lodged in the corner of my psyche, waiting for the opportune moment to attack. I had no one to make decisions for me and to tell me what to do. For the first time in thirty years of life, I would be making my own decisions and creating my own life. I lifted my carry-on to the overhead compartment, sat down, and fell asleep, unaware of how drastically my life would change.

The crisp 32-degree spring air tickled my ears with a delightful newness as Sue showed me around Wrigleyville first thing in the morning. For twelve years there'd been no wind whipped, disheveled hair, and not even a gentle breeze whistling in my ears. Any attempt to let my hair grow underneath my veil had been met with disapproval, if not outright reprimand from those in authority, so my hair hadn't grown out.

At a brisk even pace Sue introduced me to the neighborhood, the local stores and banks; she explained the el train and the bus line. Sue boasted of being within walking distance of the famous "Friendly Confines of Wrigley Field," Home of the Chicago Cubs, her favorite ball park, her sanctuary. She pointed out St. Benedict's and St. Thomasw's, sure I would want to attend daily Mass while living with her.

"I'll go to my own church." Sue chuckled.

"I'll go with you some day."

"I thought you hated professional sports because of the disgusting amount of money they make when people are starving."

"Yeah, but I also make it a habit to attend services with people of other religions to understand them better. If it's your church, I'll go with you."

Sue left for work at about eleven and I sat alone in the apartment with no obligation, no responsibility, and no job to keep me busy. Suddenly, as if dynamite imploded in the center of my soul, everything I knew and loved had disappeared. I had not had a paying job since 1981 except for the two years I taught in Hong Kong. I had no bank account, no credit history. Sue insisted I needed a job to find a place to live, but I couldn't live for long from a cardboard box and a foldout couch. A newspaper, map, phone book, and telephone would solve my problems.

"Any place on the north side would be okay, except in east Rogers' Park. Lots of drugs and stuff. I picked up this *Reader*; you can look for apartments and jobs. The jobs are mostly low level, not really up your alley," Sue said, handing the free local paper over before leaving for work at the bookstore.

Thumbing through the paper and phonebook, my hands started to shake as I lost my concentration. Why should anyone ever hire me? What did I have to offer? I typed about 50 words a minute. I could clean toilets. I enjoyed maintenance work to be honest. I'd done plenty of it. I'd always wanted to be a waitress. I'd taught English and could speak Chinese too. I could do that, but did I really want to? Did I have the mental stamina? Wouldn't cleaning toilets fit me better? Besides, it took me nine years to complete my BA. I had four jobs in the last year. No one would hire me. My biggest fear: I just turned thirty but had never been through a job interview in my entire life. I couldn't let the thoughts consume me. I had to make this work. My only other option would be to turn around and go back but that would be a death sentence or a jail term, "Go directly to jail. Do not pass go. Do not collect $200." The phrase would ring in my ears many times. An incentive to keep looking, to not give up and not give in.

Pen in hand, I read every ad in the classifieds, making phone call after phone call, everyone hanging up when I admitted having no experience. In the afternoon I walked around again: up Damen, down Irving Park, stopping in almost every shop along the way.

"Are you hiring?" I asked hesitantly.

"You can fill out an app."

Line after line, I filled in the blanks: Name, address, telephone number. Even these were temporary. I had no resume, no letters of reference and wouldn't know what to say if someone asked me what I'd been doing for the last 12 years. My experience so scattered, I didn't know where to begin. I'd done so much but so little. The kitchen, the retreat house cleaning, teaching,

116

teacher training, Chinese. Even as I filled out the applications, I knew I wouldn't be hired.

I headed back to Sue's apartment determined to search out temp agencies and to avoid the growing panic that I would never find a job. Suddenly, my palms slammed the cold pavement beneath me, my knees hit the ground, and I narrowly missed slamming my head. I hadn't noticed an uneven patch of cement until I stood up to brush myself off and keep myself from crying. When I saw the rip in my pant knee, I burst into tears. Feeling foolish for crying over a pair of pants, my chest began to tighten. The further I walked, the more I cried. Almost hyperventilating, I reached the front door, my life falling apart before my eyes.

I couldn't live with Sue forever; it would drive us both crazy. We were too different. Sue didn't have any food in the house, except for her morning Pepsi, a few slices of white bread and cold cuts, and Tabasco sauce. I needed fruits and vegetables. Sue climbed in bed by 8:30 to get to work by 6:30 every morning, and I stayed up reading anything I got my hands on. Sue loved the Cubs and hanging out at bars. I hated pro-sports and drank only hot water. With every ounce of energy and determination I could muster, I picked up the phone book. Calling temp agencies I'd heard about, I arranged two appointments for the next day and planned to meet Sue at the bookstore to open a bank account and withdraw money.

I had to choose, from my meager wardrobe, what might be appropriate for an interview. Not seeing my name on Sue's mailbox, UPS sent my two boxes back to Oregon. I only owned my freshly torn pants, a simple brown cotton smock dress, a few shirts and the flowery pink skirt and cap sleeve blouse I'd worn to Loyed's wedding. I had no shoes but Birkenstocks.

"You must be Jude," the woman asked as I walked in the door.

"Yes."

"Good. We'll start with a typing test and move on from there. You do realize you need professional attire, right?" The woman seemed almost afraid to shake my hand as she looked me over with disdain.

"I just moved from Oregon. My boxes of clothes will arrive tomorrow."

Looking at the other three women in the office, I saw dark blues and grays, polyester dress suits, nylons and high heels. I hadn't picked clothes out since 1981. My tastes were stunted. I sat in Birkenstocks and a flowered skirt. I'd worn nothing but Birkenstocks for almost three years. Birkenstocks symbolized my commitment to simplicity. Could I give that up? One pair fits all occasions. My habit had been appropriate anywhere. It drew occasional stares, but I never appeared too casual or too dressed up. Inappropriately dressed on the beach, at the zoo, playing basketball or riding my bike, but never too casual. Now, my first attempt at professional attire failed. Years of feeling insecure and inept flooded in, as if I'd returned to junior high and been snubbed by the popular girls, uncertain I wanted to be comfortable in the snug, mini-skirt outfits these women wore. By the time I sat down at the computer, the familiar odor began to rise from my chest, the sweat beading up under my arms, the odor seeping through my short sleeved blouse. I walked out feeling like Pigpen, only my outright stench replaced his dust cloud. I had entered a sophisticated, middle class world I knew nothing about and wondered if I would ever be able to survive.

As I rushed to my second appointment I tried to regain confidence. I learn two kinds of Chinese, taught myself Chinese computer in DOS, taught hundreds of people English, and managed an institutional kitchen at eighteen, but failed to get a simple job in an office or bussing tables. I needed confidence. God led me to Chicago. God would have to keep guiding my steps.

Waiting in the lobby of Banner Temp Agency for my tests, I opened my daily affirmation book. The short, simple words of encouragement uplifted, consoled and encouraged me for months. I opened to the current date to read: *"I move towards my goal with faith and trust that my journey will become clear with each step. My progress is perfect. I need only move in the right direction."*

I owned two pieces of identification, a passport and a fifteen-year-old California driver's license. I needed to deposit a certified bank check and I needed access to the cash immediately. They would have to ignore the current address requirement. They had to waive the seven-day hold. I needed a permanent address to get money but needed money to get a permanent address. Refusing to panic in front of Sue, I flipped to the back of the passport, showing the clerk a picture of myself in habit and veil.

"I just left the convent. If you can't trust a nun, who can you trust?" I felt totally ashamed for appealing to his religious side just to open a bank account. I'd never used my habit to my benefit before. I walked out with a debit card in hand. A debit card. Imagine. For twelve years I asked permission for fifty cents to buy a soda on a hot afternoon. Every penny had to be accounted for on a daily basis in a little notepad kept by the house superior. Now, I had a card to withdraw money at whim. I went straight back to Sue's, opened one of the notepads I kept for journaling, and began my familiar accounting method. I had to account for each penny as I had in the convent or I'd be completely lost. The only difference: this time, I didn't have to ask permission.

Confident something would come of at least one of the temp agencies, I moved on to finding a place to live. The next morning, I arranged to look at an apartment on the north side of Chicago. Riding the Howard-Dan Ryan train to the Morse stop, I walked to Damen. The noise, litter and people hanging out on the streets reminded me a little of home, the home I'd left long ago, and I felt ashamed of my own nervousness.

I wanted to live with homeless people on the street, but the stench of the hallways, the graffiti, and the cracks in the walls made my stomach turn. The apartment, no bigger than the bedrooms I always had in the convent, consisted of a hotel size refrigerator, an old, two burner stove and a utility sink, all hidden behind a dilapidated folding door. Is this how people really lived? Is this what I had been wanting for years? I'd wanted to be one with the poor, the outcast. But at that moment, in that tiny apartment, I wanted to vomit.

Sitting on the bus heading back to Sue's, my brain refused to shut down the self-criticism. *You want poverty, this is poverty. You want simplicity, how can you get simpler? No one should have to live like that. And it didn't feel safe. It isn't like Hong Kong where things were small and simple but not dangerous and gross. God forgive me. These are your people too. But you can't want them to live this way. No one should live this way. Francis would've. He became one with the poor. Isn't that what you wanted? You're a disgrace. What makes you so special?* With each stop sign, each red light, this litany began again.

Louise, the woman who invited me to the weekend conference, would be arriving in two hours. I had to shower and pack. On the way to Apostolic, Louise drove by the Sovereign apartment buildings, where several Sisters from their congregation were living, to show me a possible apartment she thought I might enjoy it. One block from the lake, close to the train and bus lines, and not far from Loyola University.

A glass door with brass handles greeted me after we were buzzed in by the front desk. A well-dressed elderly woman behind the counter greeted us and offered assistance. I noticed the ornate carpets, the chandeliers, the cleanliness and charm. The residents walking in and out greeted one another, exchanging smiles and getting messages from the front desk.

"Hi, I'm Louise. I don't know if you remember me. Some of the women from my congregation live here. Diane and Margaret." Louise greeted Mike, the building manager, as he approached.

"Oh, yes. Hello, how are you?"

"This is Jude. She's new in town. Just getting to know us. Do you have a space available?"

Mike took us straight up the elevator to apartment 924 and I fell in love instantly. The simple room with a side kitchenette looking east and with a great walk-in closet seemed like paradise. At least four times bigger than any room I'd ever had, with a closet just a bit smaller than my convent bedrooms.

"I have no job, no credit history but enough for first and last month's rent. I will get a job even if I have to scrub floors and toilets. I have twenty-five dollars on me right now and can bring the rest on Monday. You have to trust me." Louise and Mike gasped in disbelief at my candor.

"Can I have people in my room? Can they stay overnight?"

"It isn't college." Mike chuckled.

A shiver ran through me from embarrassment. I couldn't fathom the freedom I just walked into. I'd never been allowed to have anyone in my room, not for a minute, nor for an hour. No one would check up on me. No more lights out. The more I rolled it around in my mind, the sharper my pain. At 30, I remained as simple and sheltered as a child.

"I've never met a woman named Jude before. And I've never met someone so honest." Mike stammered. "I proposed to my wife in front of the statue of St. Jude at St. Clement's Church in Lincoln Park. My wife will kill me if I don't rent to you."

Set to move in Thursday, I needed a job. In Chicago two days, I already had my own place to live, so I decided to relax for the weekend as I met the women I hoped to spend the rest of my life with. They greeted one another with hugs, addressed each other on a first name basis, no formality, obvious warmth. They dressed as they liked and their professions ranging from teacher and nurse to professional clown and massage therapist. I heard no talk of the Holy Father or canon law. God could be a she. Mary, the Mother of Jesus, admired not so much for her virginity as for her plight as an unwed mother. The women were so healthy and free. The weekend passed quickly and I thought I'd finally found home.

Driving back to Sue's on Sunday, I imagined the Sovereign Apartments would be a brief stopover, just long enough to work out a transfer and start my new life in Apostolic within the year.

"Hey, let's take the long way back." Louise suggested.

"Sure, whatever that means."

"There's this cool, gorgeous town up here. Evanston. The houses are just fabulous. Sometimes on Sunday afternoon I drive up here just to gaze at the beauty." The awe and fascination in Louise's voice sounded like fingernails on a chalkboard, interrupting the excitement that had taken hold in my soul.

I saw only oversized, elaborate mansions. I thought of the decadence and the waste. How could someone vowed to poverty, someone with a preferential option for the poor, enjoy being surrounded by extreme luxury? Could the Apostolic's option for the poor be just on paper? The congregation managed a public housing complex on the edge of their motherhouse property. I'd seen it with my own eyes. Could both be possible?

Everything had been so perfect. The churning in my chest had to be squelched. The things these women said and did could make sense if I just thought about it. Maybe I could serve the poor but still enjoy beauty and wealth. But isn't that what my community claimed?

As we passed house after house, I realized if I didn't welcome new ways I'd be alone and lost forever, so I sat back and let the breeze wash away my hang-ups, hoping life would make sense again.

When the phone rang early Monday morning and a woman from the Banner Temp Agency offered me a job, I didn't really know how to act or what to say. Thankfully, the woman provided all of the information: long-term data entry for a daycare referral program at a bank building in Uptown. I'd start Monday. Making $8.50/hour.

I hadn't even thought about salary or what I needed to survive. I'd never needed to before, but anything had to be better than nothing. I planned to live simply as I had desired for so long.

Chicago is laid out like a sheet of graph paper. Radiating from the center point of Michigan and Madison, each block another 100 to the north, south, east, or west. 6200 North Broadway lay 62 blocks north of Madison Avenue; 4000 West Jackson, 40 blocks west of Michigan Avenue. To find any address, you simply need the coordinates. All but a few streets ran on the grid. Checking the map, I located Lawrence easily. The bank stood on the 4900 block of North Broadway. Living at 6200 North Broadway, on Granville, I would work 13 blocks south of my new apartment. A decent walk or a quick train or bus ride up and back would make life simple.

I had a place to live and a job, within a week and both so close together. Everyone said it would take months. I knew nothing happened by chance. These had to be signs God led me to Chicago and I was in the right place doing the right thing, my reassurance that everything would work out perfectly.

Sue drove me to Kmart that evening to get the basics: garbage can, broom, dustpan, dish rack, and some hangers. When I saw the big blue bean bag chair, I couldn't resist. Growing up I could never afford one. Owning something so silly over the past twelve years would have been unthinkable, improper.

My mind immediately went through the litany of questions I asked whenever I resumed permission. I barely knew how to act. I didn't have to ask anyone's permission. I didn't have to convince anyone but myself. With the swipe of my debit card and just a tinge of guilt, I bought the dark blue bag, to match the bedspread on the day bed furnished by the building manager. I'd have no real couch, but a comfortable place to read.

Waking up early Monday morning, and most mornings after that, came easy. I woke with the sunrise, drank a quart of boiling hot water, ate an apple and an orange with some oat bran, then dressed and headed south. Most mornings I sat, looking out the ninth floor window of my kitchenette. Each day brought marvels to behold as spring ripened and leaves began to cushion branches, lining the streets leading straight to the horizon. Somehow, through the years, I developed a certain affection for trees. The cycles of dormancy and new growth gave me hope. I felt my own strength stretching to the depths of my being, through the darkness of a long winter, through the depression that racked my soul, to bring forth new life within me.

I felt life awakening in so many ways but my job slowly beat me down. I completed three days' work in less than three hours. I received a new project every three days. I filled my time chatting with co-workers, but they were busy most of the day. As phones rang and keyboards click-clacked around me, my mind turned damp and soft like the rice paddies and marshlands of Asia.

"What's your son's name?" I asked my new coworker, expecting to hear Michael, James or something black, like Calvin. I had no idea I should even be thinking "African American." I had never heard the term "politically correct" and had not lived or worked with minorities, or in the United States, for so long that I had no idea they were referred to as people of color.

"Jovan," Denise said proudly, gently caressing the photo of a baby she obviously missed because of work.

"How do you spell that?" I questioned, intrigued by the odd name.

"Jovan? J-O-V-A-N. Like the perfume. You know."

"The what?"

"You've never heard of the perfume, Jovan. Where you been? Don't you ever shop girl?"

I let it go, but felt idiotic. I didn't know people named their children after perfume. I thought back to when Tina and I helped Thessie make up her daughter's name, Tunisia Ugetta. We were sixteen when we'd picked her name and I didn't realize unusual names had become the norm.

The conversation repeated itself in my head like a broken record. "Where you been? Don't you shop?" I didn't even know the name of a popular perfume. I really didn't shop but didn't tell her. I tried to keep the secret at work, but it became nearly impossible. In casual conversation I began a sentence with, "We had a Sister…" A coworker saw the silver band on my right ring finger and asked, "Are you married?" Another asked how I learned Chinese. I blew it with another co-worker the day I saw a picture of Toni Morrison tacked to Laurie's bulletin board, along with some of her poetry and newspaper clippings and asked, "Who's this?"

I heard the snickering comment, "A sheltered white girl from the suburbs," as I walked away. Growing up I felt more black than white, but someone called me a "sheltered, suburban white girl" which I considered a condemnation in itself. I couldn't relate to anyone. I didn't know the language, the vocabulary, or the people. Anger crept over me as fleas might on a mangy mutt and embarrassment gave way to frustration. As my jaw tightened and my shoulders slowly clenched near the base of my neck, the truth singed my nerve endings like a match to a fresh wick. I had become the very thing I despised. The convent managed to turn me white suburban and middle class.

I just wanted to be normal, to be one of them. I didn't want to be known as a Sister, but they talked about my clothes and my name behind my back. 'Jude,' such an odd name for a woman. Looking like I walked straight out of the 70's and far from stylish with my second-hand clothes from Oregon. I didn't know how to function as a 'normal' person. I didn't know the language. If I told them; maybe then they wouldn't look at me so strangely and some of the whispering might stop.

As I stood on the wooden platform waiting for the elevated train, my stomach muscles tightened and my entire body started shivering in the gentle breeze. The breeze, so refreshing just this morning, had taken on a biting chill, despite its warmth. I knew what came next. I began to sweat, and inside the train I began to tremble. Crossing my legs and hugging my torso in an attempt to keep from disintegrating. No matter how tightly I held on, the stench began to seep through the air. I'm sure those around me figured I was either ill or crazy. I smelled like I hadn't bathed in days. The foul odor became unmistakably my own, but all the while I felt like I shivered as if buried in snow, freezing and in fear for my life.

As the train approached the Granville station, I didn't get off. What would I do alone in my small studio apartment all night? I'd met a few people in the building. Carmel introduced herself the first day. She invited me to join gatherings of students from Loyola University, the sisters and priests studying in the Institute of Pastoral Studies, who lived in the building. I could always call Carmel, but I didn't want to be a burden. My endless rambling about my convoluted, tragic story had to be wearing thin. Allowing anyone into the pain seemed to make the pain subside momentarily, but I still ended up alone and isolated. The constant self-revelation felt as exhausting as the secrets I kept from those at work.

Lucy, one of the Apostolic's, lived just blocks away. She had invited me to come by if I needed anything. I ran as quickly as possible from the station towards Loyola's Lakefront Hall. As my eyes filled with tears and burned from the lake breeze whipping across my face, I prayed Lucy would be home and that she wouldn't judge.

By the time I reached Lucy's, the stench had settled into my clothes; my face had turned bright red and my hair damp, and every muscle ached. If only I could pretend to be sick or mentally ill, then I wouldn't have to be alone anymore. I wouldn't have to take care of myself. But I had to face my own ignorance and fears. The door opened and I crumpled to the floor like a pile of dirty laundry. Lucy not only offered me a place to relax, to shower, and to stay for the night, but an open ear and a giving heart. We talked for hours with Lucy reassuring me everything would get better. I had only been in Chicago a few weeks. I had an apartment and a job. I would slowly adjust and even begin to enjoy living alone and the freedom of being on your own. Lucy, a transfer Sister to the Apostolic's herself, knew.

I'd never lived alone, and I craved the companionship and security I'd left behind. I'd never been so free to come and go. Every time I used the phone or went out for a walk along the lake, guilt crept in because I didn't ask for permission first. Part of me feared I would totally loose it. I needed to keep control or chaos might consume me. My relaxation and leisure time had been scheduled for the last twelve years and before that I needed Mom's permission to do anything. I had never balanced a checkbook or paid my own bills. Now I stayed up as late as I wanted, bought what I wanted, and ate whatever and whenever I wanted. I panicked at the thought. If no one regulated me, could I control myself? I didn't want to be petrified. I yearned for the unimaginable day when I no longer ached for the regiment.

I woke with excitement on April 16, rushing three blocks to St. Gertrude's on the corner of Granville and Glenwood, to attend Mass before work, and to privately participate in the Devotional Renewal of Vows, my community would be. As I read the words, they slowly began to slip away:

Almighty and Eternal God I, Sister Mary Jude, now renew and confirm with my whole heart my vows of Poverty, Chastity, and Obedience made according to the Constitutions of this Congregation of Our Lady of Sorrows. I implore Thee O God of infinite goodness and mercy, by the precious blood of Jesus Christ, and through the intercession of Our Lady of Sorrows, to grant me the grace to fulfill these vows perfectly. Amen.

The formula didn't speak for my heart. I questioned if words were really necessary? Jesus knew my desire. I left Oregon, not because I rejected poverty, chastity, and obedience but because I longed to embrace these virtues more fully. Poverty meant sharing generously what I'd graciously and undeservingly been given. Chastity called for availability, vulnerability, and befriending. Obedience demanded an attentive heart, willing to discover God in the circumstances of the day. I moved to Chicago to find other women who shared my vision, others who would challenge me when I became too comfortable in mediocrity.

Even as I offered my heartfelt renewal to the gospel, I struggled with my growing desire for beauty, leisure and nurturing. I glanced around my small studio, recognizing for the first time my long-repressed love for the cozy and the comfortable. In the few short weeks living alone, I'd already begun to experiment with coordinating colors, patterns and styles in my kitchenette, bathroom, living area and the walk-in closet I'd turned into prayer space. As a young girl, growing up on welfare and living on hand-me-downs, I'd dream of a decorated bedroom with stylish sheets, a comforter and nice furniture. Dreams that seemed so impossible then, that I'd actually completely forgotten, were becoming reality at the age of thirty. Claiming poverty and simplicity, I moved towards cozy and comfortable. Surprising even me, I allowed the awareness to surface and let it go without frustration or guilt.

Later that week walking home from work, I noticed a small public library on a side street. As I headed for the door, my heart beat faster and my mind raced. At least a half hour of daily reading had been a basic requirement in the convent, not including any required reading from college instructors. I craved a good book. Lucy gave me a few Maeve Binchy novels and Carmel lent me some Robert Ludlum, neither of whom I'd ever read, but I finished them in no time. No specific titles, no authors rushed to mind, but the thought of an entire library at my fingertips thrilled me.

"I'd like to get a library card please."

"A drivers' license and two pieces of proof-of-address," the answer came like computer recording.

"I have is a passport, will that work?"

"A drivers' license and two pieces of proof-of-address," the woman said again.

"But I just want a library card; I'm not trying to buy a car!" I struggled with each word now. A simple library card proved impossible. I felt like a little child right after a long day of hard work filling buckets, carrying sand and water along the beach to create the castle of her dreams, just to have a huge, crashing wave crash it away. The tears flowed as readily and rough as the waves destroying the

125

masterpiece. My entire world had fallen apart and this five-minute exchange reinforced all of my doubts and hesitations. In tears, I sensed the lump rising in my throat and the insidious odor seeping from my pores.

Church bells rang from St. Ita's about five blocks up Broadway. I rushed in, just in time to hear the gospel. The priest described the disciples' time between Easter and Pentecost as "waiting, doing nothing." But I knew better. My heart screamed, "They weren't doing nothing! They are in an incubation period. They are maturing, getting strong. Just like I am. Wonderful adventures awaited them and now await me."

As much as my emotions swung on the pendulum of extremes, I'd already begun to reach out with the courage of the apostles after Pentecost. On Saturday I bought food for John from the street corner; yesterday I'd sat with Frank, an intelligent and well-informed person living on the street, at a local restaurant when I bought him a sandwich. I treated the transients I encountered with dignity but I had a long way to go before reaching the integrity and heart of Francis. The constant pull between fear and security, openness and safety tore at the fabric of my soul. I wanted to shout, with Jesus, "No one who comes to me will I ever reject" but I harbored fear, from being without my veil, from living alone. I had yet to grow in faith.

I wanted the deep breathing exercises, centering prayer, and my faith to be enough. I wanted to make it alone, without chocolate cake, a half-gallon of ice cream or half a dozen donuts to ease the pain. Neither my stomach nor my soul could take much more. Part of me wanted to just sit with someone and be held while I cried, but I had no more tears. My anger had dissipated. What is the point of anger, if the one who has hurt you doesn't know? Fear. Fear is futile. Nothing can keep the inevitable from happening. I just felt lonely. I had known loneliness in a crowd before, but now I knew total aloneness. I felt numb, almost comatose. I walked into my huge closet turned haven, found my prayer pillow, lit a candle and sat. I could sit for hours, possibly days and no one would ever find me. No one's life would change without me. Sure, my family might miss me in a way, but I had not lived near them for so long; it would be no huge loss. I'd been in Chicago almost two months and, except for the weekly calls from Mom, no one seemed to care. I would not even be missed until Monday, if I didn't show up for work.

My dreams that night took me back to my family, my home parish and my religious habit. I had worn the simple black dress with a scapular and veil. Now, dreaming, I wondered if I should wear it or not; if I'd done wrong by taking it off? Parishioners would not welcome me, they said, unless I became

126

an upright catholic again. Should I return to my congregation, so familiar, yet so painful?

When I woke up the next morning I was still seating in the closet. Darting from the pillow, I pulled out the ironing board, punched in a cassette, and began work. I had taken to ironing all of my clothes every Saturday morning. Lucy gave me some clothes and a few weeks earlier suggested, for a more professional look, I buy a shell to wear under a blazer she gave me. I remembered painter pants and tube dresses, but not much more. Lucy took me to Target, another new experience, to give me the ins and outs of simple fashion. She suggested appropriate interview attire, office wear and shoes. I had been wearing Birkenstocks consistently for the past three years and before that black loafers. Although I felt uncomfortable with most of the styles and could not believe the price of clothes, I bought several shells, some T-shirts and several shorts outfits that night and began experimenting with different colors and styles. I decided to organize my clothes by color in order to easily match pants or skirts to tops according to how I felt each day. Waking in an up mood I wore yellow, solemn would be blue, down to earth meant green, in need of warmth and comfort I'd wear brown. So each Saturday, standing in my walk-in closet, I ironed clothes and tried new looks and styles. Friday had been tough, but a good night's sleep cured my exhaustion. With routine and control, life felt good.

I slowly learned not to panic about leaving a glass on the nightstand or falling asleep reading a book. I didn't worry someone was checking my garbage to see if I wasted something useful. I even allowed myself an occasional afternoon nap without fear of being reprimanded. My exposure to the sisters and priests from around the world helped me confirm that living the gospel could be done without paranoia, neurosis or pettiness.

Almost as steadily, I began avoiding quiet time and reflecting in my journal. I ate too much, slept too much, read too many novels and listened to music constantly. Avoid as I might, the thoughts crept in: Will it all fall apart again? Will get sucked into an unhealthy environment because of my vulnerability? Will I eventually experience the rejection I felt with my Sisters in Hong Kong and Oregon? I'm getting scared. I'm feeling so vulnerable and at the same time so eager. I don't want time and space. I won't be disillusioned in the end. My hopes won't be crushed. I wanted to just join and get on with my life.

On the walk to Mass the next morning the Wizard of Oz came to mind. Dorothy, Lion, Scarecrow and Tin Man spent so much time and energy searching for the wizard to give them what they desired. In the end, he showed them they possessed what they were looking for within themselves. I spent months, maybe a year, if not twelve years, agonizing over what to do. I never trusted myself. I talked to spiritual directors, priests, friends, even virtual strangers. I had been hesitant to say anything, to return to the States, hesitant about taking a year off to seek transfer and scared to move to Chicago. I wanted the transfer to work. I wanted to be a Apostolic, of that I remained certain.

I found my path, loving myself, knowing that I had something to offer to others, to the Apostolic's, to the church, and to the world. I didn't need to look outside myself or to anyone else to tell me what to do. I needed to take care of myself, get back on track with my prayer life, eat right, and choose life. Meditation is where I listen for answers. Letting go of my own fears and doubts and insecurities allowed me to open my channels to hear and to know what I needed to do. I spent time meditating that night, determined to reach within and listen to God in the stillness. My reading from *A Time for Joy* spoke to my desire: *If we have to determine which of two courses to take, we ask God for inspiration, an intuitive thought or decision. Then we relax and take it easy, and we are often surprised how often the right answers come after we have tried this for a while.* - Bill Wilson AA

Lucy invited me to spend the next weekend in Wisconsin with three or four other women from Apostolic. We drove up on Friday afternoon with no real agenda and no schedule. We spent the weekend going for long walks in the woods, relaxing in front of the fireplace, and playing match after match of Rummikub. Every round brought another interesting conversation. Topics of speculation and wonder, not absolutes and should's. Every time Lucy shared some opinion I felt as if she gave voice to the depths of my own soul.

"If you were picking a Native American name, what would it be?" Lucy offered as we played.

Finally, I found other women who enjoyed conversation in the midst of a game. Women who were not out for cut throat, uptight competition. As the night ended, I asked about plans for Sunday Mass. Everyone looked at me as if I just announced I had cancer. They'd all be together for brunch. No one had plans for Mass. My comfort level began to shake. My insides tightened and confusion mounted. As my defenses went up, I tried to justify the women staring at me, and began questioning my own convictions. At the same time, I searched for the church address and schedule in the phone book. I would walk so as not to disturb anyone else's plans. Any attempts to dodge self-incrimination were futile.

Would my practice of Sunday Mass, something so basic to Catholicism, be challenged if I got closer to these women? Would I be respected or would I be pressured? Would these women support me or would I live by their convictions rather than my own? As I dosed off, my worries entered my reams, causing frustration and fear. I woke in tears and wondering if I'd get to Mass. If I didn't go, I'd be allowing others to dictate my conscience. I'd be compromising my integrity, letting go of something prematurely. The Scripture, "You will worship in spirit and in truth," kept popping into my mind. As I got ready to leave, I noticed Lucy, dressed and waiting for me. Not sure if I should feel supported or humored, I simply thanked her.

Mass left me feeling more distressed than refreshed. The empty ritual lacked community, lacked life. Feeling depressed and angry with the Church, I questioned how the faithful are expected to grow spiritually when offered such trash. The music, prayers, and homily lacked spiritual nutrition like fast food lacked nutrients. Leaving Wisconsin that afternoon, I wondered if needed intellectual conversion. Did I hold on to my strict Catholicism for fear of letting yet one more thing go? I wished desperately for someone to tell me what to do but knew I had to find the answers within myself.

That night I sat with my jigsaw puzzle, thinking. I often approached life as I did the jigsaw. Separate by category. Edges formed one pile, middles with only holes another, and mixed middles still another. Compartmentalize and then attack. Piece by piece, create a replica of what's in the picture. I'd lived in the Church for so many years to not know what things should look like. But still, the struggle to make all of the pieces fit could be endless. Every time I thought I had it right, something didn't match. The total commitment I thought I'd find with the habit and strict community life had lacked any real substance; the freedom demonstrated by the Apostolic's slowly seemed to be more New Age than Catholic. I wanted to let go of the outward show and the rituals that made no sense. I wanted to be free. How would I justify not going to church? What would others say? I couldn't let go just because Lucy had, but holding on had more to do with what Mom or others might say than of letting go of something important to me.

After another long, uneventful day doing nothing at work, feeling useless and still confused about the weekend, I headed to catch the 5:30 Mass at St. Ita's. I hurried towards the comfort of something familiar and a sense of salvation. Regiment could keep me from crumbling. As I pulled the heavy wooden door open carefully so as not to disturb those praying inside, the smells, sights and sounds of everything church is, overwhelmed me. Squeaking kneelers, candles burning, fresh cut mums at the foot of the altar, dim lights and conspicuous silence. Old familiar faces seemed to be jutting out from every corner to welcome me home. Anthony, Therese, Bernadette, Martin, Francis, Patrick, Joseph and Mary. The Communion of Saints. Each statue reminded me of someone both dear to me and painfully lost.

"Let us begin, in the name of the Father, the Son, and the Holy Spirit." The booming voice of the priest called me back to the moment. "Lord, have mercy. Christ, have mercy. Lord, have mercy." I found myself slipping in and out of the present to all the pain those who taught me to rely on the mercy of the Lord had caused.

Did what the Sisters think really matter? I lived with these women for twelve years. I'd grown up with them. They shaped and molded me. With them I shared sorrow and joy. Now I struggled to live the gospel more fully, to practice all we prayed about and studied for so long, and they rejected me, unable to understand and unwilling to try. I felt like screaming, "Screw you! If you don't care, I don't care!" They would do nothing to help me discern God's will because as far as they were concerned, God willed that I remain in the congregation. They allowed me to make final vows. God spoke through them; they couldn't be wrong.

I stood in front of the Blessed Sacrament, longing for peace and reconciliation, but felt betrayed and forsaken. I could no longer offer up my sacrifices with Jesus. I could take the hypocrisy no more. As I robotically and methodically repeated prayers and followed ritual, memories shook me like a 6.8 earthquake. Feeling the walls and the stone cold statues closing in on me, surrounding me, calling my name and reminding me to be humble, be charitable, be chaste, be obedient, I stumbled to the nearest door, holding my chest almost in a panic. I would never return. The institution made no sense. With certainty it had nothing to do with Lucy, and with great pain, I let it go.

In just two months, I comfortably moved from present to past tense. I spoke of my former congregation and the community I came from. Awkward as it sounded, I remained a Franciscan Sister but without a congregation, with no community to call my own. Still legally bound to the congregation, I lived in isolation. Except for a simple housewarming package I'd received in the mail, I heard nothing from the Sisters unless I made contact. I kept them informed of my address and phone number, sent copies of the official credential evaluations I'd paid to be processed, and let them know I'd be undergoing the psychological assessment necessary for all transfer candidates to the Apostolic's.

Louise arranged the psychological assessment for June 9, two months after my arrival in Chicago. The only professional psychological assessment I'd experienced had been conducted by Sr. Thomas's sister, Nancy the day after my return to the United States from Hong Kong. Nancy dredged up every joy and pain, and every memory, and even introduced the idea of sexual abuse, then left. The encounter had been bizarre and troubling.

130

I wondered if the same thing would happen again with this psychological assessment. Now that my life had fallen apart and made little sense; now that I struggled to begin again, to be an adult, to make life changing decisions. Could I open myself to the possibility of rejection and disappointment again? And keep trusting, searching for good, loving people? Could I believe not every dad ran off and not all congregations just wanted to add numbers?

The pre-session package arrived in the mail a few weeks prior to the assessment. I needed to complete biographical information and six inventories before the session: relationship to each parent, dealing with anger, spirituality, intimacy, finances, depression. Did I include too much, not enough? Did I bring up subjects that might cause questioning or concern? Not sure what to feel, I mailed it right away to avoid constant revisions.

As I walked from the train to the office building in Oak Park I noticed a sign which read, "Sponsored by the Apostolic Franciscans." The overwhelming sense of connection and pride I felt surprised me. I had begun, in recent days, to ponder the possibilities: "Hi, I'm Sister Jude, a Apostolic Franciscan." "Hello, I'm a Franciscan with the Apostolic Sisters."

I thought of my dream from the night before. The statue of St. Jude sitting with his hand turned upwards in expectation, which Sr. Ruth gave me years before, crashed to the ground, shattering into innumerable pieces. Did the statue stand for my self-image as Jude, for my patient openness, for my quest for sanctity or my pursuit of religious life? Could the constant prayer from my novitiate days, that God break me if that is what it took to make me a saint, finally be realized through this struggle?

Except for the slight gnawing question "Are they too New Age for me?" I liked everything about the Apostolic's. They stood for concern for the poor, empowering the oppressed, bringing good to the earth. They embodied what I desired. The assessment would just be a formality.

Usual pleasantries with John and Charlaine briefly describing their professional backgrounds came first.

"Let's begin with your family history," John offered. "You mentioned you didn't really know your father."

Here we go again, I thought. Everyone thinks my world revolves around the fact that my father left me. I've gotten over it. I didn't dare say it, but literally tasted the temptation. Instead, I recounted the feelings of an abandoned child, the anger, the guilt, and the apathy. Sharing how I came to consider God my father in literal sense and how my whole existence became a search for a relationship with my true father, I recognized, more than ever before, how naïve I sounded. They moved on to my mother, which although not as common a topic for conversation, seemed to me to be just as ridiculous. I hoped they would bring up my most difficult life experience, the convent. But they seemed to be avoiding the topic. Everyone wanted to discuss my childhood. But my world no longer revolved around my father's abandonment and my mother's emotional distance. I wanted to transfer to another congregation, and felt strongly the discussion should be about finding out what went wrong in my former congregation.

During the ride home I turned the conversation over in my mind like kneading a ball of dough. Turn, fold, press and push. Turn, fold, press and push. They'd asked me briefly about the convent and my attitude towards authority, and the more I kneaded it, the more frustrated I became. Would anyone ever believe, unless they'd been there, the coercion and manipulation that went on behind the convent walls? Yes, young and impressionable, I allowed, maybe even welcomed the degradation and humiliation. I wanted desperately for everyone to understand how much I had grown and how much more I understood about the world, the church, and myself. I didn't have issues with legitimate authority and I didn't rebel just to get attention.

That night Lucy called me to watch a lightning storm over Lake Michigan. As usual, we met at the lake behind Loyola's library. Sitting on the huge rocks in the humid night air, we shared joy and pain.

"How did it go? I don't want details because I'll read the assessment write-up at committee, but are you okay with it all?" Lucy wasted no time letting me know, off the bat, about her role on the committee reviewing my request and that everything would be official business now. I stretched the truth a bit to tell her it went well, and my mind floated across the lake in front of me to Sr. Thomas's voice as I avoided thinking Lucy befriended me just to evaluate me. I couldn't believe she could be so manipulative and I didn't want a simple sentence to change my life forever as it had before.

"Do you realize I know nothing about the eighties? How many thirty-year-old women, born and raised in California, are totally ignorant of anything after 1981? I feel like I was frozen in time in the seventies and thawed out in 1994. I have twelve years of my life missing. I'm older, but in so many ways, I am still an ignorant eighteen-year-old, just out of high school. When will I ever catch up? I finished college, but never had a real college life with parties or the dating experience. I never even had a real graduation celebration. I never cultivated friendships either. That's the thing I miss most. I have no connections. People always talk about a friend they've known since high school or college, and I don't have any peers."

Lucy let me go on, without much comment except for me to be patient, as I burst into tears. "I just have nothing in common with anyone. I'm no

132

ood at the shallow, small talk. I need philosophical, meaningful encounters. I eed stimulation, reflection and fascination. I can't talk politics or ntertainment because I'm totally clueless. What is left?" Conversations with ucy often wound in and around the range of emotions running rampant ithin me, until she brought them to an end and I reluctantly headed home, nging for the next visit.

The next night, my brother Daniel called and I panicked, wondering who died at he needed to call me in the middle of the day. "Hey, huh, Janet. I mean Jude. ou still go by Jude right? Anyway, huh, this is Dan."

As Dan's voice cracked, I blurted, "What's wrong?"

"Nothin' really. I just need to tell you something." Dan's pause lasted forever. "I found Dad."

"When, how, what happened, where?" I couldn't listen fast enough and Dan efinitely didn't talk quickly enough.

"You know we just went on this trip to Disneyland, right?.

"We drove from there up to Las Vegas. But we had this accident. The car rapped out. I took it as an omen that maybe we shouldn't go. Maybe we weren't eant to meet. But I swear this angel helped us out. This man came from owhere. Said he'd fix the whole thing. He took us home. All seven kids, Leah and e. They fed us pizza and let us swim in their pool. The whole time, he worked n the car. I told him what we were doing in Nevada. They encouraged us to keep oing, to find Dad. He fixed the car in no time and we took off. We ended up in as Vegas on Fathers' Day."

I usually appreciated Dan's ability to tell a good story, but in the moment it st frustrated me. I just needed to know what happened when he met Dad?

"So, we get there, and the apartment gates are shut. I parked the car, jumped a ence, found the apartment and rang the doorbell. Nobody answered. At 6:30 in e damn morning, nobody answered. I figured someone had to be there. I ropped on the stair thinkin', now what?

"As I sat, getting pretty pissed, I heard this cough. A simple cough but I knew is cough. I hadn't really thought about what I'd say or do at that moment. I'd ehearsed it a million times in my mind over the years, but none of it seemed right the moment. Before I could think, he stood in front of me.

"'I just stuck out my hand and said, 'Happy Father's Day. Long time no see.' He just said, 'Well, hi. How did you get here?' and shook my hand.

"My past and my future changed forever. Then, I remembered Leah and the ids waiting in the car. He told me to go get them and we all went in to meet enny who'd been asleep. We chatted and talked for hours. They fed us breakfast.

133

Freakin' unbelievable. He's a great guy. And Jenny is wonderful. The kids loved it. We took pictures. And you know what? He writes poetry."

"Are you kidding? I can't believe it."

"I knew you'd trip 'cause you write, too. He's got some stuff published. Under Loyed Arnold. Can you believe it? He published under his own name."

"Did you ask him about anything, why he did it?"

I remembered how ticked Dan got when I told him about my trip to Iowa just three years earlier when I learned Dad lived in Las Vegas, and about Jenny. He'd been livid. Now he seemed cool and welcoming.

"No, I didn't ask anything. I just figured I'd take it from where it is now. We'll see what happens. My problem now is if I should tell anyone else. I don't want people showin' up to get all mad or to fight with him. They had no idea what we were doing in Las Vegas. The thing is, I can't keep the kids from talkin' about meeting Grandpa. They loved him."

"You gonna tell Mom?"

"I gotta sit with it all for a while, write to him, call him more, see where it goes. Then I'll tell people."

"Can I get his address and phone number."

"I better check with him first. Dan hesitated. "See if it is okay. I'm not sure what kind of contact he wants. I know he doesn't want people confronting him. He kinda said that outright."

"Well, ask him. But you know I've prayed for his peace and tried to find him for so long; I won't screw it up."

After hanging up the phone, I sat in the middle of the floor where I'd been putting on my shoes when the phone rang. Life would not be so simple anymore. All of the sudden, in an instant, I could no longer say, 'He left me at seven and we have no idea where he is.' With one phone call, I became the abandoned child who found her father twenty-three years later.

So many times strangers and even well intentioned friends, including some of the Sisters, suggested he might come back. They questioned, as I had as a child, what my mother would do if he returned? I learned through the years to use my mother's response, 'He won't." Although he didn't return on his own, my Dad was back and I had no idea what to do next.

"Lucy, Daniel found my dad."

"Really? That's good, right?" Lucy's dispassionate response surprised me, until realized she hadn't known me long enough to appreciate the importance of my announcement. I tried again; "Can you believe it? I've waited for years! I never believed it would happen! It's so incredible. I actually might meet my father, my dad. I don't even remember him, now we might meet. Man, my dad."

Lucy remained unenthused, almost uninterested. I tried to tell her about his poetry, how he fed Dan and his family, how he's a nice guy, but as my enthusiasm and excitement seemed to echo in the vacuum left by Lucy's lack of engagement, I realized no one could completely understand, except maybe Myrna, the first person I ever told he left. I don't know why I didn't call Myrna. I had absolutely no one with whom I could share my newfound joy. I would be silly to think anyone in Chicago would really understand or care. I hadn't known Lucy long enough for her to understand how profound this moment felt for me. I found my Dad, but only after I lost everyone else.

Sr. Thomas and Sr. Ruth might remember the many books on the healing of memories I'd read, but they always accused me of being overly emotional. Sr. Thomas insisted I just accept my abandonment as God's will. God set me up for a vocation and I should be grateful.

"Maybe since you offered this great sacrifice," one of the Chinese Sisters, had offered shortly after I made final vows, "God will bless you now and your dad will come back." I could never convince them Dad's return may not be a blessing, especially for my mother.

The irony of his returning only after I left struck me even as I grappled with the discomfort brought on by my conversation with Lucy. I sat on my bed attempting to ignore the old tapes running through my mind. My insecurities and suspicions made me question if Lucy had only befriended me with the hopes I might become a Apostolic. She'd become somewhat distant since the psych evaluation and her reaction to the news of my father only furthered my concern that she didn't really like me, for me.

Trying to give Lucy the benefit of the doubt, I reminded myself of the times Sr. Thomas made me go to bed in the middle of a vocation crisis. As the superior Sr. Thomas showed concern for my health, work, and family, but only because she had to, not because she loved me. As soon as Sr. Thomas stopped being the superior, she also stopped caring. I realized her indifference the day I raced home from the Natural Medicine doctor for lunch to celebrate the feast of St. Jude and to share the good news that I didn't have cancer.

Everyone had been worried because many of my symptoms were similar to Sr. Veronica's: stomach troubles, fatigue, aches and pains. The doctor promised I had no serious illness but needed to cut down stress and change eating habits. Everyone who saw me asked about the doctor's visit immediately. With five minutes to spare before lunch, I sat thumbing through the newspaper. When Sr. Thomas approached the table without greeting, I said, "I just got back from the doctor."

"Oh, yeah, I know."

"Aren't you going to ask what happened?"

"You need to go talk to Sr. Joanne. I'm not your superior anymore."

Every kind word, every expression of concern or admission of care I'd ever received from Sr. Thomas, instantly meant nothing. My joy suddenly disappeared. Sr. Thomas did what she had to as the superior, out of obligation. She never cared; she'd only lied. The phrases kept ringing in my ears like an echo of the many times I'd been told to go to bed, to let it go for the night, that things would be different in the morning.

But what happened with Lucy? Had the psyche evaluation gone poorly? Had they already held one of those meetings superiors have to discuss matters, without letting the people involved know? Or had I just smothered Lucy like I tended to do? Had I so relied on her friendship, attention and companionship and become so infatuated with her that I scared her off? Trying to fend off the voices discrediting Lucy, the woman who had done so much for me since I arrived in Chicago, I followed the advice she gave me before we hung up; I sat down at the computer and began a journal entry:

Dear Dad,
Dan just called to tell me he and his family just met you.

Even as I tried to write, I didn't know what to say. I didn't know what to say to my own dad. So much time and energy I'd spent forgiving him. Whenever someone gave me gift money, I offered a Mass stipend to pray for his peace.

I have no hard feelings. I love you and I pray for your peace every day. At least I had for most of my life. I couldn't promise at that point in time, even after learning about his new family and what he and his new wife Jenny did to her daughter, that I prayed for his peace anymore.

I'd really like to get to know you and to let you get to know me. What could I tell a man I hardly knew?

I actually think we have a great deal in common. Dan said you write poetry. I do, too. I'm a pretty good cook, and from what I heard all my life, you are too. And most of all, just as you made a major life decision that turned your world upside down, so have I. Do you realize I spent 12 years in a convent? I left last March and live in Chicago now.

Writing to a complete stranger proved difficult. He had not been there when I needed him, to ask advice, to hold my hand, to check out the guys I dated, to see me off on my first date, to congratulate me on my first communion, confirmation, graduation, entrance to the convent, first vows, and final vows. He never knew I was a cheerleader in fourth grade; that I went to Hillcrest for sixth grade; and in eighth grade I helped on yearbook staff and became the student body president. Could I tell him about high school, my boyfriends, my drinking, and my best friends? He didn't yell at me because he loved me and cared about me and didn't want to lose me, like dads are supposed to do for their little girls. Could I ask advice or redo all the firsts he missed? Could I share my memories of Taiwan and Hong Kong? Or tell him about all the women I lived with in the convent, those who left and those who died? Could I let him in now? Could I let him share without asking him 'Why?'

My life and feelings couldn't be summarized in a simple letter. What could I possibly say to the man who made one decision that influenced my entire personality; the man whose faded memory shaped my life, invaded my prayer, and haunted my soul. I wanted to say everything but had nothing to say.

Shuffling papers, punching number after number into my pocket calculator, counting and recounting, I looked for some answer. How had I gotten into this financial mess? More importantly, how would I get myself out? Continually punching the same keys, arriving at the same answer, I thought of the old definition of insanity: repeatedly doing the same thing, but expecting a different result.

As I sat growing more and more anxious about what I needed to do to survive the next few weeks, Carmel called to invite me for a walk. Carmel's relaxed, witty demeanor made me comfortable and I enjoyed her company. We headed south along Lake Michigan as usual. Children played in the sand, bikers whizzed by, kites dotted the crisp blue sky, and boats swayed in the gentle lake breeze. All the while I attempted to forget my pending doom.

Lake Michigan had been my salvation many days. Long walks at sunrise kept my hopes up. The crash of waves matched the emotions crashing against my soul as I walked, sometimes for hours. Longing for something to occupy my brain, anything to think about so I wouldn't go completely numb; trying not to think so I wouldn't go completely crazy. Scenes that usually filled me with wonder and gratitude left me vapid. I tried to exchange small talk, attempting to carry on a simple conversation.

Carmel noticed. "Are you okay? Did something happen?"

Barely holding back tears, "I screwed up my money."

"What happened? What do you mean by 'screwed up'?" Carmel seemed sympathetic and genuinely concerned.

"The Sisters gave me $3000 when I left. I've made about $3000 more since March. I haven't spent an unaccounted for penny. I've kept a log of all the money I've spent and made, like we had to in Hong Kong. Six-thousand dollars and I have nothing to show for it."

"What do you mean, 'nothing to show for it'?" Carmel sounded almost angry. "You've rented an apartment, bought clothes at mostly second-hand stores, paid bills you never did before, paid for your own transportation and walked most places. You've not only fed yourself, but you've fed others. You have lived simply and carefully. Do you really believe you have nothing to show? You are starting life over!"

"I'm starting life over, but failed at my first attempt to balance a budget. I've bought too much I don't need."

"Like what?"

"Junk food, those house plants, the extra dishes and my prayer pillow, the T.V. and stuff I bought from Lorraine before she flew back to Ireland. I could name a million things I shouldn't have bought, and I didn't really need, I just wanted."

Beginning to pick apart everything I'd accomplished, I accused myself of living luxuriously when I'd said I wanted to live simply and for others. It's what I'd said, but I realized at that moment it wouldn't work without community. Each time I walked down Granville towards the train or the store, I dreamt of all the possibilities for the empty storefronts. Small unkempt children holding the hands of obviously drug-addicted mothers would prompt a 'that would make a great tutorial center' response; the men eager for food, money, and possibly drugs of sorts, led me to a 'that corner store would be perfect as a soup kitchen' thought. I longed to 'go about doing good,' like Jesus did, but if I worried about my own survival from day to day and month to month, what could I possibly do for others?

I needed community for more than financial reasons; I needed the community for emotional support as well. I needed an identity to give me the strength and the courage to do what I desired. I needed someone to encourage me. I could call myself a religious, a Franciscan, a missionary. My clothes alone made a statement before I ever spoke a word. Now, I melted away in the crowd, alone. Unattached and uncertain.

"You're still a member of your congregation, can't they help you out?" Carmel proposed innocently.

"Are you kidding? I practically had to sue them to get the $3000 they finally gave me. As far as they're concerned, I'm on my own."

"What about your mom or your family?"

"No, they don't have it either."

"I can have you over for dinner sometimes if it would help. Just don't beat yourself up. You've come this far; you'll figure something out. God will provide."

Mom always claimed, "God will provide." Whenever we ran out of money near the end of the month or an unexpected expense popped up, she gave her tried-and-true answer: 'God will provide.' Carmel ended with the words I least wanted to hear. I felt as if my life were repeating itself. I knew the struggles of not having enough money as a child, of growing up on welfare, of wearing classmates' hand-me-downs and of receiving the box of canned goods collected at church each Thanksgiving.

I'd always wondered how my mom balanced the humility with the pride. Mom accepted donations from parishioners but got angry when I brought home food a friend gave me. Mom insisted "God will provide." Deep down I wanted to believe more than I believed anything else. I wanted to trust. But right now, I simply felt angry and wanted to find some way to punish myself for wasting money and failing at my constant attempt to reach sanctity.

I claimed I wanted true and pure simplicity. But my reality began to sink in. I could not stand up to defend the homeless and the helpless when I had never defended myself. I let the Sisters walk all over me for years. I spent most of my waking hours doing things for other people; doing anything; doing, just to keep from thinking. I couldn't let myself think too much. Thoughts led to feelings. Feelings led to pain.

Redirecting my personal feelings to efforts and ideals for other people, didn't seem as painful. As much as I hated to admit it, I needed something beyond myself to cling to, to fight for. Even as I refused to shave my legs or wear nylons, or I arranged appointments and outings without asking, I did it all in the name of women's rights or the essence of obedience, not personal freedom.

Yeah, I'd purchased a sandwich or two for people who were asking for food, but I blew my first real chance to live simply and poorly, to live with and for the poor in that little apartment on Damen. Instead I lived at the Sovereign, with a closet full of colorful clothes and a room adorned with potted plants and matching pillows. I had extra food stashed in my cupboard and plenty of food in the fridge. A far cry from the life I envisioned the day I left Oregon content with a wok, a bowl and a set of chopsticks. Could my love of poverty all be a big farce? The possibility both frightened and angered me. Carmel told me I should trust God, but I would trust God later. I needed to survive for now and I couldn't be such a living contradiction. I had serious questions to face.

Daniel finally sent Dad's address and phone number along with pictures they'd taken on their visit. Dad gave permission to give his number as long as no questions were asked. I had no questions, just a desire to know him. He looked much shorter than I remembered. He appeared bald and chubby standing next to his wife and his eighteen-year-old son, my half-brother Teddy, with blonde hair, blue eyes and glasses. I'd only seen the 1931 wedding picture and a few candids Grandma brought when she moved in. I'd totally forgotten what he looked like until that moment. I held in my hand the closest, quickest way to connect with my father after twenty-three years: 607-934-0245. I could pick up the phone and call him, if I wanted to pay for a long distance call in the middle of the day.

I picked up the latest Robert Ludlum novel Carmel lent me, opened it and started to read. After reading and rereading the first three lines five or six times, my eyes kept wandering to the phone number sitting next to me. I dropped the book and walked into the kitchenette thinking I'd get a bite to eat. I had some day old donuts, some baby carrots, and a bag of chips. I didn't want to eat. Pigging out would smother the excitement and anticipation I enjoyed for the first time in years. A walk would keep my spirits up, and my mind off the phone number sitting in front of me. Tying my shoes, I stared at the phone. I couldn't resist. My hands shook and my teeth chattered as I picked up the receiver and dialed.

The southern drawl on the end of the line surprised me. I'd completely forgotten my father came from Arkansas.

"Hi. This is your daughter, Janet, but I go by Jude now."

"Well, hello."

"Daniel gave me your phone number so I thought I'd call to say hello."

"Yeah."

"You know I live in Chicago now? I recently left the convent after almost thirteen years. I moved here about three months ago."

"I knew you were a nun. What order were you with?"

"Franciscan."

"Oh, yeah."

"Daniel said you write poetry. I do too."

"Maybe we can share some poems. I could send you some. If you want."

He seemed hesitant, almost shy. I'd never thought of him as shy and I wouldn't let his anxiety smother my own joy.

"Great. I'd love it. I'll try to send you some. What are your poems about?"

"All sorts of stuff. Holidays. Religion. Family."

I felt as if I were suspended in space watching myself chat with this stranger on the other end of the phone. My father, who abandoned me, wrote poems about family. Interesting. Did he just say he wrote about religion because I'd been in the convent? I couldn't stop the cynic within but tried to keep a light tone and an upbeat voice.

"I better get going. This is long distance. Can we keep in touch?"

"Sure. I'd like that. I have never wanted to push myself on anyone. I have my own little world. I'd like to let you into my circle if you want, but I don't really reach out. I guess I just don't want to be pushy."

He didn't want to be pushy? He couldn't really reach out? He had his own little world? I tried not to think anything negative. He had to have his reasons. I didn't care. Finally hearing his voice and getting the chance to know him after all these years excited me.

I cut the conversation short to take control of the little voice within me tempting me to be the negative cynic. I prayed for his peace and happiness all my life. I needed to just be happy my prayers had been answered. Hanging up, I headed towards the door and straight for the lake. I walked north, towards Loyola. I had nowhere to be, but I just didn't want to be inside my own head. The immensity of the lake seemed to swallow me whole. I walked, almost meditatively, for about an hour before turning around and heading home.

The answering machine flickered with a missed call and I hoped maybe Lucy called; we hadn't spoken in days.

"Hi. Janet. This is your dad. After we hung up I realized I didn't say Happy Birthday when we talked. So, Happy Birthday. Sorry I'm such a knuckle head."

July 8th is Tina's birthday, not mine. He'd gotten mixed up. I almost got angry. What the heck, he didn't even know my birthday. But I couldn't risk being angry. Besides, after twenty-three years did I really expected him to remember my birthday? I called him back to clarify he had the wrong child and offered to send his greetings to Tina instead.

"I remember now. Tina got so angry because your mother planned to take her Trick-or-Treating but instead Tina got stuck with me."

My birthday had always been a sore point because Dad made everyone sing 'Happy Birthday' and eat cake before they could trick-or-treat. My siblings hated the rule and my usual cake flavor of choice, Betty Crocker's Cherry Chip. Every year, my siblings made fun of me. With my lisp, which lingered well into my tenth year, the ch- came out sounding more like a cstchth-. Cstchtherry Cstchthip cake. Once the family actually sang Happy Birthday and ate cake without me because they wanted to go trick-or-treating and I had a phone call.

In the convent, we never celebrated birthdays; not officially anyway. On my nineteenth birthday Sr. Ruth and the novitiate members gathered in the recreation room with pink pig noses made of construction paper in honor of Halloween and my childhood nickname, Arnie Pig. We had ice cream and Sr. Ruth allowed me to eat mine with potato chips, one of my favorite midnight snacks in high school.

On my twenty-first birthday, for Halloween, the novitiate members put together a "Holy House" in the hallways of one of the retreat house buildings. Rather than scary faces and spooky noises, we drew silhouettes of the Saints for the walls and we each dressed up as our patron Saint. The professed Sisters walked through in the dark, wooing and awing at the edifying figures as we all chanted the Litany of the Saints over and over again.

No wild parties, no drinks, no bar hopping. Instead I spent my twenty-first birthday dressed in a green bathrobe with a paper flame on top of my head chanting 'pray for us' after the names of countless men and women like Sylvester and Anastasia. A Litany of the Saints replaced any drinking songs or even the traditional "Happy Birthday." I represented St. Jude, patron of hopeless and impossible cases. I pledged to be responsible to pray for all of those out drinking, using drugs and blaspheming the Holy Spirit. I convinced myself I had plenty to be thankful for on this birthday; I need nothing more.

Occasionally Sisters said 'Happy Birthday' to one another and families sometimes sent cards and gifts but my family followed the rules. I made certain any cards or well wishes happened on October 28, the feast of St. Jude. By my thirtieth birthday, I'd returned to the United States and lived in Colma, been accused of being mentally ill and become an outcast amongst most of the Sisters. I also began sharing some of the convent community 'secrets' with my family. When October rolled around, I asked my siblings and their spouses to celebrate my birthday with me at Chevy's, one of my favorite Mexican Restaurants. Without the chaos of what our family gatherings with dozens of nieces and nephews had become, and in what I considered a safe environment for the first time in more than ten years, I reclaimed me just a little bit more.

"Hi. I'm Janet," I offered as I walked into the office of Sr. Camilla Burns, director of the Institute of Pastoral Studies. Even as the words left my lips, I didn't believe my ears. Janet. I hadn't been called Janet, by anyone, for twelve years. Yet, at that moment, I reclaimed and owned Janet unconditionally.

"What can I do for you, Janet?" Camilla invited me to have a seat.

"I'm not sure. I'd like to study in the program here, but I'm not sure how to go about it. Can I take classes in September? Is there any financial aid?" I early had no idea of what to say. I had met so many folks at the Sovereign in the program, I had to find out more. I'd heard about a liberal, even radical program at the University of Loyola, Chicago and thought it would help me better discern the direction my life would take. I needed to see other facets of the church before joining the Apostolic's and letting my community go.

"Well, why don't you tell me a bit about yourself? How did you hear about us and why are you interested?" Camilla gave direction to the conversation quickly and easily.

"I'm actually a Franciscan Sister, officially. I've been on a leave of absence, since the end of March. I moved to Chicago in April."

"Which Franciscan? We have many faculty and students who are Franciscan."

"I'm from the Franciscan Missionary Sisters of Our Lady of Sorrows. Very long name for a very small group, mainly on the West Coast and in Asia. There are only about fifty in the world."

"Really?" Camilla sounded intrigued and I wondered how much of my story I'd have to tell this time.

"Anyway, the group is very conservative. I think IPS might be good for me to learn more about the larger church and the more progressive aspects of it, especially in the U.S. I came back from Asia last year. I'd been in Hong Kong and Taiwan for six and a half years."

"Wow! How conservative, exactly?"

"Let's put it this way. Until just this very minute when I introduced myself, I went by Sr. Mary Jude, and until this past April I wore a habit and veil everywhere. I didn't own any other clothes. We lived in community, prayed together three times a day, had scheduled meditation and spiritual reading time and worked only in community apostolates. We couldn't see a spiritual director and our superior chose our confessor. I am thirty years old but still needed to ask permission to go for a walk, even on community property."

As I spoke I marveled at how quickly I mastered the art of summary according to my audience.

"Were you cloistered?"

"No. We worked in the public, but we weren't supposed to study theology and we were treated like children."

"I can't believe it. When was this?"

"I entered in 1982."

"Unbelievable. You look great right now. You must be holding up incredibly."

"Thanks. Anyway, I really need to study or something, to move into the Church of the 90's, so I don't make decisions with lopsided information."

"I understand. Unfortunately, I'm afraid it's too late for September. You can take an evening course or two, but we have no more financial aid. If you apply for next year, then we'd possibly offer graduate assistantship and scholarships."

"So, nothing for September?"

"No, but I can promise to keep my ears open for job possibilities. Job announcements come by my desk all the time. We actually keep a file in the front office. What do you do? What are you interested in?" Camilla seemed enthusiastic and eager to help.

"I'm a teacher and I love working with teens. I've done parish work, school work and retreat work, but I'll do absolutely anything. Really!"

I walked home hopeful, wondering what I would do come September. With each step, literally, I convinced myself it would work out. As my shoe hit the pavement beneath me, I repeated a positive affirmation, trying not to panic. I would make it work. By September I might well be a member of the Apostolic Franciscans. I had two weeks to find something before a new part-time job started in Chinatown.

Musing over my sudden name change as I walked into my apartment, I noticed the answering machine blinking. Racing to press the button, I heard Camilla, "Janet, great news. Sr. Beatrice, the principal of Good Counsel High School just called to say she desperately needed a Campus Minister for September. I told her about you. Call her this afternoon. Let me know what happens." Not sure if I should jump for joy or fall on my knees in gratitude, I dialed the number and set up an interview the next morning.

As the bus approached the corner of Peterson and Pulaski the next morning, I saw gorgeous tree-lined, luscious green lawns, manicured bushes, a stone bridge over a small creek, a Marian shrine, and a huge chapel in the center lay before me. I identified immediately the motherhouse for Sisters, and finally, the school building all pointing towards a statue of St. Francis with a sign saying, "Peace Zone." Peace. For years I'd prayed for peace. Peace for my father, in the world, in my community, within my own soul. The prayer rolled from my mind almost unconsciously: "Lord, make me an instrument of your peace. Where there is hatred, let me sow love, injury, pardon; doubt, faith; despair, hope; darkness, light…" At Good Counsel I could surround myself with the spirit of St. Francis every day.

Double-checking I hadn't gotten too nervous finding my way, I sniffed carefully. I had no trouble with body odor in weeks. I'd been feeling confident and secure. Life had rarely been so good. This job would be perfect for me: Campus Ministry for an all girls' school of 800. I knew the Franciscan spirit;

I'd fire them up for the gospel. I felt confident I'd get the job. I'd finish my work in Chinatown in August and then return to my ministry.

"Hello, you must be Sr. Janet," the extended hand brought me back to reality. "Hello. Sr. Beatrice, right?" Standing before me I saw a very tall slim woman, with snow white curls visible from the edges of her brown veil. She wore a simplified brown dress with a scapular over the shoulders. The habit struck me. The Sisters who ran Good Counsel still wore a simple brown habit. For many this meant nothing. For me, it spoke volumes. Volumes about conservatism and what I'd left behind. Most Sisters were no longer in the habit. Anyone familiar with church circles knew the habit represented the letter of the law, hanging on every word spoken by the Pope, blaming God's will for everything and anything instead of taking personal responsibility for bad choices. "Just don't get nervous. You can do this. Maybe it isn't that bad," I tried to calm myself. I actually believed the habit held value for the sake of poverty and simplicity. I never had to worry about what to wear. Maybe Sr. Beatrice felt the same.

I drew quickly on my enthusiasm for spreading the gospel, my love for teenagers, and my experience with retreats, teen groups, confirmation classes and Bible-studies I held in Hong Kong and Taiwan to convince her I could bring them together. No, I'd never led a choir, but I knew how to spot a leader and let them lead. Sr. Beatrice needed to discuss my hiring with Sr. Eileen, my assistant, and the administrative team. As a vowed religious transferring to the Apostolic's as soon as all formalities were taken care of, I request to be introduced to the students as Sr. Janet.

My mind immediately began planning for the new position. "All creation paused when you were born." I'd use the poster from when I taught sixth grade for the first bulletin board; I'd let these girls know God loved and cared for them. I would bring the message of the gospel to them, not expect them to come to it. I'd meet them with everything I had to offer. I would challenge them to live life to the fullest; to choose life over all else and to always be grateful. Like a blaze burning uncontrollably, ideas jumped and danced around the grey matter of my brain leaving nothing in its wake. My mind always raced constantly from one insight to the next, or at least it had until a few months ago. They hadn't outright offered me the job, but I certainly met the qualifications for the position and they were running out of time. The fog that had settled around me cleared with the morning's interview. I welcomed me back.

I wanted to call Lucy with the good news before she left for Australia for the month. My whole life seemed to revolve around Lucy, who had become the one I turned to for affirmation, a kind of permission, and a sense of approval. I waited for her calls and wondered what she might think or say about everything I did.

Every time I mentioned her, Mom said something negative. 'You saw her last night and you're having dinner with her again? Isn't it a bit much?' But Mom always challenged my friendships. 'Why are you always calling? If they want to talk, they'll call you.' and 'No one wants to come to our house. You always invite them and they always have an excuse.' I resisted the negative tapes running through my mind. I still feared letting go and being independent, and avoided the pain of loneliness. The more I contemplated the possibilities, the more trepidation set in.

I tried to remember the image of the narrow gate that had been popping into my prayer. Only I could walk my path, relying on myself for affirmation and on my God for guidance. Others may be walking along beside me, but at each turn in the road, and every new possibility, I needed pass through my own narrow gate. By listening to my own heart and paying attention to my gut for guidance, I would know what to do and when to do it. I didn't call anyone. Instead, I spent the day celebrating my success and my dreams solo.

Sunday morning, I walked to Mass at Loyola's Madonna del Strada. I enjoyed the lively music, the challenging sermons and the community I'd developed. Lucy and four other Apostolic Sisters sitting on the opposite side of the chapel caught my eye. Immediately, I longed for their company, for a connection. No matter how many others I greeted, my eye kept wandering back to them, wondering if they noticed me or if they wished I sat with them. My longing to be with them boiled over into fear of rejection by the end of the communion meditation. I began to recognize I had been seeking my identity and grasping fulfillment outside of myself again. This only opened the door for me to be set aside, abandoned, and disposable yet again.

I awkwardly approached them after Mass. My skin sticky, I dared not lift my arms or take off my sweater. I didn't want to be rejected. Years of childhood fears tumbled into my psyche, along with the hours I sat on my front porch hoping a guy might come along and notice me.

They lightened up when I told them to call me Janet, happy I'd given up the man's name, leaving me to wonder if they would accept me for who I am or would I just adjust to their liberal, progressive ways to please them as I'd adopted the more conservative ways to please the other Sisters. I needed to find my true self, not just substitute one set of expectations for another.

"You wanna work here. I can only pay you minimum wage, but I really need the help." Sue offered a chance of a lifetime. I hadn't even mentioned my financial struggles.

"I've never done retail, but I'm sure I can. I've always wanted to." I filled out the paperwork on the spot. As I filled the blanks, I explained my return to my given name. "Jude just made no sense anymore. It had been bothering me for a few weeks. I'm not really impossible or hopeless. And I'm not a man. After I talked to Dad, I let it go."

I needed to claim my own goodness and worthiness. I had to let go of the negativity the name Jude carried. A part of me will always be Jude, but I needed to be Janet. Perhaps Sr. Janet for now, but for the most part, simply Janet.

"Who's the big bald black guy that anyone wanted to read his book?" I pointed to a display at the front of the store.

"Are you kidding? You really don't know Michael Jordan?"

"A basketball player, I guess, but what's so special about him?"

"He's only the greatest basketball player ever, with the Chicago Bulls."

"Is that the Chicago team?"

"Where've you been, China?"

My secret wouldn't be easy to keep, but I didn't want everyone here to know. I wanted to make friends with normal people and not be the odd one out, the intriguing weird one.

"As a matter of fact I lived in Hong Kong until about a year ago. Besides, I never pay attention to pro sports."

A customer provided distraction just at the right moment but a few days later, a woman came rushing in on her lunch break; "Do you have the newest Martha Stewart?"

"What's a Martha Stew...?"

"Right this way ma'am," Before I finished, Elizabeth came rushing around the counter. Both women looked at me, appalled, as if I'd been accused of child abuse or murder. Completing her rescue mission, Elizabeth returned to the counter, "You don't know who Martha Stewart is? You don't know the expert in home décor and all things domestic?"

"Nope. I guess not."

I prayed no one saw the mental beating I inflicted on myself in these situations. I felt completely stupid and wondered how many times I would be faced with my own ignorance? Would I ever be normal again? No matter what I read, how much television I watched, or who I talked to, nothing recaptured the twelve years I'd left behind.

As I straightened the books and vacuumed the carpets each night, I took sneak peaks at titles like *Joy of Sex* and *Sensual Massage*. I spent the most time in the

147

back corner right behind the computer section. With the store at the center of the loop, Chicago's business district, people packed the aisles at lunch and left the computer books a mess in their hurry to get back to work. I could act like I needed to shelve the computer books but skim and scan other titles while no one looked. I placed myself strategically between the cameras and mirrors to devour a paragraph here and a page there. I'd never even considered nor imagined most of the scenes being described. I couldn't paint a picture in my mind's eye because I had little idea what it all meant. I felt the flush rise in my cheeks but partly because of being deathly afraid of getting caught. What if someone knew? What else could explain the warm feeling rising to my chest? It took time for me to realize, or maybe admit, these words were unlocking doors I shut long ago been. I felt so ignorant and so naïve.

I never experienced sex, and I literally knew very little about the mechanics of sexual intercourse or what much of the surrounding vocabulary meant. I supposed I learned it in high school sex ed class, but I'd been so opposed to sex before marriage then, so I didn't feel the need to really pay attention. I couldn't tell anyone and I couldn't ask. I just secretly searched for books that might explain and perhaps satiate my burning desire to know. Somehow, I wanted to understand and to discover my own sexuality. As I straightened books each evening and, like a member of an audience, watched my mind dance with the intricacies of sensual curiosity, I could not ignore reality. Perhaps I couldn't be true to my vow of chastity.

Walking along the Montrose harbor with Carmel, stopping to marvel at the gorgeous orange shades of the setting sun, melting like sherbet before our eyes, my longing for intimacy could barely be contained, nor could my guilt.

"When I see a sunset like this, I just dream of a man wrapping his arms around me. It seems so romantic. I don't know why I never felt like this before. I always gave praise to God and sang hymns of gratitude. I don't want to feel this longing for romance. I shouldn't feel it."

"It's possible to praise God while a man has his arms wrapped around you. It's okay to want that; you do know that, don't you?" Carmel didn't judge. "You know that you can recognize the romance without acting out sexually, too."

"But we were never given an opportunity to find a balance. From the moment I entered the convent, I couldn't even write letters to male friends, much less let them hug me."

"Just because the women you lived with couldn't handle their sensuality, doesn't make it wrong for you to explore." Her voice became unmistakably firm.

"But I don't know if I want to just explore without acting. I wonder if I really ant to act on it. I wonder if I want to have a relationship with a man. Every time man walks up to the counter at the book store, I flirt, check his ring finger and art wondering if maybe he's THE ONE."

"Marriage then. You are thinking about marriage?"

"No, I'm here to transfer to the Apostolic's; to serve the poor and work with ie homeless." I didn't want to give up my desire or the sacrifice I made years ago.

"You need to decide. That's why you are here and not on the West Coast, isn't ?" Carmel offered. "Leave yourself open or you might make the same mistakes ou already have. Trust God, She'll show you the way."

Carmel, like most of the Apostolic's, referred to God as She. I didn't mind the :minine. Whatever made people comfortable. God, in my mind, is beyond ender. God as Father had always held a special meaning, but God as Mother nally began to take hold in my heart. I used He and She interchangeably epending on who I talked to or prayed with.

With Louise and Sally I didn't even refer to God anymore. They spoke of the upreme Being, the Universe, and the Cosmos. After seeing the movie *Little uddha* they began discussing the idea of reincarnation and resurrection. I listened ith interest and awe as Sally shared her views of Jesus.

"Jesus is the best example we have of how to live. Divine or not, he had omething going for him."

"Why is Jesus better than Buddha?" Louise questioned.

These types of philosophical and theological discussions reminded me of my wn family, but no one in my family ever really questioned the divinity of Jesus. .espect and tolerance for other religions is one thing; believing in Buddhism as iuch as Christianity another. But being a vowed religious and not believing Jesus God, made no sense. Refusing to believe my ears, I chopped the tomatoes and roccoli for dinner, trying to focus on the sound of the knife hitting the cutting oard while I watched O.J. Simpson leading police officers on a chase down the ighway in a white SUV on television, rather than join the conversation going on ehind me.

In late July, John and Charlaine finally called to arrange a meeting to go over ieir psychological assessment. I'd have a better handle on the timeline of my life fter hearing their assessment. Maybe my official transfer process would begin efore school started; then I wouldn't just be Sr. Janet with no congregation. I ould be Sr. Janet, Apostolic Franciscan. I passed the hospital once again glancing t the sign, "Sponsored by the Apostolic Franciscans" and remembered I hadn't lost my vocation; I simply desired to be true to it. I had not failed, I needed to transfer to succeed.

"Before we begin, we'd like you to take a few minutes to read the summary notes we'll send to the Apostolic's," John handed me a packet of papers.

They left me alone to read the report. Skimming as quickly as possible to find the important parts, certain phrases caught my attention: *talked easily and expansively … looks for humor when uncomfortable… writing skills are excellent.* Their writing skills were atrocious, so being impressed with mine did not come as a surprise to me.

…raised in San Francisco…bipolar disordered father …mother's attention only when she was sick…subsequent pattern. When we were sick we got to stay on the couch and dictate what everyone else watched on T.V. I appreciated that, but what child in a family of eight wouldn't? And I enjoyed the special foods and the pitchers of tea Mom made when I got sick. Again, who wouldn't? Being sick felt kind of like having a birthday. You got your way. But I hadn't developed a pattern. Once in a while illness afforded special attention in the convent; someone might bring soup to your room, but I definitely had no pattern of developing illness for attention. I wondered if they really listened to me or if they simply checked prefabricated little boxes they fit people into for diagnostic purposes.

Janet dated a boy whom she describes as having been in love with her and she viewed as her best friend. He reportedly committed suicide after she entered the convent.

They make it sound like Vernon committed suicide because I entered the convent. How crazy is that? I never said he loved me. I said I thought I loved Vernon, a lost soul I thought I somehow had the power and obligation to save, but I never thought he loved me. I had to clarify this section for sure. Did they listen at all?

Began to experience a physical breakdown from the stress and requested a leave …a heightened unconscious somatic reaction to stress from her childhood discovery that physical illness would bring her comfort. What? The physical breakdown had nothing to do with looking for comfort. And the leave had nothing to do with the physical breakdown. These people are coo-coo.

I hadn't even begun the "Issues" section and I didn't want to. They'd screwed up on real basic stuff just in the biographical summary. What would they say about my issues?

Her capacity to screen and deflect unpleasant emotions and experiences out of consciousness is highly developed. Out of consciousness. Didn't I live with the pain of being abandoned, of close friends dying, of relatives being sick, and all the rap that went on in the convent? Who didn't screen unpleasant emotion? I'd be sycho by now, or alcoholic, if I didn't.

*For this reason, she does not register her anger or depression easily...*register epression? I had been told not to. Especially in the convent. Anger was rowned upon; depression unacceptable; everything offered up. Sr. Thomas colded me every time I cried. When people left or even died, she said if I trusted iod I shouldn't cry. Crying meant I lacked faith. But these two psychos didn't ant to hear anything about my life in the convent. They just wanted to hear bout my childhood.

...maintains a highly optimistic and idealistic view of life which sets her up for isillusionment. Thinking people who claim to live the gospel should at least be a ttle better at it than those who don't, this is being idealistic. Call me Pollyanna.

*... thinking style is simultaneous and associational...*No way. I am one of the most ogical people I know. Yeah, my mind races, I think about a lot of stuff; but that's ot bad. I had to be simultaneous and associational in their meeting -- they asked ie to convey my entire life, in all its complexity, on a few sheets of paper. And iey never once let me explain the situation in the convent.

*... emotional experience is cyclical ... submissive and dependent on others for affection, ttention ...*Well, sort of. The first section I agreed with. I'd learned this about iyself in the Enneagram class. I needed, even craved, attention and affection.

*... fear of abandonment compels her to have her major decisions made by others ...self-ramatizing to obtain much needed attention ...*Maybe that had been true, but not iaymore.

...denying all disturbing emotions ... characteristic for persons with Janet's personality to el empty and to fear that [if] others get too close to her, they will discover her lack of real ubstance ... Who said I had no real substance. I didn't fear getting close to people nd I never said I lacked substance.

Janet recapitulated her rebellion against her mother recently with her community; being isillusioned in both cases with the possibility she will ever have her nurturance needs met. They arely listened to my stories of the convent. How can they figure I left just out of ebellion or because I felt sorry for myself? Disillusioned? They make my mom ound like a monster. She raised eight kids by herself. She put us through Catholic chool. She did her best to keep us out of trouble. Who said my needs weren't iet? They're imposing some middle class idea of what a mother should be. What id they expect? Man, these people are whacked.

Her more current preoccupation with physical intimacy reflects the same nurturance need and ould lead to the same disillusionment... So I'll never find love or happiness, just ecause my father left me and my mom ignored me? I'm not helpless. I can take

151

care of myself. Haven't I shown that? Yeah, it'd be nice to share with someone, but I'm not desperate.

Janet's preoccupation with pleasing others and gaining their approval has robbed her of a sense of her own identity throughout her life. Her present preoccupation centers on the conflict between her deep seated need for attachment to others and her striving for real autonomy for the basis of her identity. While she has recently begun to challenge her reliance on others, Janet has considerable amount of autonomous development to achieve before she can be sure she will not replay the same dependency-rebellion pattern with another authority system. Robbed of my own identity throughout life? Have I never really known myself?

As much as it hurt to think along these lines, I knew, deep down it had to be true. I tried to establish various identities for myself. Eighth grade student body president. The girl who wore the scarf every single day of freshman year. The one who didn't eat chocolate and refused to wear make-up throughout junior high and much of high school. If people really liked me, I claimed, I didn't need to wear make-up. They'd take me for me.

Can't attachment and autonomy co-exist? Am I doomed to be forever oppressed or forever alone? Would I never have a normal, healthy relationship?

Entering another religious community at this time may not be in her best developmental interests. They didn't recommend I transfer to the Apostolic's. Period.

My chest felt as if a wad of chewing gum replaced my heart. They didn't even know me. After one or two hours they determined I had 'no sense of self.' They concluded I clung to the idea of community to avoid autonomy. They wanted to focus on my mother, my father and Vernon. They wouldn't listen to the positive events in my life. How well I'd done in the kitchen, in University, even as a sixth grade teacher. They wouldn't listen to the sickness I finally realized surrounded me in the convent.

Tears welled up as I boarded the train. Louise claimed the assessment did not determine the next step, but when she received this assessment the transfer process would be over. Some outside authority would again dictate who I would be. Assessment in hand, I headed to Lucy's for dinner. I tried to remain calm and to appear relaxed as we visited but I felt my intestinal tract tighten when I realized Lucy already heard about the report. They already sent one to the community and Lucy, being on the committee, already read about my being 'associational', 'lacking a sense of self'; in dire need of autonomy before community life would be viable.

"Do you really think these things are true?" I asked, realizing this question confirmed much of what they claimed; I needed others' approval.

"I think maybe they have some truth, but definitely not the whole truth."

"You think I am like this, really?" I gagged on my own question.

"To a certain extent." Lucy felt cold and distant.

I could barely handle my own vulnerability. This made me sound so bad. hey didn't hear any of my convent stories. They lumped all of it together as bellion to authority. How could an insecure person have stood up to her ongregation, to the stigma of being a failure, and to the likes of Sr. Thomas?

"So, do you think it would be bad for me to transfer?" I hated to be so direct, ut I couldn't handle the uncertainty.

"Well, it's not my decision of course. You should talk to Louise and some of ne others more, but you should consider what they say. They are the rofessionals." I couldn't believe Lucy's lack of interest. She'd been so ompassionate, so caring at the beginning. The bike rides, the nights spent on the ke watching lightning storms, hours of Rummikub and simple dinners. She saved ne from the brink of insanity so many times.

"Yeah, I guess. Whatever happens is God's will." I kept smiling and laughing we ate but I left by 9 o'clock, giving me plenty of time to call Suzanne.

"I got my psychological assessment back."

"Really, and?"

"They claim I'm not very logical. Can you believe it?"

"Is that all they say?" Suzanne wanted more information before she ommented. She listened intently to my concerns and asked me to fax a copy so ne could read the whole thing. "With bits and pieces it's difficult to judge its ccuracy."

"I just need to know if I'm completely ignorant. Am I really that sick? They ad to exaggerate; they twisted things."

I felt drained. I'd been proud of my self-awareness and my willingness to flect and be brutally honest with myself. Self-reflection temporarily depressed ne most of the time, but I sprang back to begin working on my weak points, nproving whatever the issue at hand. I couldn't stand to think I didn't know nyself.

all, 1994
ood Counsel High School

I forgot my neck being covered by a veil for twelve years left it susceptible to ne sun. I'd only been out at the park for about three hours but my stomach renched violently each time I vomited from the sun poisoning and the xcruciating pain. I'd already eaten at least twenty carrots as the natural medicine doctor suggested. The sting subsided but left blisters that looked like huge hickies on my neck. And worse, I school started in two days.

Listening each morning to the Louise Hayes tapes I'd received from Nora convinced me to send forth blessing to all those I would meet each day, to create an open and peaceful environment wherever I went. As the air entered my lungs and expanded in my chest, I felt the peace invading my soul. I would be here, with and for these girls. St. Francis would be my inspiration. I would be an instrument of peace. Before the students arrived for the Opening Day prayer services, I sent forth blessings around the room and beyond the walls to the students as they prepared for school. As the moment neared for the girls to arrive, I asked the Spirit to guide my thoughts and words. I remembered the blisters on my neck and wondered how the students might react. Students entered with a side glance, giving my shin length, navy blue skirt and simple blouse, my knee high nylons and my Birkenstocks more than a once over. They'd all heard briefly of Sr. Janet in the school newsletter, and just by looking at me, they saw I did not belong to the Felician order.

"Good morning. I'm Sr. Janet, your new Campus Minister. Before we get started, I just want to point out these are not hickies on my neck; I just have a really bad sun burn."

After allowing the guffaws to subside, I continued in a sincere tone. "I invite you to join us in prayer. But if, for whatever reason, you do not want to pray, I ask that you sit quietly, respecting the atmosphere of prayer and the neighbor who may be sitting beside you. I prayed only that the prayers, music and readings touch the hearts of at least one or two of these young girls. Most of the groups listened intently and entered into the spirit of prayer, at least on the surface. Only one session flopped. The girls chatted, giggled, and some even slept their way through the entire service. I took mental notes for the future, and offered the failure as an opportunity to learn and grow as a guide on the journey.

Sr. Eileen didn't like it, but apparently she didn't plan to like much of anything I did. My predecessor, apparently, had been perfect and would be sorely missed. Sr. Eileen wanted me to scold the students, to force them to listen, to make them participate. I had to trust myself. My job was to create an environment of trust, community and Christian action.

On the feast day of St. Francis in early October, the Sisters invited me to morning Mass and to join them for breakfast. I watched the elderly Sisters and listened to the conversations of the women surrounding me and my head began to spin. Except for the fact that these women wore brown habits instead of black, I could have been back in my congregation. The older Sisters gathered round me like fruit flies to a ripe banana in the heat of summer, each attempting to coax me into transferring to their order. I wanted to simply say, no chance in hell would I ever be one of them; but that would be harsh. Sr. Eileen, Sr. Beatrice and the others were as conniving, manipulative and dysfunctional as the group of women I'd left behind.

I asked why Sr. Eileen hadn't been appointed Campus Minister. She gave me some explanation about how she liked being the assistant, without the added responsibility because she had duties at the convent, and how this would be her last year at the school. I quickly realized she and Sr. Beatrice had history. I didn't know where or when their toxic animosity began, but I soon got pinned between them like paper in a clip. Whenever one appreciated something I did, the other definitely became furious. The mind games had begun and if I wanted to survive, I'd have to learn to manipulate all of the rules myself until I could get out.

"Hello, is Corrine there? It's long distance from America." I finally felt comfortable enough with my finances to call Corrine, the only person besides Sr. Nathaniel in Hong Kong, who knew why I returned to the States. Corrine knew my struggles and stayed by my side, supporting me through it all.

"Hello. This is Corrine. Is this Sr. Jude?" I heard the excitement in Corrine's voice.

"Yes. But I'm going by Sr. Janet now. I decided to return to my baptismal name."

"Wonderful. How are you, really?"

"I'm good."

"Are you doing well? I have missed you so much and I pray for you every day. What is happening?" Corrine stumbled over her words with excitement and I relaxed in the warmth of a distant friend.

"I am in Chicago now. I am looking to transfer to another community. But I'm not sure what will be happening. It is so complicated." I didn't know where to begin; I didn't realize how much changed; how much I'd grown since leaving Hong Kong.

"Are you following your heart? Are you happy?" Corrine's sincerity ripped at my soul. Corrine knew me as a prudish, uptight, traditional, submissive Sr. Jude and still seemed to love me.

"I am happy. Most days. It's been hard some days."

"Of course. You're going through major life changes. Be kind to yourself."

"How are Anita and the boys?" I changed the subject before I broke down.

"Everyone here is great. Have you heard from the Sisters at all?"

"No. They don't want to hear from me. They're still pretty angry."

"I don't want to upset you but I think you should know I saw Sr. Nathaniel in TaiPo a few weeks ago. When I asked about you she said in her mind you didn't exist and she walked away. I couldn't believe it; but you know that is her anger? You've done nothing wrong. You know that, don't you?"

"She said I didn't exist?" I could barely repeat the words. Sr. Nathaniel considered me dead. My friend and confidant hated me. No wonder she didn't respond to the few letters I'd written. She didn't care. The rest of the conversation continued in a blur. Sr. Nathaniel now despised me. The one person who shared so much with me, who held me when I cried and hugged me when I smiled, and for whom I did the same, now considered me dead, non-existent. What did they say or do to make Sr. Nathaniel so bitter?

I went straight to the kitchen; opened the refrigerator, then the cupboard. Looking back and forth; I needed something, anything, to eat. Sugar, chocolate, ice cream. I'd been too good; my house had been clear of all junk food for over a week. I found nothing but I wouldn't make it through the night without something. I grabbed a sweater and headed down to the elevator. By the time I reached the Dominick's around the corner my tears dried on my cheeks. Luckily I hadn't run in to anyone. I couldn't talk. Not tonight.

I headed straight for the freezer section hoping some ice cream would be on sale. Passing the sweet rolls, I snatched up my favorite cinnamon rolls before I could change my mind. I could pig out this once. I'd been so good but now I needed some comfort. I stood staring at my choices: rocky road, chocolate mint, peanut brittle parfait. Two for seven dollars. Three fifty a half gallon. I agonized over every choice. Which flavor and deal would be best?

Holding on to the edge of the freezer case, I stood, frozen with pain, for what seemed to be forever. Blinking back to reality, I let go of the freezer case and turned around. Walking away from the freezer and back down the aisle where I'd picked up the sweet rolls, I dropped them on the shelf and headed towards the exit. I wouldn't do this to myself. I wouldn't let their hatred destroy me.

I marched across the parking lot, about to cross the street to head home, when my body jerked around. I needed ice cream. I didn't have to be perfect. I could eat just a little; I didn't have to eat the whole thing. God would forgive me for slipping this once. As my foot triggered the automatic door to let me back into the supermarket, I stopped again.

Did I really want to give in? Or did I want to stand firm. My choice to leave the convent did not invalidate anyone else's choice to stay. If it did, they had problems. I did what I to do. Sr. Nathaniel would have to do the same if she wanted peace. I spent my life making reparation for vague insidious sins. Would I do it again? Would I destroy myself so Sr. Nathaniel would be vindicated? Would I punish myself for finally listening to my gut, trusting my own conscience, believing and loving me with all of my imperfections, not for what I did or did not do? I stepped away from the door and with less determination but with freedom in my gait, I headed home.

My alarm rang at six just like every other morning. I slapped the snooze and dozed. Six-fifteen, same thing. Six-thirty, six-forty-five. By seven thirty I knew I'd never make it to work on time so I called in sick, grateful no one answered so I didn't have to explain myself. When I rolled over the next time, the clock read noon.

My soul weighed heavy on my chest as I lay exhausted on the floor knowing I needed to get up today or I might never. I had no reason now and would have no better reason tomorrow or the next day. Except for missing work, my absence would not be noticed by anyone. The people I'd called family for twelve years, my Sisters, considered me dead. I had no one or nothing to keep me going. I didn't see the point of going to work to face the same kind of crap. I could have stayed in the convent for all the dysfunction, backstabbing, and hostility Sr. Beatrice and Sr. Eileen showed me.

Like a teaspoon being swallowed by a huge bowl of cake batter, the pain seemed to sink deeper into my soul. I couldn't grab hold to pull it out. I could only cry. I cried like I hadn't cried in weeks, maybe even a month. How could Sr. Nathaniel be so hateful? What did I do to deserve it? My shoulders shook and my stomach tightened and I felt myself quickly being engulfed in panic, hyperventilating as I lost control.

My arm stretched towards the phone cord lying feet away knowing I couldn't be alone.

"Hmph, hmph, He – ll – ll –o, Carmel."

"Who is this, what is it? May I help you?"

"It's …hmph…J..j…j…a..a..a..n…n..et."

"I will be right there. Janet. Wait for me. I will be right there."

Carmel pushed opened the door, grabbed my shoulders and hugged me as tightly as possible. "It's okay. Ssshh."

We stood, motionless except for the slight rocking to and fro, in the doorway to my apartment, for at least ten minutes. Carmel held my head as she might a new born baby and I knew I'd done the right thing.

"You'll be alright. Shall we sit now?" Carmel's voice, with its strong Australian accent, felt soft and gentle as she led me towards the chair. "Would you like some water? What happened?"

"I don't know. I just panicked. I'm sorry."

"Hi, are you a new student?" I asked approaching the young man sitting in the high back lounge chair. Having only one evening class this semester, I didn't know all of the Loyola students in the building.

"No, not really. I live on the ninth floor, but I saw a party and thought I'd drop in."

He looked so young and stood about five feet tall; he even had a slight lisp to accompany his prematurely balding head, wire-rimmed glasses, and apparently bold naivety. The manager, Mike reserved one of the breakout lobbies on the ground floor of the building for the growing population of IPS students who requested a place to gather for homework, discussions and prayer services.

The young man didn't stay, but Dan and I ran into each other in the hall, the elevator, or the mail room almost daily and our friendship developed into bike rides together on the lake a couple of times a week and hanging out to eat and watch TV. Dan worked as a receptionist at a mental health clinic in Evanston, a place mostly for families in trouble, but the therapists, in his words were, 'all really cool and they had a sliding scale and everything'. One cloudy Saturday afternoon we hopped on the train to go see the place; we played tag on the boulders lining the lake and drank hot chocolate on the ride back home. I felt young, almost childish for the first time in a long time.

"Over the phone you mentioned you need a therapist familiar with Jung and respectful of your Catholic faith. We'll chat today but if for whatever reason you don't feel comfortable with me and want to speak to someone else, we can make arrangements."

"Okay. Well, yeah, I'm taking a class right now about Jung. I've been working a lot with my dreams, and making some important decisions. I just want to keep going in that direction."

"Understandable. What about the issue of religion?"

"Well, that's a bit more complicated. I just left the convent. I'm starting life over after twelve years as a Franciscan Sister. I just need someone who understands, or at least respects the Church enough to not get all mixed up in Church issues instead of my issues."

"I'm not actually Catholic. I am Jewish. I know quite a bit about Catholicism, but more importantly, I respect my clients' journeys in faith as much as I do my own."

"Great, that's what I need."

Irene didn't flinch when I said I'd just left the convent. Her jaw didn't drop with a 'wow' or 'really' following closely behind. Irene felt warm, almost cozy. Young and pretty. She came across so normal, not the typical clinical feel I got with previous counselors. I'd been meeting with Sr. Jeannie for spiritual direction, on the advice of a teacher at IPS, since late August, but spiritual direction and therapy are different. I needed therapy.

Jeannie asked to see the biographical summary Nancy wrote back in Oregon, and the psychological assessment done for the Apostolic's, but she didn't seem to help me dig underneath the surface. I didn't need to keep telling interesting stories; I needed to figure out what the stories meant, why I allowed them to happen, and how to create new ones. I needed someone to push and pull, even drag me into the recesses of my soul, kicking and screaming if need be, to unveil the secrets hidden within. My gut liked Irene. The twenty-dollar weekly sliding scale fee would be much more manageable than the seventy-five dollars I'd been paying Jeannie.

According to Jung, our dreams are the key to unlocking the psyche where we can learn about our deepest desires and longings. I'd been keeping track and trying to analyze them for a few months as part of my homework assignments but the teacher gave no individual time to each student. I spilled my guts on paper and hoping my reflections made sense. I'd been agonizing over one particular dream for weeks.

On October 6th for my journal assignment I wrote:

I am in an unfamiliar hospital setting at the start of the dream. Several of my family members are there because my sister, Karen, is sick. She is dying from stomach cancer. She cannot eat. As we speak with her, the nurse comes in and out of the room. It's obvious Karen is very calm. She is resigned to the reality of her impending death and she does not get emotionally upset or express any fear or sadness. As I talk to my mom and the others outside the room, I want to convince them Karen should not be so calm. She must be running from the reality of her situation. I am afraid she is covering up or refusing to let her emotions surface. I am afraid she is intellectualizing the entire situation so as to remain strong and invulnerable. I want to yell and scream and get her to break down. At the same time, I am afraid of saying anything because I vividly remember the blame I received when Sr. Veronica was dying and I tried to be upfront about it. I awoke from the dream without speaking openly with Karen about her situation.

Some immediate connections: Karen had gallbladder surgery a few months ago. In high school she had a near fatal car accident. Did Karen represent me in any way?

159

Throughout childhood people called me Karen or Tina, and constantly compared me to them. I verbally attacked many people, teachers included, for not using my correct name. I insisted on being my own person. But later, as I moved away from home, even when people didn't know I had a sister, others still called me Karen on many occasions. I concluded I must look like a 'Karen.' So, with this dream I wondered if Karen represents some part of me that others see and I don't. In many ways Karen is connected to spirituality, church and religious attitudes in my mind. Before her accident in high school, Karen experienced her share of rebellion. 'Born again' after the accident, she adhered faithfully to Catholic teaching; and she tried to make me do the same. I had just begun to follow in her wild footsteps, and did not want to give up my crazy lifestyle. In this, she represented someone who went from one extreme to the other. She had been a rebel and now turned into a Jesus freak.

After her marriage, Karen relaxed in her practices, left the Church for an evangelical group, and eventually returned to the Church. She seems to represent someone who can remain a Catholic and have enough of her own autonomy to practice without needing to be perfect. She seems to allow her expression of faith to be freeing not binding.

I connected to my own understanding of the institutional church and all of the struggles I am presently experiencing. Strictly following letter of law – incorporating spirit and allowing for growth and challenge – a growing sense of frustration and disgust with some laws and customs

Karen is someone who can handle everything, not only in my dream, but in real life. She'd managed to cope with her second son being treated for cancer from 4 months to 2 years old, at the age of 20. She manages to get involved in a million volunteer service projects at church and school and the American Cancer Society. I've often wondered if Karen isn't trying to run from some reality, some pain. I've dreamt once before Karen was dying and knew Karen represented me in some way. I have been at everyone's service but neglected myself. I have always been strong, handled things maturely, like my mother and all of my siblings before me. Falling apart is not in the Arnold's DNA. My domestic affairs – my interior life and my own needs – repressed, ignored, put last on the list of priorities.

Something is dying. Trying to balance extremes – not being at the disposal of others to my own detriment. My need to remain strong is dying – let myself breakdown -- remain functional at work, keep afloat socially – balance budget, eat healthy, look into various options for the future – and inwardly I scream for all of it to end. As much as I want to let the shell fall away, I cherish its existence. Not wanting to be blamed for confronting Karen in the dream, like when I confronted Sr. Veronica in life. Do I have a guilt trip for my own dying process? Attempts to care for self and not be a workaholic; incorporate healthy exercise and eating, I am pressured by others. Reprimanded by superiors, called selfish and separatist – same as at home before entrance or on home visits. Mom always expected me to help set up and clean up at family gatherings, to be at everyone's disposal.

Biblical Connection: Story of Jacob and Esau - Karen is the one who claimed "Janet's going to heaven" -- I have been struggling with that declaration since childhood… Is this the part that must die? Did I sell my birthright – in allowing this prediction to dictate my life choices? Have I allowed others' expectations to take over to the point I identify more with Karen than with Janet?

Do I need to listen to the voice urging me to not be afraid to speak out and confront my own transformation process? The voice crying for attention: Let yourself take care of yourself, let yourself be vulnerable. Let yourself question and challenge your own rigid, perfectionist interpretations. Old me is dying. I am letting go of the familiar, what others see in me, what I have tried so hard to become. Is my being a 'Sister', staunch adherent to rules, overly conscientious, servant of all – is this the Karen in me that must die? Why am I afraid to confront her with the emotion? Unless grain of wheat dies – what is death? Is the dream challenging me to let things go or to be cautious?

"Have you ever hugged a tree?"

Dan chuckled as we walked along Lake Michigan.

"Just take a deep breath. The energies from the depth of the earth have healing properties." I leaned against the tree and stretched my arms around the large trunk.

"What? You're crazy."

"No. For real. I hug a tree every day. It is good for body and soul." The gurgling on my left side released the emotional block just under my ribs. Dan did some crazy things in his day, but had no intention to hug a tree; instead he challenged me to a climbing contest. Up for the challenge, I grabbed the nearest branch and started climbing, grateful for the chance to relax and act silly with a friend.

Dan and I biked or walked together, sometimes for hours, checking out store fronts, commenting on passers-by, told stories from our childhood and wondered what life might look like in the near future for both of us. And we laughed, alot. Dan dropped out of the local Bible school recently but put off returning to face his family and his rural Michigan town. With a good job at the Family Institute in Evanston he wanted to make it in the big city on his own.

"Let's grab a video." I suggested.

"We can have some spaghetti for dinner. I have the sauce if you have the noodles." We sat on the floor, noodle bowl in hand, eating and watching the Prince of Tides. I felt comfortable as we leaned against each other and our sore legs relaxed. The excitement rose in my chest as my cheeks turned a warm pink. I wanted to kiss him, to touch his hand, to have him hold me. I couldn't make a move, so I asked awkwardly, "Wanna kiss me?"

161

Dan's leg and lip shook excitedly. "I promised myself and God I wouldn't kiss a girl unless I am ready to marry. That's the true Christian way. Kissing leads to sex."

"You said you're curious about sex and you haven't had a girlfriend for years."

"I wish I could. I like you. But I'm going to remain a virgin until I'm married." Dan stood up and headed towards the door. "I gotta go. Bye."

I went limp, grabbed my pillow, sunk my face deeply into it and cried. Feeling thirteen all over again, I questioned: Am I pretty enough, sexy enough, desirable at all, will a man ever want me?

Gerry from my Jung class rejected me just days earlier. Partners in class, we'd opened up on an intimate emotional level. After class we walked along the lake for hours and returned to my apartment. Leaning against the armchair as we sat on the floor chatting, Gerry massaged my shoulders. His strong, manly hands pushed and rubbed, pulled and prodded away my tension. He gently pushed my hair off my neck and kissed me. As I turned around to return the gesture, our lips met tenderly. He drew me to himself with supple kisses, his lips pressing against mine until he abruptly pulled back and sprang to his feet.

"I'm sorry. I shouldn't have done that." He whispered.

"It's okay. It's good."

"No, no. I can't. You know I can't. Not right now."

"Are you sure?"

"I am firm in my commitment. I am a priest. I want, no I have to, be true to that. I am sorry."

He secured the door quietly behind his back, leaving me alone. He desired me but his vocation as a priest and missionary compelled him. He wouldn't surrender to temptation. A morsel of my deepest soul admired his courage; courage I could not muster for myself. My vow of chastity now twice tarnished led to nothing. I buckled in pain.

Boarding the train with the senior class girls, I remembered the electricity and excitement of my own senior retreat: an overnight experience, away from home, with boys from the brother school. The reflection questions triggered meaningful, deep conversations that went on for months beyond the retreat and the walls of the classroom, into hours of phone conversations and journal entries. I felt almost as giddy as them; not only for them, but for me. I'd be spending my 31st birthday with these young women I'd chatted with in the hallways, with whom I'd shared my story. They'd asked why I became a Sister, why I'd left my order, what I'd learned. I spoke carefully not wanting to make my agenda theirs. I encouraged seeking God's will and following the inner voice God gave each of them. I spoke of always choosing what brought life, of not being afraid to admit mistakes and make changes. I had to do the same.

The questions and exercises for the students held no surprises: facing the fears of the unknown future, making important life choices without complete knowledge of what lies ahead. Each chance I got, I headed to the chapel, intent on reflecting for myself. Just after lunch they presented a simple task: your personal view of God.

The image of the cat from my thirty-day retreat kept rising to the surface of my mind and emotion. I sat on the lawn, with the Bible, preparing to begin a meditation when a cat climbed in my lap. I'd always been afraid of cats but as a Franciscan, I struggled to acknowledge all of creation as my sister and brother, reconciled in Christ. When I saw the cat I wanted desperately to push it away, to be left alone with God. But as I sat, the cat became a metaphor for my relationship to God. The cat nestled in my lap as I nestled in the lap of God. Each time I moved, the cat fidgeted and only settled down when the initial shock subsided. Each time God moved in my life I begin 'clawing' and 'scratching' and trying to defend myself until I finally acquiesces in the protective lap of my God. After dinner my meditation spilled out, without hesitation or an erasure.

I cry and cry for help
Yet no one hears
Through the laughter or sees
In the smile, the pain
Will I ever know the place?
That niche where I may blossom;
The soil in which I'll thrive?
Instead, I push on: getting things done,
Accomplishing tasks given to me,
Inside, the empty hollow
Yearns for fullness, for connectedness,
Meaning and purpose.
Am I running, trying to dodge
The reality of my own emptiness?

I couldn't resist the conviction rising in my chest. I knelt in the chapel and penned a letter.

Dear Archbishop Levada,

After much prayer and continual discernment, I am writing to request a dispensation from my vows with the Franciscan Missionary Sisters of Our Lady of Sorrows. I can no longer faithfully fulfill my vows and believe firmly God is calling me to move on with my life.

Sincerely in Christ,

Sr. Mary Jude Arnold, O.S.F. (Janet Arnold)

I walked directly to the small mail box at the retreat house office. I couldn't hang on to it; I might waver. To further my resolve, I knocked on the office door the day we returned to school. I spoke quickly and firmly, not wanting to waver as I spoke. "I just wanted to let you know up front, I wrote asking for a dispensation from my vows."

"Oh, really? So, you've made a decision."

"Yes. I thought you should know, when the dispensation comes through, I will no longer be using the title Sister."

"What do you want to be called?" Sr. Beatrice seemed surprised.

"Ms. Arnold."

"I would rather you just keep the title for this year. Next year you can change it so you don't confuse the students. We don't want a scandal."

"I can't do that. Choosing to get a dispensation isn't a bad example; maybe it's a good one." An unmistakable tension and vulnerability coated every word as my voice cracked. Sr. Beatrice, like Sr. Thomas or Sr. Fatima, thought she could control me.

"As a non-religious, I am leaving myself open to dating."

"Well, I guess that's okay."

I wanted to tell her outright I didn't need her permission or even her advice, but I simply said, "I will change my name to avoid rumors or confusion if students see me."

"If they see you on a date, you can explain it to them then. All the students don't need to know." Beatrice's naivety astonished me.

"I can't do that. No one would believe me. Especially if they don't approach me, they'd just start rumors. What kind of scandal would that be? My dispensation isn't final yet, but after Christmas I'm sure it will be and I will tell the students to call me Ms. Arnold."

I stood up, said good-bye and left the room walking quickly down the hall to the small chapel near the main doors, my place of refuge whenever I couldn't preach the party line or defend another teacher's actions in front of the students. I focused on my breath and turned to Jesus in the Blessed Sacrament to make sense of the chaos.

Pulling the mail from the tiny box, I noticed the return address and ran to the elevator. I wanted to read this letter from the Archdiocese of Chicago in privacy.

Dear Ms. Arnold,

I am writing to inform you Cardinal Bernardin has received your request for a dispensation from your religious vows from the Archbishop of Portland, Oregon and after prayer and discernment has agreed to accept your request.

Please call the office at 312-333-4455 to arrange an appointment for signing the necessary paperwork.

Sr. Mary Jude, gone forever. Finished. Done. Period.

Unsure of the emotions welling inside, I sat down on the edge of my bed, heart pounding and knees shaking. Twelve years; my life; everything officially ended with this letter and I was officially Ms. Janet Arnold.

No longer in limbo, I didn't know if I should celebrate or mourn. Could emptiness coexist with joy? I didn't need to convince myself. Peace and joy permeated the center of my soul. I faced no fear and no more uncertainty. I needed to celebrate. Now. By myself. Without anyone. I couldn't share my personal moment yet. I dropped the letter on my bed, slipped on my shoes and headed for the door. Sure the grin on my face would invite questions I'd rather not answer, I hoped not run into anyone as I pushed open the front door and darted across the street.

"Do I need an appointment to get my ears pierced?" I asked the woman behind the counter.

"We can take you now. Have a seat here."

For most people an ear piercing might seem insignificant, but with the simple needle gun to my earlobe, I unpeeled years of prudish buildup. For years my low, almost no maintenance, attitude had kept me comfortably androgynous. Now I had no black habit to hide behind, no baggy clothes. I wore clothes that conformed to my shapely body and styled my hair after each wash. I even wore cut offs and a sports bra for my bike rides down the lake. I didn't feel so guilty when I flirted either; it felt almost natural. I'd been good at it in my teens and wanted to perfect it again. I claimed my feminine self, finally.

Walking into the dark chapel for choir practice that night allowed me time to settle and center myself before the crowd came. Would anyone notice my pierced ears? They all knew I'd just left the convent, but in the past two months, I'd only gotten to really know Fred, on the afternoon he asked to borrow *Care of the Soul* by

Thomas Moore. We sat for hours on my apartment floor sharing stories of childhood and attempts at recovering from our pain. We spoke on the phone every day and saw each other several times a week, going to movies and out to dinner. We took long walks along the lake, spent hours sitting on my apartment floor holding hands as we chatted. We spoke openly and honestly about *Care of the Soul*, the twelve steps and the *Big Book*. I accompanied him to the vet when his cat got sick and by his side as he attended the information workshop about the graduate program he hoped to apply for.

I only wished the dispensation had come through a week earlier because then maybe Wednesday night would have ended differently. After a romantic dinner, slow dancing in his living room, and cuddling on the couch, he invited me to stay the night but promptly rolled over to fall asleep. Thursday morning, he barely look at me and he hadn't called me since. As it stood, I felt awkward; almost offended.

Surprisingly, he greeted me with his typical smile and hug at the end of practice. Holding me at arms' length he noticed the studs in my ears almost instantly.

"You look particularly happy tonight. Good news?"

"My dispensation came through. I'm not a Sister anymore."

"Wonderful. Great. Congratulations."

With his arm around my shoulder we walked towards the Open Ace Tavern with the rest of the crowd. Choir practice usually ended with an hour or so at the free buffet.

"Did you have a good Thanksgiving dinner?" I couldn't say what I really wanted to. Not yet.

"No big arguments. That's a step. What about your aunt's?

"Nothing special."

I ordered steaming hot water at the bar as usual. Most of the others ordered beer to go with the spicy chicken wings and lasagna.

"Well, everybody, Janet's dispensation came through today. She's not a nun anymore. We should celebrate with something more than water. What'ya say?" Fred brought me to the center of attention. Attention I didn't want.

"You need something stronger. How about hot chocolate with a little rum; nothing too strong?"

Fred's suggestion angered me. We'd shared stories; he knew my history. I drank nothing but hot water, ever. I stood up to everyone else along the way, but standing up to the choir members proved impossible. I gave in to unrelenting pressure and ordered a hot chocolate with rum. Standing at the dark, dimly lit bar table, I sipped down the warmth of the drink and swallowed the emotions raging in my soul. By the time I got home, my throat was swollen and I had a hacking cough. I had to confront Fred or I'd be full blown sick by morning.

I picked up the phone and dialed.

"You know how I told you I get a sore throat if I have something I really want to say to someone but I can't say it?"

"Yeah."

"Well, I have to talk to you."

"What about?"

"What happened Wednesday night. Or should I say Thursday morning."

"I just couldn't do it. I'm so sorry."

"Do what? You're the one who kissed me."

"I'm so sorry."

"Am I a terrible kisser? What happened?"

"I don't know. I just couldn't do it."

"At dinner you called us soul mates. You held my hand, caressed my fingers, and stared into my eyes. You kept your arm around me as we walked and danced to candle light. We laid together in your bed. I know I'm out of practice dating, but please explain to me how I messed up."

"You didn't mess up. I did."

"Aren't most of those things what people do on dates? But it all meant nothing to you. I am stupid I guess."

"You weren't being stupid. I sent mixed messages, I guess."

The pain in my throat began receding as Fred admitted his mistakes from last week and at the bar. I enjoyed Fred's company and needed his friendship more than a relationship.

At brunch after Mass, I noticed Fred not only sat next to Leanne, but pulled out her chair and kept his arm around her back the entire time. When he kissed her in front of everyone, I knew Leanne meant something more. Why didn't he just tell me he had a girlfriend? Did this just come up since Wednesday or had he been playing me?

As hard as it might be, I wouldn't run my fingers through his curly, golden hair or stare into his soft blue eyes again. I would admire his gorgeous white teeth and buff shoulders from a distance through phone calls only. Dinner, maybe. Nothing more. We would simply be friends. Besides, I longed for fulfillment and completion not just a relationship. Jesus always offered union and Advent spoke to the longing. Ultimate union and satisfaction could only be found in Christ.

"O Come, O Come, Emmanuel and ransom captive Israel that mourns in lonely exile here, until the son of God appears. Rejoice, rejoice ..." My heart beckoned for the salvation,

the joy, the peace and happiness the Messiah promised with a longing almost palpable.

Mary, Mother of Jesus, conceived without stain of sin. For the feast of the Immaculate Conception I needed to figure out how to present this Church teaching to the students even if I didn't totally believe it myself anymore. Theoretically I still believed because with God all things are possible. But what did Mary's conception have to do with me or with the students at Good Counsel. We weren't born without sin. We couldn't become the Mother of Jesus like Mary. Theology needed to sense for the students, but first it must make sense for me. As I sat in the chapel waiting for inspiration and hoping for a miracle I thought of the twists and turns of my own life and calling. Had I turned my back on my true calling, my original fiat, or finally just discovering it?

Finally, it struck me. The Immaculate Conception is about God more than Mary. God prepares people for their callings. God gives the gifts. God provides the talents. God infuses each soul with the desires and dreams leading to fulfillment. God gave Mary gifts and talents, desires and dreams that allowed her "Fiat!"

Just as I said, "Let it be done to me according to God's Will," so each young lady at Good Counsel could do the same. Each is called to recognize the gift and use it to bring forth peace. I easily connected it to the Toys for Tots gifts they'd be bringing in that day. The Immaculate Conception invited students, in a simple way, to share from the blessings they received from God.

My journal entry from the airplane on December 24, 1994 read:

Here I sit on an American Airline plane waiting to return to California for Christmas. It's been thirteen years since I'd been home for Christmas. It seems so strange. I am excited to go home. Tomorrow I meet with Sr. Ruth to return my ring, and then it's off to Las Vegas to meet Dad. I'm at peace. I feel so good about where I am, who I am. I am whole and at peace. I can meet Dad just like I've met so many others and see if anything comes of it.

I hoped this year might possibly be the beginning of a new celebration? Navigating a year of disappointment, change, newness and hope had mellowed me. The excitement of finally meeting my dad continually shared space with a calm, not quite apathetic, realization that individuals moved in and out of my life, branding my soul but rarely remaining an integral part of my life. I wondered if Dad would be any different.

On Christmas morning I headed to Santa Cruz to say good-bye to the life I'd known and loved for so long. Wind whipping through the window, sun shining through the clouds, poking in and out, playing peek-a-boo through the magnificent redwoods blanketing the Santa Cruz Mountains, I gripped the gear shift at her knee as my left hand rested on the steering wheel. Music blasting from the oldies station on the radio, my confidence almost scared me, as the ring once again embracing my right ring finger for the journey clinked against the cool plastic. I would return the wedding band signifying my commitment as the Bride of Christ without ceremony or recognition; no invitations sent, no banquet prepared; no rite of passage to usher in the return, the restoration, the integration of Janet Mary Arnold.

"Don't stop thinkin' about tomorrow. Don't stop, it'll soon be here. It'll be here better than before; yesterday's gone, yesterday's gone."

The words of the familiar Fleetwood Mac song boosted my spirits higher, grateful for the serendipitous music. God must have known I needed it. I lived on what others' might call coincidences. I believed little life moments have a purpose and nothing happens by chance. Every song I heard in the supermarket, every word spoken by a stranger, every thought that struck me as I washed dishes or even used the toilet, were God moments. Insights and intuitions meant, for me, God filled the hole in the center of my soul, a sweet spot that otherwise gets stuffed with my obsessions, addictions and fears.

I felt like I was falling in love. Not with someone else, not even with God, but with myself. I cared about how I looked and what I wore; I even considered trying make-up. I'd died to myself almost thirteen years earlier on these narrow, winding roads. I wanted to reclaim my right to be happy, to dream. Returning the ring and saying my final goodbyes would bring the closure I needed to keep moving on.

I pulled into the driveway at the Hill, where Sr. Ruth insisted we meet. The retreat house would be too public. We could talk at the Hill and I would disappear without disrupting the lives of the others.

"Hello, Janet. How are you? Your hair is getting so long." Sr. Ruth greeted me with open arms but as the conversation progressed, I realized nothing really changed. Sr. Ruth felt the other Sisters weren't emotionally ready to see me because not enough time had passed. I made some very bold moves when I left and stirred up so much emotion and controversy. Sr. Ruth just wanted to give the Sisters time to heal. Her plans were blown when Sr. Francis and Sr. Theresa Ann walked by as we sat on the deck. All the Sisters would know I'd been there, so Sr. Ruth agreed to let me head down to the retreat house. Tom's dog house still sat in the corner just outside the office door, garbage cans lined the back walkway to the

169

kitchen, and stacks of dishes sat on the counter ready for the next buffet line at dinner.

Sr. Daphne, Sr. Phillip and Sr. Julianne sat in the guest dining room when I walked through. They all stood to greet me with no apparent anger or warmth. I felt at home and out of place simultaneously. Sights, smells, sounds hadn't changed. Even the tablecloths looked exactly the same. I'd washed dishes, folded laundry, cooked, run errands, broken bread, and prayed with these women who greeted me with the awkwardness of strangers. Our relationship had changed.

Memories flooded my thoughts but without judgment or pain or bitterness. I practically felt the numbness in my wrist from the carpal tunnel I'd acquired thanks to the hundreds of jars of apple sauce I made from the fruit of the apple orchard at the bottom of the hill. Games of soccer and Frisbee; Stations of the Cross; pulling weeds; washing windows; a basketball hoop put up at my request on an old empty cement block at the end of the property; guitar playing on the deck in rainy weather; games of canasta; heart-wrenching conversations with Sr. Ruth; the stationery bike where I rode two miles each day just to see how long it would theoretically take to get back home; sweeping pine needles from the driveway; bathing the dogs; cleaning cars; reciting the rosary; buffing floors and waiting for relatives to come visit.

In many ways I loved being a Sister. I loved being of service to others. I'd been praised for my adaptability to language, culture and food in Taiwan and Hong Kong. I loved being the young, jovial, vivacious American. I loved most of the Sisters with whom I lived; the others I loved through tolerance, as my roadmap to heaven. I loved the simple, symbolic habit: a sign of service and commitment and part of my poverty, a sign of availability. I held no regrets, but I couldn't deny some anger lingered.

On the road back to Karen's I thought of Sr. Theresa Ann. We'd lived, or I might say, co-existed, with struggle and tension, for six years in Hong Kong. Sr. Theresa Ann grated on my every nerve almost daily. Not only did we clash during the day, but Sr. Theresa Ann invaded my dreams where I lashed out at her both verbally and physically. For a long time, I considered the dreams a release of justifiable anger everyone felt towards Sr. Theresa Ann for the way she set herself apart, and slightly above, everyone else. She refused to join us for meals, resisted all correction of her Cantonese skills, and tried desperately to Americanize the elementary school in Hong Kong. Could Sr. Theresa Ann be a reflection of my shadow, like we discussed in the Jung class? Sr. Theresa Ann embodied the independence and courage of conviction I lacked. So

170

tent on pleasing my superiors, and others, even if I had the courage to confront
omeone or express strong opinions, I never acted on them if the superior
isagreed. Instead, I got depressed and confused, becoming the struggling child
ho needed guidance, prayer and understanding to resist the 'temptations of the
evil' rather than to risk disapproval.

When I no longer crushed my own personality for the sake of not being
onsidered rebellious, I saw Sr. Theresa Ann simply claimed her right to be treated
s an autonomous adult – something I feared because of those who interpreted
ommunity and obedience as conformity in all things. Sr. Theresa Ann had been
oing what I subconsciously wanted to do from the start. She achieved
dependence and autonomy without falling into the temptation of pure rebellion.
couldn't possibly have stood up to the sneers or survived being completely
stracized within community. I knew, in the deepest crevices of my heart and
ind I did the right thing returning the ring and moving on.

Sitting in Karen's living room surrounded by family, I floated in a twilight
one between absence and presence, like a soul hovering above the room where
y body lay dying. Physically present, I carried on conversations and performed
enial functions, but I watched every action, heard every word, and examined
ch detail from a distance outside myself.

"So I might buy a car. Any suggestions?" I offered a benign topic, but the
onversation slowly escalated to a full blown discussion on the pros and cons of
ed-over-new with depreciation and blue book values and different insurance and
r companies. I just listened and hoped someday to not be so ignorant or so
competent. I slumped into the chair as the onslaught of my inadequacy
erwhelmed me.

From the kitchen Mom called me. "What?" I yelled, not wanting to budge.
om marched into the room, dish towel in hand, insisting that I help clean up.

"Why me? What about everybody else?" I tried to stand my ground at first,
ing to confirm my self-worth and not go clean up. Did it always have to be me?
wanted to visit just once without living by others' expectations. On Mom's
cond attack, I weakened. Unable to resist, I got up, went into the kitchen,
ming and on the verge of tears, and ignored anyone's attempts to console me. I
ded up locked in the bathroom in tears. Memories of the last gathering at
aren's house that ended the same way added to my feelings of frustration and
lure. Leaning against the bathroom door sobbing, I cringed as Leslie, and then
na, came in the opposite door.

"You have to know your mom must be feeling betrayed and abandoned by
u." Leslie had a strange way of trying to console me.

171

"What!"

"Well, after all she's done for you – and Loyed feels the same way – you went to find your Dad. You are the one who started it all right? It's a slap in the face to them. She took care of you all your life. And Loyed did his best to take your dad's place. And now you go to hunt him down. Don't you expect her to take it out on you?"

Tina escorted Leslie out of the bathroom almost slamming the door behind her. "Don't listen to her. Nothing is your fault. She doesn't even really know us. You know Mom always does this to you."

Attempting to tune out the accusations being leveled at me, and avoiding the pain of knowing I was best loved for the work I did, I tuned in to Karen's conversation on the other side of the wall.

"Did you ever stop to think maybe Janet's had a hard day? She's been basically alone in Chicago for almost a year; she flew in last night and drove straight to Santa Cruz this morning to return her ring. Don't you think there is some emotion attached to that? She's had a rough day. Doesn't she deserve some rest?"

"She decided to do all of that, no one told her to. How is it so emotional? That's crazy." Mom sounded flabbergasted. I splashed water on my face, returned to the kitchen, and finished the clean-up in silence.

Sitting alone in the back seat of the minivan the next day on the road, I tried to regain my sense of self. I wanted to be my own best friend, to be whole. I felt whole and centered. Not quite consciously, I now "expected" God to bring someone into my life. At the same time I didn't want it. I wanted to spend evenings alone to read a book, do needlepoint, play guitar – work on my writing.

"What are we doing?" Karen asked incredulously as we headed over the hill and into Las Vegas. "Do we really want to be here? We don't have to go."

"I know what you mean. Let's stop a second." Tina sounded nervous.

I kept my foot on the gas pedal, ignoring the hesitation in their voices. "What do you mean? What's the big deal? We're just meeting a man we don't know. I do that kind of thing all the time. I've met plenty of new people in the past few months."

"But he's our dad. Did you ever think you'd see him again?" Karen choked on her own words.

I turned into the driveway of the apartment complex. "This is it. You comin'?"

I led the way and rang the doorbell. Karen and Tina held hands as they waited, standing slightly behind me, still invisible when our dad opened the door.

"Well, hello. Come in. Let me see. You're Karen, you're Tina and you're Janet, right?" He said, pointing to each of us correctly.

As my father's arms reached around my shoulders to embrace me, the damning thoughts crashed through my mind screaming, "Did he sexually abuse me, ever? Did he?"

I never said a word and I refused to let the questions flavor the conversations exploding around me. Nancy planted the thoughts in my brain but I had no evidence, no reason to believe them, except for some odd phases I'd gone through in childhood. I could not condemn this man for something so ridiculous.

"Janet had a lisp ... Janet loved Cherry Chip cake ... Janet got drunk once and fell down some stairs.... Janet spent twelve years in a convent." The convoluted conversations spilling from the lips of my sisters all entailed stories of my life, apparently so nervous they couldn't talk about themselves, they felt safest talking about me.

"The thing I remember most about you is how so many times when I asked what you were doing, and you'd say, 'I wanted to ... whatever ... but no!' You always had to do what Karen or Tina or one of the older kids wanted 'cause they were bigger. You never got your way."

As my father reminisced, sharing one of the very few stories he remembered of my childhood days, I remembered saying this, all the time. The reality hit that this simple sentence, spoken at such a young age and so often in my early years, planted a seed and took root in my soul; this became my essence without even realizing it. My life to that point had been a continual recurrence of the same script. I gave up my basic wishes, my daily desires and my lifetime dreams constantly because someone else had another wish, desire or dream. It began with choosing which game to play with my sisters but it became much more complex. My desire to please and to be a part of the crowd led me down roads I would not necessarily have chosen to travel, if I'd only listened to my heart.

The father I hadn't seen for twenty-two years had stolen my dreams and desires when he chose to never return home. At that very moment I recovered my lost sense of self. I no longer had to do what others wanted if I didn't. I no longer had to put my wishes aside just because of another's idea. I possessed the power to choose.

I studied the wall of photos from the life Dad led since leaving us; I read his poetry and thumbed through the photo albums Teddy, his eighteen-year-old son, pulled from the hall closet.

"Hey, Grandma had this picture of you." I looked closely at my father lying on a blanket in 1952. Turning to Teddy, "Did you ever wonder whose arm this is?" I pointed to the arm of a baby lying in the corner of the picture.

"No, not really." Teddy muttered.

"That's Regina's arm. Didn't you ever ask about his life before he married your Mom?" I spoke with a chuckle in an attempt to not sound too harsh, but I found it hard to believe Teddy had never been curious.

Dad appeared to be a kind, gentle man with a loving wife and child. I couldn't argue that point. I couldn't see the monster I heard about who kicked Loyed down a hill or slapped Dan across the face for saying, "Shit." He didn't appear manic-depressive or angry or sarcastic or distant. I wanted to say we bonded as if we'd never been apart; like I never lost the daddy I loved. But I couldn't. I accepted him as I accepted all those who entered my life within the past year, with open arms and a non-judgmental attitude. I planned to keep in touch, eager to read more poetry and share life with him. I'd see how our relationship developed over time.

"So, how did it go?" Mom asked the night I arrived home.

"Good. We had a good time. He's interesting." I remained nonchalant.

"Is he still so emotional? He used to be such a cry baby. Just like you. You're a lot alike." Mom's words cut sharply but I didn't bite. I couldn't.

Mom had already accused me of "pulling a Dad" during our monthly phone call when I still lived in Hong Kong. I mustered all of my courage to confide in my mother. I planned to surrender my passport and remain in Hong Kong in solidarity with the people preparing for the Chinese takeover in 1997. I needed someone to understand and accept me – even if I questioned my commitment to the community. I needed to know that even if everyone else rejected me, someone still loved me as I attempted to discover and follow the will of God in my life.

"God is calling me to work among the poor, but I'm sure the community won't let me. I've tried to bring up the subject, but it's impossible."

"So what are you going to do?" Mom's question encouraged me to divulge more than I originally planned.

"I'll stay in Hong Kong but move out on my own to figure things out."

"So, you're going to pull a Dad, huh? Just run off when things get tough?" My mother's anger had been clearly audible.

"I'm not running off. Anyway, I'm just trying to figure out what to do. I'm not sure what'll happen."

The conversation lasted just minutes but I never forgot the accusation. "Pull a Dad." I always thought the incubator created the barrier separating my mother and me, but perhaps I constantly reminded her of the pain she suffered at the hands of my father. Maybe the guilt I carried for my father's leaving had been well-founded. I refused to entertain the thought back in psyche class when my professor suggested it, but maybe my entering the convent had been an attempt to fulfill my mother's unfulfilled dream, some unconscious or subconscious desire to say sorry for destroying my mother's life.

The Sisters often suggested God might reward me for making final vows by bringing my father back. Maybe God finally saw fit to reward me for following my own dreams instead of the dreams of my mother or the prophecy of my sister or the desires of everyone else. I would never know the answers to the maybe. I simply knew I must be genuine, authentic, and real; whether that meant crying or laughing, make-up or no make-up, being a teacher or an airline stewardess. No matter what my dreams or my daily reality, I no longer needed to continually say no to myself to make others happy.

"Whatever. He seems nice enough to me." I walked up the stairs and closed the bedroom door.

"You look concerned today. Is something bothering you?" Irene asked gently. I didn't realize it showed.

"Billy and I fooled around the other night." I choked back tears.

"Are you upset about that?"

"Yes and no. He's been giving me a guilt trip ever since."

"A guilt trip?"

"He's a fundamentalist Christian. He says we're wrong to give in to the flesh. He keeps saying we sinned."

"Do you feel like you've sinned?"

"No, not really. I had to get over the hump. I really like to banter with him about the Gospel. I miss talking about Jesus. But as we talked, I just kept staring at him. I wanted him to hold me.

"I muddled up my desire for spiritual union with physical attraction. I spent my entire adult life searching for some sort of mystical union as the Bride of Christ. 'Like a deer longs for running streams, so my soul pines for you, my God.' But this time the longing turned physical.

"I preached about the body and soul being one, but for the first time I felt it. As he held me in his arms, one gentle touch led to another. I didn't want to stop. He never said he did either. He had a great time as far as I could tell.

"But when I saw him the next day he got all mopey and quiet. He started talkin' about how we sinned. I tried to comfort him a little; but then I got mad. I really don't think I sinned."

175

"Did you?" Irene cracked a smile.

"I don't know. Nothing really happened in the end. But he has this 'no touching before marriage' thing like that guy Dan I told you about."

"How do you feel?"

"Guilty, of course. And mad."

"Mad at whom?"

"Mostly him. For making me feel so guilty. But I don't have a vow of chastity anymore. I am free to explore."

"How do you feel about yourself?"

"I feel good. I feel like I'm letting go of hang ups, like I'm not just doing things because someone else says I should."

"Is that important to you? The should's?"

"My whole life has been one big should. I've gotta do what I want."

"Without any boundaries?"

"Well that's what I'm afraid of. I don't know if I can control myself. My mom always called Dad a womanizer. Maybe I'll have the same kind of sex drive once I let it out of the bag."

"Do you really think so?"

"I don't know. I'm afraid of the all or nothing tendency I seem to have."

"Maybe you need to work on not being so extreme."

"I guess so."

"Remember it doesn't have to be all or nothing. We've gone over this before. You can eat one doughnut without eating a dozen."

"Besides, he's engaged anyway."

"He's engaged?"

"Oh, I didn't tell you? Yeah. Supposedly. I feel like I'm back in high school. The same thing happened with Vernon. He had another girl living with him but still wanted to get me in bed with him."

"So, what do you think?"

"What do you mean?"

"Why do you think you allowed yourself to get in this triangle again?"

"To teach me some lesson I didn't learn the first time around."

"What might that lesson be?"

"Self-respect. I shouldn't let myself be the 'other' girl."

"Why do you think you really got involved with Billy in the first place?"

"What do you mean?"

"What deeper need did you fulfill, beyond the physical urge?"

"I appreciate someone is interested in me."

"Do you believe that now? Did it work?"

176

"Not really. He's using me. I could be anyone off the street."

"So you're dispensable?"

I sat, stunned. Sr. Thomas switched me from place to place, and job to job, to meet some community need, and always reminded me everyone is indispensable. Her exact words were, "Remember, no one is indispensable."

Sr. Thomas wanted me to know I could easily be replaced and never get too proud. I worked hard; followed all of the rules; and fulfilled expectations with very little resistance. I just wanted to know I had value. Like a paper plate or a napkin, I could easily be replaced. My dad threw me away. Vernon threw me away. My community threw me aside. Now Billy could too.

As the train sped down the tracks towards home, my determination to stay away from Billy turned to dust and the voices questioning my worth and whether or not anybody cared about me got louder and louder. Just before the doors closed at the Loyola station, I hopped off. The Dunkin' Donuts downstairs closed in ten minutes. Donuts could take away the pain. A half a dozen. No, a dozen. I'd get a great deal on a dozen at closing time.

Glazed, old-fashioned and jelly donuts sat on the floor in front of me as I leaned forward on my folded knees in the middle of the floor, trying to remain calm. I bought the donuts but I didn't have to eat them all. I had choices.

I stared at the donuts and said softly, "What pain are you trying to shove down? What am I avoiding?"

I could make a list: fear, sadness, frustration, anger, guilt, loneliness, worthless, disrespected … and check it twice.

Looking at the box of donuts, I closed the lid, put them on the dining room table and sat down in my prayer corner and wrote in my journal:

Don't be afraid to listen to the depths of your heart telling you what you want out of life. You have been searching, seeking, experimenting. This is great! It is wonderful. You deserve a good, healthy, happy life. Only you can get it for you. Only you know what can really make you happy. Don't give up now. Don't turn back. It is so hard to feel so open to rejection, lacking confidence in the classroom, not having any direction — exposing my story so often, having people be fascinated, then feeling dropped, abandoned, alone. Don't be afraid to apply to the Airlines, to apply for a credit card, to apply for an Illinois Teachers' Certification, to go ice-skating, skiing, to the movies, or on vacation ALONE. Love casts out all fear. Love yourself.

A local adult education center sponsored a one-day ski trip. I rented the skis, attended the introductory lesson and headed up the slope. Almost landing on my face attempting to jump off the lift, I composed myself, said a prayer and pushed off. Within ten feet of takeoff I spread my legs, stabbed the poker into the ground and landed on my butt. Every ten feet or so until I reached the bottom I landed in the same, cold position. At the lodge, I returned my skis, bought a cup of hot chocolate, found a chair near the window, and sat until the bus reloaded to head back to the city. On the return trip I struck up a conversation with John, the tall blonde guy, next to me.

"Do you eat sushi?" He asked as we gathered our belongings.

"Yes, do you?"

"There's a great place on Belmont, you want to get some."

My nervousness about getting into John's car took second to my excitement that someone asked me to dinner. By the end of dinner, as we headed to the movie theater any anticipation completely disappeared. After a walk under the moonlight on the lake, he drove me home, parked the car and walked me to my room. As we sat on my daybed, the only furniture I had, he leaned over to kiss me and drew me, around the waist, towards him. The warmth of his hands sent chills up and down my spine as I longed to give myself to him. We fell back unto the bed and my hands shifted to his chest as I pushed him away. "I can't do this. Not tonight. Next time, okay?" Looking dejected, John said he understood, picked up his jacket and closed the door behind him. I called him the next evening after waiting for his call all day. He never answered the phone or returned my calls.

Sara, my newfound neighbor friend, and I planned a night out at Shoeless Joe's sports bar to help me forget about John. I wore white legging pants, a maroon turtle neck and a champagne, rose sweater touching just below my butt. From the moment I walked in I hit the dance floor with barely time to return to the table for a drink before the next guy asked me to dance. Towards the end of the night, Eric repeatedly asked me to dance. With each song he moved closer to me until we danced ourselves into a dark corner, pawing and groping each other uncontrollably. "Let's go to my car," he panted between kisses. "Or we could go back to my hotel room if you want." I didn't, or couldn't answer. I didn't want to resist the fire taking over my body. Finally, I managed, "I gotta tell Sara."

"Are you sure you want to do that Janet, really?" Sara's concern was unmistakable. "Think about it sweetie. You don't really know him."

I walked, weak kneed, back to his table, wrote down my number and took his. "Call me tomorrow," I said as I headed with Sara towards the exit.

My mind knew I did the right thing, until he didn't call me the next day. I picked up his information to see if he wanted to finish where we'd left off.

"Hello, is Eric there?" I spoke clearly despite my shaking hand.

"No Eric at this number. You have the wrong number."

"I'm sorry."

I hung up, devastated he gave me a fake phone number. Why hadn't I just gone with him? Why did I stop? What really scared me? Sex? Why couldn't I loosen up and stop being such a prude? Did it have to be all or nothing? The self-ridicule escalated until I sat, sobbing into my pillow. Rocking back and forth on my bed, I wanted to explode. Why couldn't I just be crazy and wild, just once? Why did I always have to do the wise, mature thing?

Believing only Irene could talk me through the turmoil, the downward spiral inhabiting my thoughts, I called.

"Hello. Irene, this is Janet. I'm sorry to bother you at home but I really need to talk…" I rattled on in stream of consciousness fashion for some time when Irene finally broke in.

"Janet, it is ten forty-five pm. You cannot do this. You can get control. This is not an emergency." Irene spoke with a firm, intentional tone. She refused to travel the path of superficial insanity with me like a college roommate or best friend might. I should not have called her. I tried to explain myself but recognized I probably saved my own life by not leaving with him. "Call me at the office between noon and two tomorrow. You will be okay. Good night."

All I could think was *Crap. Crap. Crap. Why had I called Irene? How ridiculous. I would knock the mess out of any student who attempted to go to the car or hotel room of a perfect stranger. Did being thirty give me permission to be stupid and go from a vow of chastity to a one-night stand?*

I'd resisted John right in my own apartment but I just wanted to be wild. I wanted to do something crazy. I couldn't stand the constraints I had placed upon myself for so long. I stood up, walked to the freezer, pulled out the half gallon of Caramel Marble Fudge from the other night, stood at the sink, and gulped it down in under three minutes. I took a few deep breathes, climbed in bed and fell asleep.

Sara went out of town the next weekend and let me use her car for the weekend which meant I could wear the fancy teal colored business suit I'd picked up at the second hand shop down the street to work that Friday. Everyone commented on how professional and extraordinary I looked. Passing auto row on the way home, I swung into the used car lot.

"Hello, may I help you?"

"I hope so. I know absolutely nothing about cars or how to buy one, but I think I want one. I know how much I can afford and that's not much. Can you help me?" My candor seemed to startle Tom, the salesman.

"Don't tell too many people that. But I'm honest, so I'll do what I can."

He showed me into the office to figure out what price range I could look into and then led me to a Ford Escort and a Plymouth Sundance. The moment I opened the door to the forest green Sundance the cup holder under the dashboard caught my eye as an absolutely perfect fit for the large pink cup for the hot water I drank eight times a day.

I needed a thousand dollars down and the car would be mine. I'd agonized for months over buying a car. I'd discussed it with family at Christmas and with Irene numerous times. What would it say about my commitment to poverty if I owned a car? Could I still consider religious life an option? Could I manage financially? What about maintenance? I knew nothing about cars. Each time I presented some obstacle to purchasing a car, Irene challenged my reasoning. With each discussion Irene pushed me towards some revelation, but I didn't know what. I could not fathom the deeper, hidden meaning of buying a car.

"Didn't you tell me after your dad left they found his car abandoned in an airport parking lot?" Irene finally posed the question.

"Yeah. So?"

"Couldn't your hesitation over the car stem from the fear you're going to 'pull a Dad' as your mother phrased it?"

Did my relationship with cars mirror my relationship to my dad? Did buying a car force me to confront my fear of abandonment, challenge me to put down roots, and release the hold my dad's leaving had on my past, present and future.

I needed a way to get the down payment. I told Mom all about it during our regular Saturday morning phone call.

"You need to be realistic and practical," Mom had a knack for sucking the energy from me – my hopes for a car, like a popped balloon, quickly deflated.

"I'm sure I can manage, I just have to figure something out." I didn't want to cry on the phone but the thoughts snowballed into negativity: Doesn't anyone believe in me? Am I just a crazy dreamer? Is it all just a fantasy?

"You've always wanted a Dad around to make your life easier." Mom's words burned like jalapeno pepper salsa rubbed across the eyes.

I wanted connectedness, roots, understanding, and support – not money. What child wouldn't want a dad around? Dads should be around.

"What do you mean? I never thought that?" I didn't want an argument, but I
uldn't just hang up.

"You had dreams that couldn't come true. You're a romantic. Just like
ad."

"Okay. Whatever. I gotta go."

Just like Dad. Mom had said it at least three times. Maybe I had to face the
ct we shared a great deal in common. I realized maybe he could help. I called to
are with him the same thing I'd told Mom: I found a great car and needed a
ousand dollars. Any ideas?

"You have to follow your dreams. Don't let a little obstacle get in your way."

"We can't give you the money, but we could lend it to you if you can pay it
ck on a regular basis. We could work something out. What do you think?"

"Really? Could you? I will definitely pay you back. A little each month. I could
obably send about fifty or seventy-five dollars, depending on my car payment.
ow. Are you sure? That's really great. Thank you so much."

How different life may have been if only I had the input of someone so much
e myself; someone who didn't step on my dreams the moment I shared them.
ears welled in my eyes as I realized he hadn't been around because he did the
ry thing he now told me I needed to do: follow my dreams; do what I wanted,
t what others said I should do.

I called Tom at the dealership immediately. "I'll have the down payment by
onday. Can you hold the Sundance for me? I'll fill out paper work; give you
enty dollars or something. Can you please just hold it?"

"I really can't hold it, legally. But I'll tell the guys not to push anyone towards
Anyway, I close in an hour and we're not open on Sunday. I'm sure it'll still be
ere. Don't worry." Tom sounded sincere.

I thanked him and believed if God wanted me to have the car, I would.

Sunday I planned a mini day of recollection in an attempt to focus and
group, allowing my journal to listen to the secrets of my heart without comment,
ithout judgment, without giving opinion. I needed the silence to hear my own
oice over others'.

April 24, 1995

*What is this little ache inside? The feeling like someone is squeezing my heart,
twisting, turning attempting to squelch the fire burning within. I sit with the dull pain
waiting for tears to come — the well rising in my throat that wants to scream. Just let
me be at peace. Let go of me. Let me settle down and be still. Let me be rooted and
grounded — moving in one direction. I'm sick of looking back, going over and over*

what went wrong; telling my story; figuring things out. I want to just be, to move towards something else; to not be the ex-nun.

Why am I so afraid of making money? Why is this car such a big hurtle to jump? Why do I constantly feel like I'm stepping out of my boundaries by thinking about buying a car, making more money, investing, dressing up, being business-like. Why do I convince myself I can't handle numbers or finances or insurance claim forms, etc. I've always done very well in Math and Science. I even liked them in high school. Why or what has convinced me otherwise? What am I afraid of? I have an IQ of 140. I am not stupid. I'm gonna do it now. I'm gonna buy a car and I'm gonna make money.

I want to dream again. To dust off the dreams I once had. I know I have to reach within to pursue a new goal, to follow a new dream. I have to believe in myself. I do believe in myself. I believe in me.

What are my dreams? Not what I've claimed for twelve years. What are my real dreams? I used to want the whole white picket fence with decorated rooms, like matching furniture and wall to wall carpet. A home. Not an apartment. Not a war zone. Not a ghetto like I grew up in. I wanted a family. A real family. I use to dream of being a good wife and mother. So good my husband wouldn't leave; so good my children would always have their dad.

Can I give up my dreams of working with the poor, of living a life of poverty, chastity and obedience? Can I give up my desire to be a saint? That's what I've wanted for twelve years. I've just wanted to be a saint. Why? What's all that about? Had my junior college psyche teacher been right? Had I become a nun because Mom always wanted to be one? Did I live her dream to make her happy? Did I think it might undo her pain? Or make up for her loss? Or did I hope to avoid ending up like her?

What are the dreams buried beneath the busyness of my daily life; beneath the layers of year upon year? How am I called to cherish my own giftedness and be gift to others? Forget that. What do I want; what would really make me happy?

Wholeness and Integration: Attentiveness to body, mind, spirit so caring and nurturing one doesn't lead to neglect of another; exercise, eating right, fresh air, sleep, intellectual growth and challenge, meditation, healthy relationships, positive thoughts, service, a career I enjoy, and a hobby.

Sitting before Jesus in my prayers, I allow myself to dream, to look into my future, to create a fantasy. It isn't easy allowing myself to dream. I've become so detached from my own desires; but I want to do it, I won't let myself back down. I'll ask simple questions. What will my life look like? Where will I live? Marriage? Kids? Work? Will I ever be able to let go of the need to be poor? To be less than others? To put myself down? Could I have a nice house without being a greedy, selfish middle class snob? Does it have to be all or nothing? No. I can have a life and still have God. I don't have to be ashamed of having a life.

I want to live in a house with matching furniture and fixtures, with an upstairs and a downstairs with room for hobbies, study, exercise – a yard of some kind, with a rock path for my foot massage – with a clothesline; a car – a stereo system; a beautiful kitchen where I can bake, create meals, entertain. A person of service – running a soup kitchen or tutoring program – making a difference in people's lives. I want a house. I just want to be normal.

Normal. What did normal people do? Most of the singles at St. Clement's ₁ent weekends bar hopping, so I did too, with Sara, with Becky, with girls from ₁oir. I dressed to show just enough of my slim, sexy curves to make men ₁onder, and I mastered the art of flirting. My usual cup of hot water in hand, I ₁ayed to the music until one guy after another led me to the dance floor. But I ₁ted it. I hated drawing attention to my body rather than my soul. I couldn't ₁hom the emptiness and apathy that must have enveloped the individuals I met ₁ch weekend. The loneliness and longing for connection seeped from the pores ˙ these poor lost souls dug at the recesses of my own. I longed for deep ₁nversation and soul searching discussions. I ached at the thought of living my ₁e so superficially. I laughed at their jokes and tried to contribute to the ₁eaninglessness of it all. Playing football at midnight on the Evanston ₁achfront, falling and shouting, acting as drunk as the people around me made ₁e feel like a kid again, especially when the cops drove us off with a spotlight. I ₁d fun, for a minute but got home feeling empty and out of place.

Someone out there had to want what I did; I just had to find him.

"Single white male seeking female; age 30-35; for sincere, romantic relationship…SWM ₁king F for long walks on the lake, bike riding, and a good time…SM, professional seeking ₁me in F for companionship and fun…" The personal ads in the Reader seemed to ₁ve someone for everyone. Why couldn't I find someone? I searched for ₁hristian radio stations and Catholic dating services to find somebody who could ₁ soul searching and fun at the same time; someone unafraid to peel off the ₁tificial layer that kept the world out and the pain in.

I needed to find the one who respected my concern for health; who wouldn't ₁iticize me for not eating late dinner, or for drinking only hot water, or for being ₁getarian and staying away from too much white sugar. Would I ever find ₁meone to support my efforts to be whole?

183

Brandon, my first date from the personals, sounded perfect. *"SWM seeking SWF. Mid-thirties. Professional. Enjoys long walks on the lake, reading, biking, and conversation. If you are interested in the same, call."*

Should I tell him my history or not? How long could I avoid it? What would I say? My mind raced as I walked from the El stop towards the bar. Would this be the man I'd marry?

I managed to stay calm and confident. I didn't smell anything, even under my arms, as I stepped off the train.

Perched on his pedestal, his tall slender physique mirrored the disdain and disappointment visible in his eyes when he saw me. Apparently I did not meet his standards of beauty. Determined not to scare him off by my body odor, I took a deep breath, forcing myself to silently articulate: *I am worthy of love. I am loveable.* Confident in my own person, I would play no games and have no hidden agendas. Right up front, I shared I'd been a Franciscan nun for twelve years, left looking for more commitment to the gospel, and decided to step completely outside of the whole thing to rediscover me. He admitted finding it all very intriguing, spoke about his position as warehouse manager in some western suburb, and within ten minutes, politely excused himself for the long drive home.

I reveled in the fact that I arrived home, still smelling fresh and clean. I hadn't allowed the outright rejection by this young man to demean my sense of self-worth. I didn't want to hide from my own reality. I had a great body and a great soul. Yeah, my nose may have been a little too big or my hair a bit frizzy and I may not be the most attractive or classy person on the planet, but I didn't need anyone who judged me so quickly. Maybe the next guy would be different.

We met at Leona's, another public place, just up the street. Steven kept our phone conversation brief, but sounded eager to meet me.

"Sara, I've got to talk to you." I swung the door open.

"I thought you had the thing with the guy from the ads tonight."

"I just did. The worst thirty minutes I've ever spent in my entire life. You'd never believe what I just went through. The guy had absolutely no personality. None. We said maybe six things to each other. I couldn't drag words out of him."

"What do you expect?" Billy, who saw me barge into Sara's apartment and snuck in behind me, interrupted. "The guy took out a personal ad. Guys like that are complete losers or out for sex. You got what you asked for."

"Oh, let's listen to the expert. Suppose you're right, then I'm a loser too, 'cause I answered the ads."

"Don't be crazy, Janet." Sara, always the supportive affirming friend, insisted I be careful and always meet in a very public place, but she would never call me desperate. "There's nothing wrong with trying something new. You never know."

"Well, now I know. I can't do this anymore. It's no better than the bar hopping. It's a waste of time."

I tried not to think too much about the failed dates. No regrets. I decided I would regret nothing. I had only choice. I had to be about choice. I'd given over my power to choose for so long, I decided to no longer chastise myself if a choice I made turned out badly. I would make mistakes and I would choose again. No fault. No regret. No should's or shouldn'ts. Just choices.

I would not be a victim nor would I be held hostage by anyone or anything. I'd said this many times before, but after sitting in Irene's women's therapy group that week, my words had to become my reality or I would end up like the women around me. *He's constantly forgetting to take out the garbage... The other day he called me a bitch in front of my kids ... Every time we argue he puts me down, says I'm stupid...*" As each woman spoke, I heard my own story of manipulation, oppression and pettiness in the convent. Complaints of dishwashers loaded wrongly and arguments over non-issues provided the noise these women needed to cover the insecurity and the self-hatred making them tick.

I wanted to scream, *Just get out! Don't do this to yourself. Get out.* I got out; they could too. I never wanted to allow myself to be caught in the cycle of dysfunction again. I left the room, having said almost nothing, moving forward on my journey, not backwards. Positive I could not surround myself with women who had not yet accessed the courage hidden beneath layers of shame, guilt and longing to be loved, I walked to my car knowing I wouldn't revisit this group. Someday I may be able to help women in this position, but my sole intention at the moment needed to be keeping my own fragile existence from crumbling.

"Can I see you in my office?" Sr. Beatrice had called me to her office. "We need to discuss next year."

"What do you mean?" I feigned naiveté, forcing Sr. Beatrice to be straightforward.

"Well, I'm handing out contracts this week, but before I prepare yours, I wondered if you really think this is the best place for you?" Sr. Beatrice's eyes almost implored me.

I had expected this. I had already applied to study full time at IPS, but waiting for an acceptance letter, hadn't told Beatrice.

"What do you mean the best place for me? I do a good job, the students all like me and I've done nothing wrong." I wouldn't give up so easily. I would make

185

Beatrice own her dissatisfaction and be honest. If Sr. Beatrice didn't want me to return she should say so.

"Well, you don't seem to be happy here. Since you left the convent, you seem to have other priorities. Are you sure you don't want to do something else with your talents and experience? I'm just concerned for you." Beatrice might have been Sr. Simon's evil twin.

"You know I love the girls. You can't stand they love me too. You hate I don't give demerits, but give so many angel cards. You've had it out for me since I got my dispensation. It's okay. I understand. I'm gonna go ahead and quit. You don't have to ask me to leave. You don't even have to pretend to be concerned for me. I respect you enough to be honest. I will not be returning next year."

As all color drained from Sr. Beatrice's already sullen face, I turned and walked out of the office.

"I just quit." I said walking into a coworker's office.

"You have to make a plan, what if you don't get another job? What will you do? You can't be so foolish; you might end up on the street." Cindy and Becky spoke almost in unison, trying to convince me to renege.

"I know I can't stay here. It's too much like the community I left: too much manipulation and dysfunction. Something will come up. I found an apartment and a job within a week of being in Chicago. God's taken care of me this far, will it stop now? I'll find something if IPS falls through. I'll die if I stay here."

Walking into the IPS office, I met Mary Anne sitting at her desk. "Can I see you for a moment?"

"Sure, what can I do for you?"

"I just received my acceptance letter. I'm really excited. But I need to find out what my schedule will be as soon as possible because, with only a partial scholarship, I've got to get another job."

"Would it be helpful if you had a full scholarship?" Mary Anne spoke in a very matter of fact tone.

"Yes, of course." I didn't want to get my hopes up but I could scarcely contain my excitement.

"Well, actually, I just discovered I have one half scholarship that will remain unused. I could offer it to you. I'm sure Camilla would approve." Mary Anne finally cracked a smile.

"Wow. That's great. Really? You'll give me a full time assistantship, like that?"

"Yes."

I couldn't say thank you enough. Studying Theology and Scripture in a pastoral, contemplative setting would allow me to find my place in the church, to integrate all the pieces of my life, and to create meaning and sense.

That weekend I wrote letters to Sr. Ruth and Louise expressing my certainty that this year would be one of growth and personal discovery. I'd worked through my issues, mourned my losses and acknowledged my faults. I'd rebelled and returned to my senses. By the end of the year my IPS courses would be finished and I would certainly know exactly which direction my life would take: a return to community, a life of private service or marriage. I remained open to whichever path God showed me, as long as I retained some sense of personal dignity and autonomy.

I might sacrifice my life in poverty, chastity and obedience again, but I'd reclaimed my conscience and my self-respect and will never hand them over to another human being again.

It was important that you find an anchor, a safe harbor where you could allay anxiety and find some predictability and respectability for your personhood. And it is strange, but I sense you needed to enter that congregation – from there you would eventually find your anchor within yourself – but for those years in your 20's, you needed to develop a sense of self that linked to the larger identity of the group. Despite its rigidity and narrow vision of life, the congregation gave you the opportunity to grow and grow you did – you outgrew the congregation – they couldn't offer you any more life-giving energy, so you left and you had to, as you now know.

- Words of an IPS professor

"Hi, I'm Bob and I'm an alcohol…." The teachers roared. I'd have little trouble getting along with this new coworker and happy he would teach the twelve students assigned to me on Wednesdays.

"Do you have a cabinet I can leave my stuff in?"

"Not really. I don't have space." Willie barely looked at me, the encounter less than amicable.

We spoke briefly about arrangements for Wednesday's classes but otherwise exchanged only collegial small talk until the afternoon in mid-September when we waited together for a department meeting. We discovered that we were both vegetarian, ate tons of rice, and had a devotion to St. Jude. I suggested he buy a rice cooker in Chinatown, but when he didn't find one in the price range I'd mentioned, he asked for help.

"I don't cook at the priest's place today, or next Wednesday."

"I work Wednesday. Why don't we go tonight? I'll pick you up at four."

"Good. Okay. I'm at the corner of Granville and Kenmore."

"Ya. I'll find it."

I wore my forest green thermal shirt and green stretch pants. I felt sexy at one hundred and ten pounds. I had no guilt, no shame and no imaginary fingers pointing in my face to warn me against being a slut or giving up on my dreams. Standing in the front lobby, keeping my eye out for his silver CRX, I almost chuckled over how far I'd come in the past year and a half.

Dropping into the passenger's seat, I relaxed as we visited at least six stores that evening. Willie never did find just the right deal on the rice cooker, although neither of us minded. With classic R&B for background music, we chatted our way into each other's lives and hearts. I met his family, his friends, and his church community. We spent every evening together bowling, walking along the lake, holding hands and staring into one another's eyes.

On October 28, 1995, on the feast of St. Jude, kneeling at the National Shrine of St. Jude on Chicago's south side, Willie proposed to me. We married on February 10, 1996. Fourteen years, almost to the day, that I'd left home to enter the Franciscan Missionary Sisters of Our Lady of Sorrows.

The desire, hidden in the depth of my heart, never spoken or written in a journal, or voiced concretely in my mind, would finally coming true. I could finally answer, aloud, the question I asked myself as I sat, halfway across the world in a chapel in Hong Kong, before I visited the Natural Medicine Doctor three years earlier: *What one desire do you have before you die?*

"I want to have a child."

49965117R00109

Made in the USA
Lexington, KY
27 February 2016